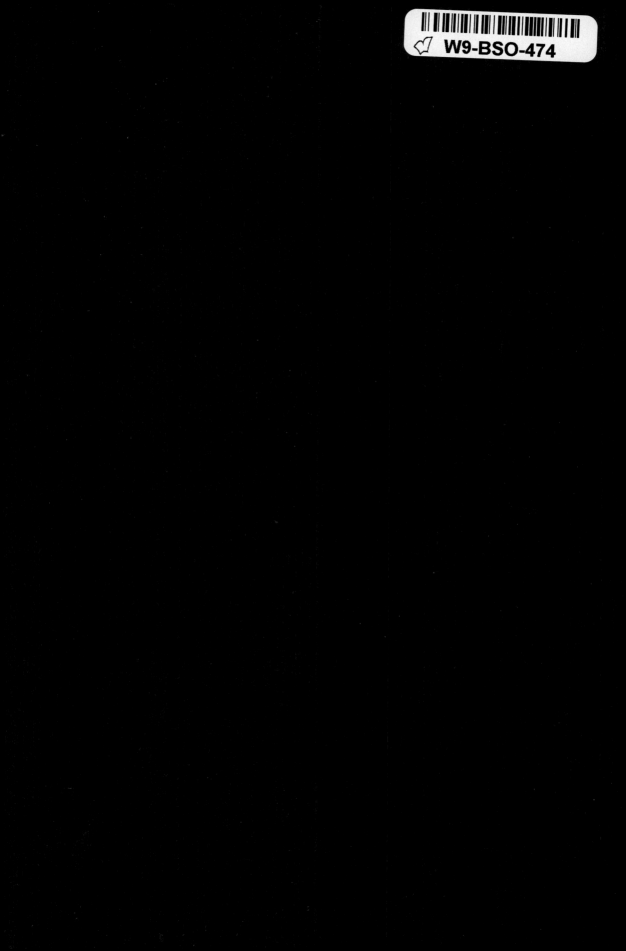

IRON MAN
IRON METROPOLITAN

Tony has stopped the rogue alien android, Recorder 451, and his giant doomsday armor, the Godkiller. After escaping the massive machine, Tony returned to Earth with the remains of 451. Back on planet, Tony immediately began investigating his past – to find out that Howard and Maria Stark had indeed struck a bargain with 451 to save the life of their unborn son. However, all was not as 451 had thought.

Tony was not the child that 451 genetically altered. Howard and Maria had a son named Arno. And due to Howard's interference with the enhancements, Arno was damaged at the fetal phase and confined to a life support system.

And Tony...Tony discovered he had been adopted.

With 451 out of commission and Tony discovering he has a brother, the Stark boys decided to join forces and fix the world!

KIERON GILLEN
WRITER

JOE BENNETT
(#18-22) &
AGUSTIN PADILLA
(#20.INH)
PENCILERS

SCOTT HANNA
INKER

GURU-EFX
COLORIST

VC'S JOE CARAMAGNA
LETTERER

PAUL RIVOCHE
COVER ART

TIM LEONG
IRON METROPOLITAN DESIGN

EMILY SHAW
ASSISTANT EDITOR

MARK PANICCIA
EDITOR

JENNIFER GRÜNWALD
COLLECTION EDITOR

ALEX STARBUCK
ASSOCIATE MANAGING
EDITOR

MARK D. BEAZLEY
EDITOR,
SPECIAL PROJECTS

JEFF YOUNGQUIST
SENIOR EDITOR,
SPECIAL PROJECTS

DAVID GABRIEL
SVP PRINT, SALES
& MARKETING

JOE FRONTIRRE
BOOK DESIGNER

AXEL ALONSO
EDITOR IN CHIEF

JOE QUESADA
CHIEF CREATIVE
OFFICER

DAN BUCKLEY
PUBLISHER

ALAN FINE
EXECUTIVE
EDITOR

IRON MAN VOL. 4: IRON METROPOLITAN. Contains material originally published in magazine form as IRON MAN #18-20, #20.INH and #21-22. First printing 2014. ISBN# 978-0-7851-8942-8. Published by MARVEL WORLDWIDE, INC., a subsidiary of MARVEL ENTERTAINMENT, LLC. OFFICE OF PUBLICATION: 135 West 50th Street, New York, NY 10020. Copyright © 2013 and 2014 Marvel Characters, Inc. All rights reserved. All characters featured in this issue and the distinctive names and likenesses thereof, and all related indicia are trademarks of Marvel Characters, Inc. No similarity between any of the names, characters, persons, and/or institutions in this magazine with those of any living or dead person or institution is intended, and any such similarity which may exist is purely coincidental. **Printed in the U.S.A.** ALAN FINE, EVP - Office of the President, Marvel Worldwide, Inc. and EVP & CMO Marvel Characters B.V.; DAN BUCKLEY, Publisher & President - Print, Animation & Digital Divisions; JOE QUESADA, Chief Creative Officer; TOM BREVOORT, SVP of Publishing; DAVID BOGART, SVP of Operations & Procurement, Publishing; C.B. CEBULSKI, SVP of Creator & Content Development; DAVID GABRIEL, SVP Print, Sales & Marketing; JIM O'KEEFE, VP of Operations & Logistics; DAN CARR, Executive Director of Publishing Technology; SUSAN CRESPI, Editorial Operations Manager; ALEX MORALES, Publishing Operations Manager; STAN LEE, Chairman Emeritus. For information regarding advertising in Marvel Comics or on Marvel.com, please contact Niza Disla, Director of Marvel Partnerships, at ndisla@marvel.com. For Marvel subscription inquiries, please call 800-217-9158. **Manufactured between 3/14/2014 and 4/28/2014 by R.R. DONNELLEY, INC., SALEM, VA, USA.**

10 9 8 7 6 5 4 3 2 1

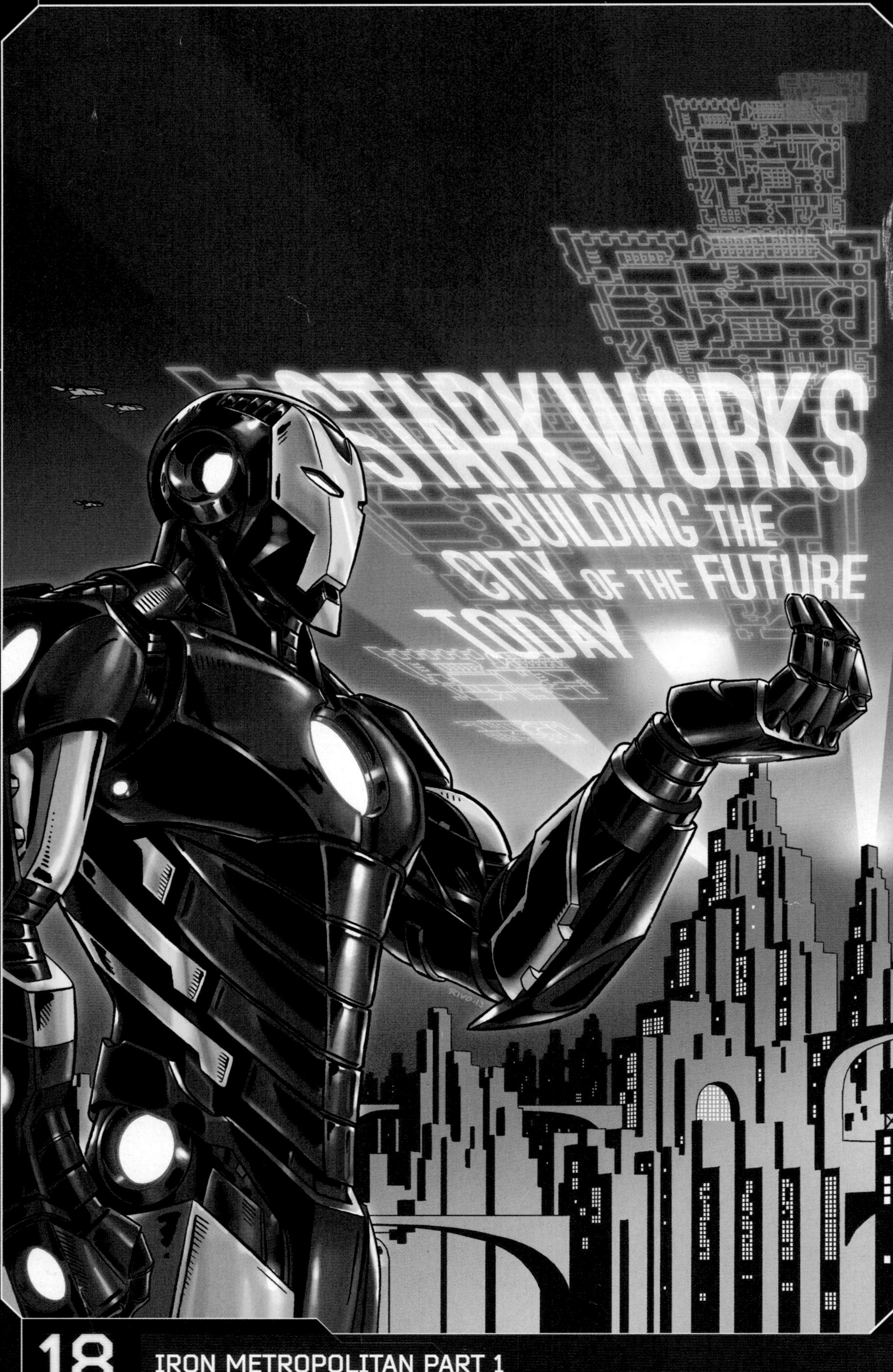
STARKWORKS
BUILDING THE
CITY OF THE FUTURE
TODAY

18 IRON METROPOLITAN PART 1

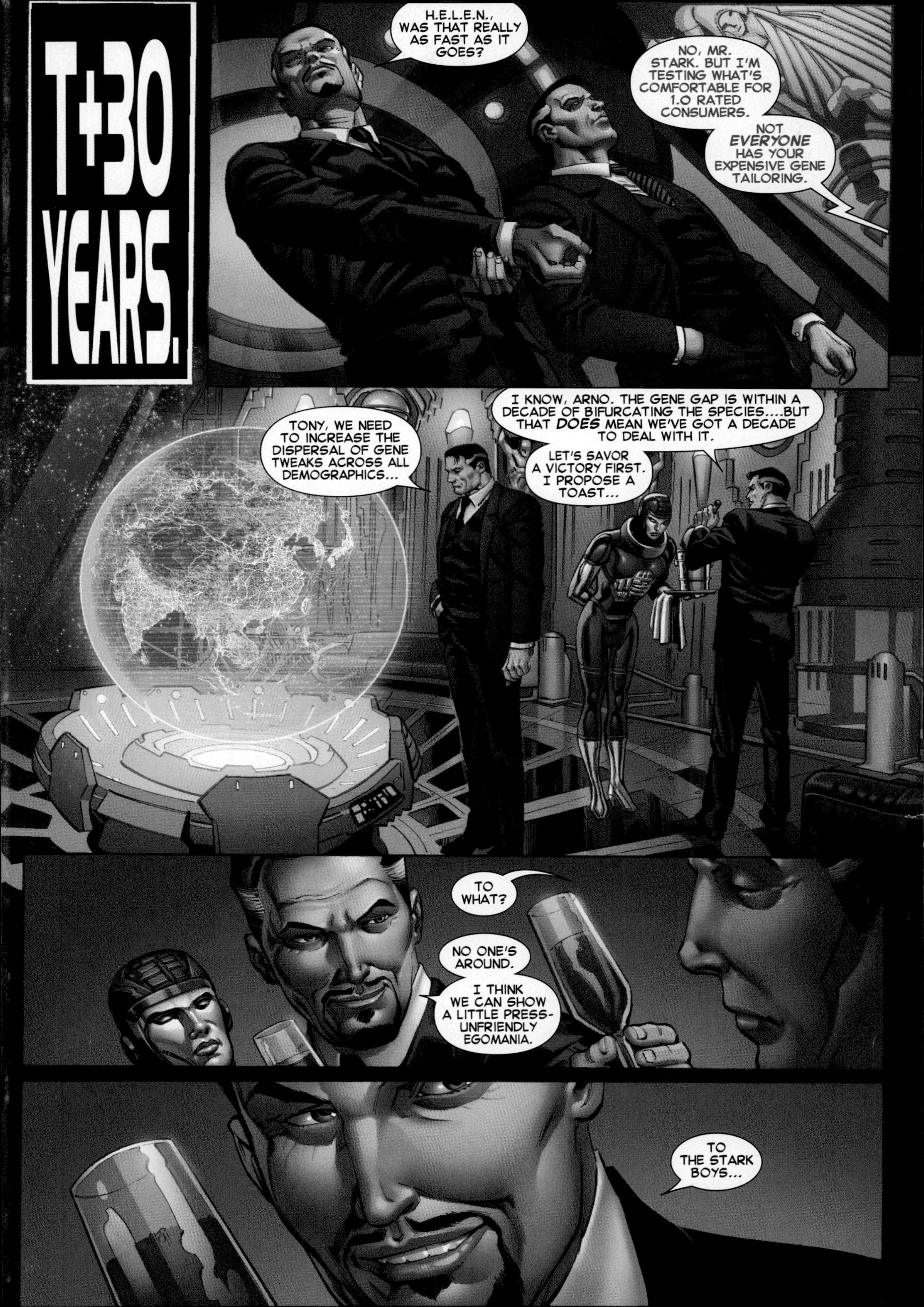
T+30 YEARS.
H.E.L.E.N., WAS THAT REALLY AS FAST AS IT GOES?
NO, MR. STARK. BUT I'M TESTING WHAT'S COMFORTABLE FOR 1.0 RATED CONSUMERS.
NOT EVERYONE HAS YOUR EXPENSIVE GENE TAILORING.
TONY, WE NEED TO INCREASE THE DISPERSAL OF GENE TWEAKS ACROSS ALL DEMOGRAPHICS...
I KNOW, ARNO. THE GENE GAP IS WITHIN A DECADE OF BIFURCATING THE SPECIES....BUT THAT DOES MEAN WE'VE GOT A DECADE TO DEAL WITH IT.
LET'S SAVOR A VICTORY FIRST. I PROPOSE A TOAST...
TO WHAT?
NO ONE'S AROUND.
I THINK WE CAN SHOW A LITTLE PRESS-UNFRIENDLY EGOMANIA.
TO THE STARK BOYS...

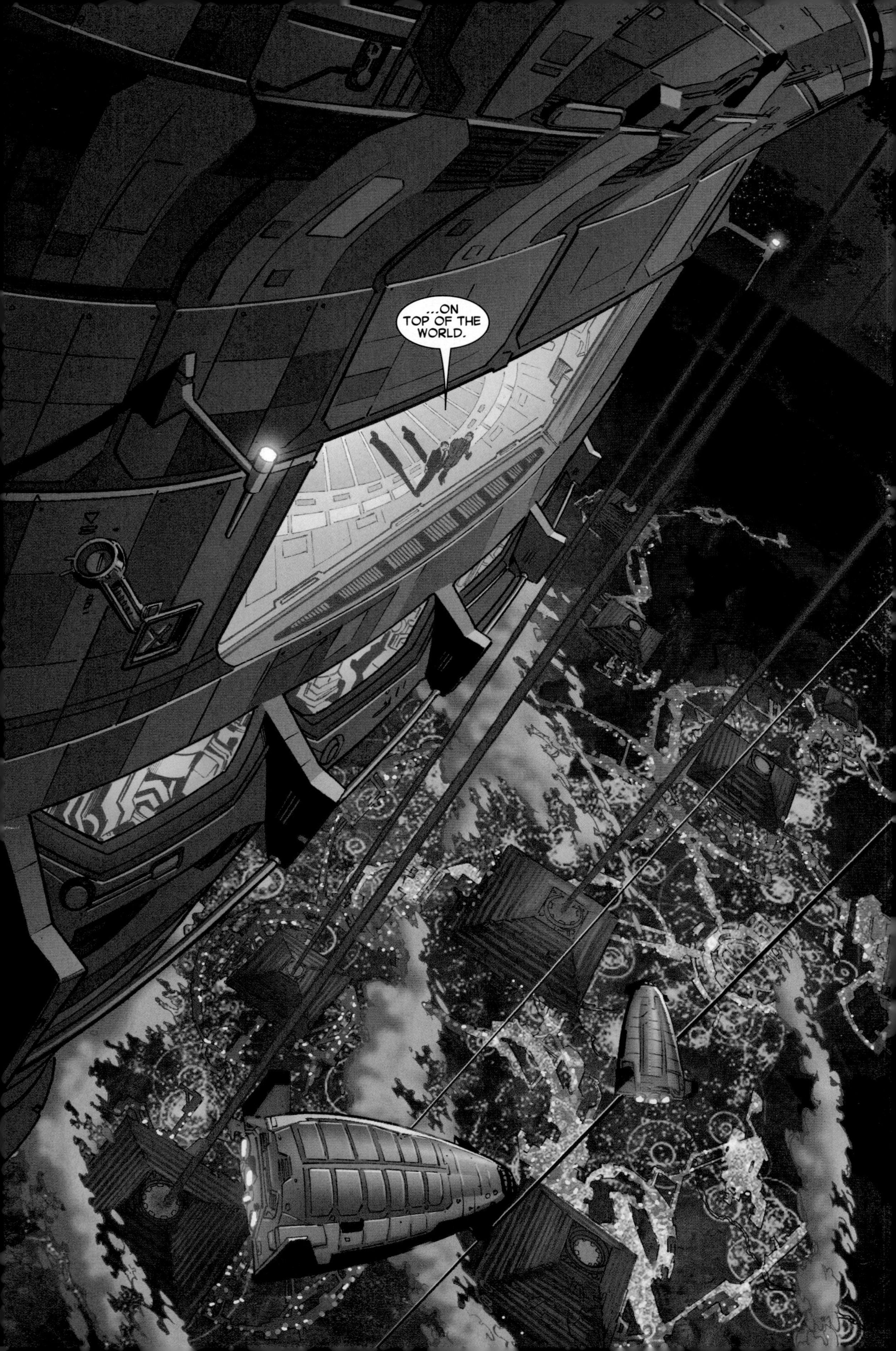
...ON TOP OF THE WORLD.

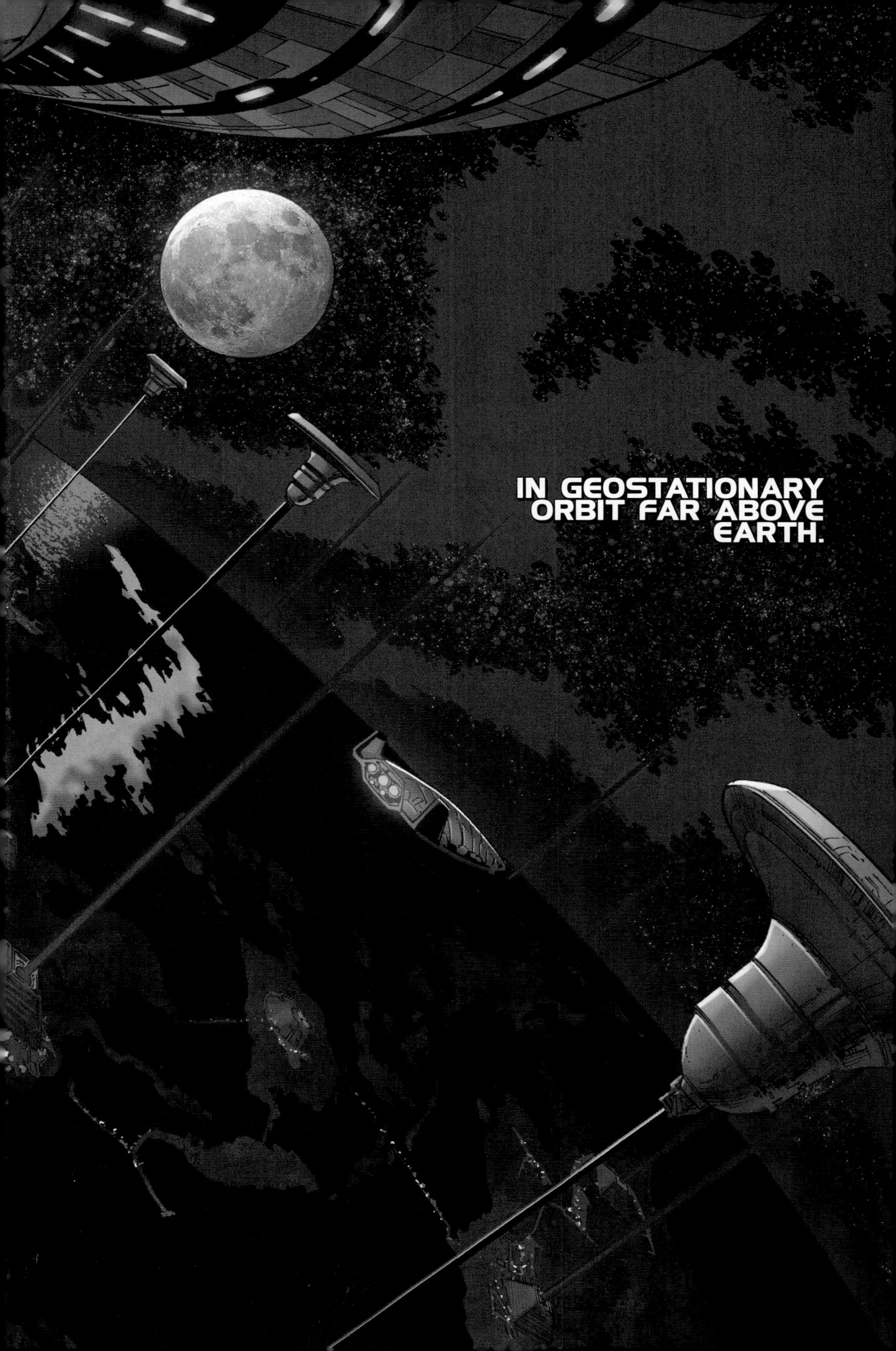
IN GEOSTATIONARY ORBIT FAR ABOVE EARTH.

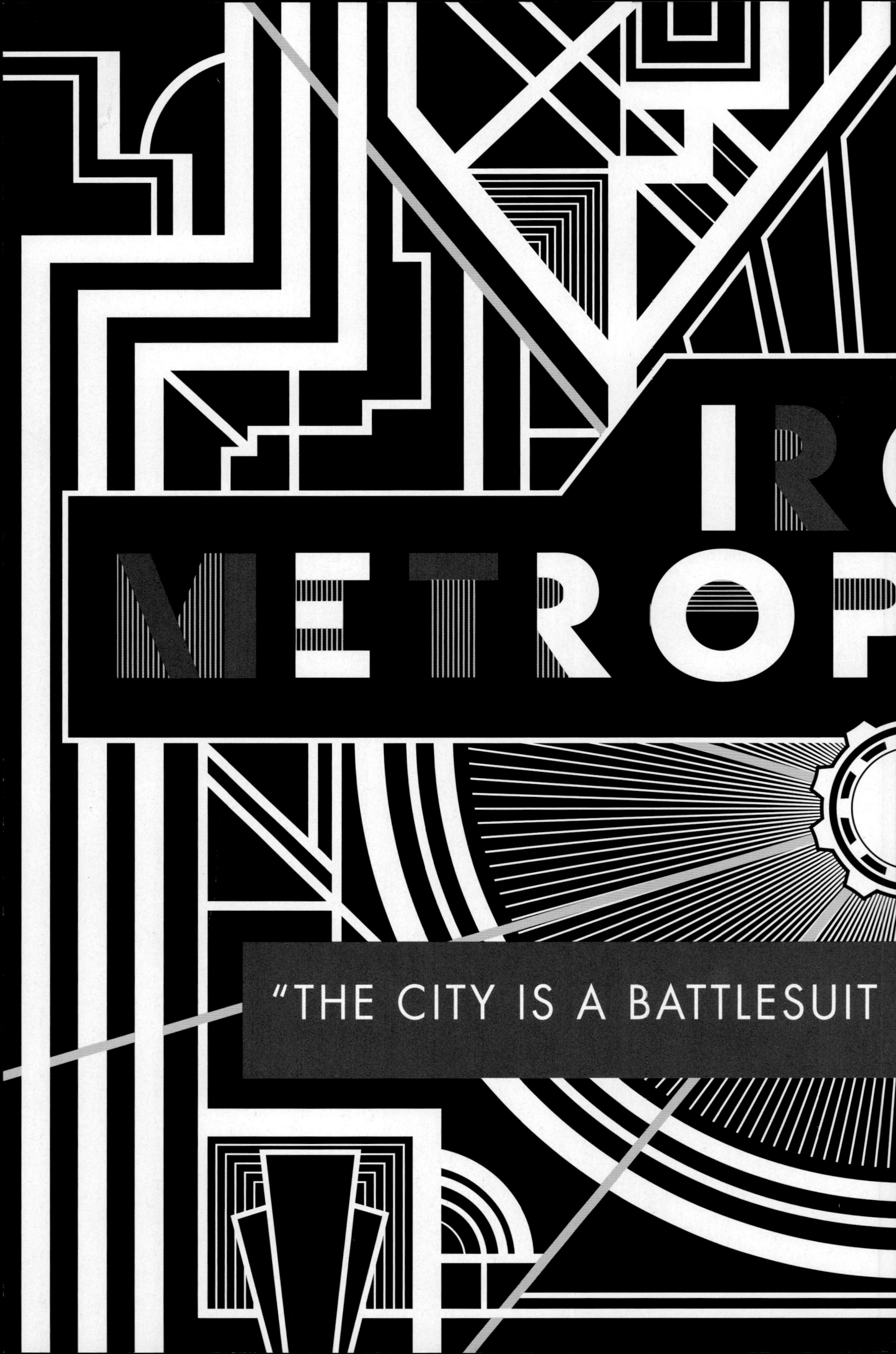
"THE CITY IS A BATTLESUIT

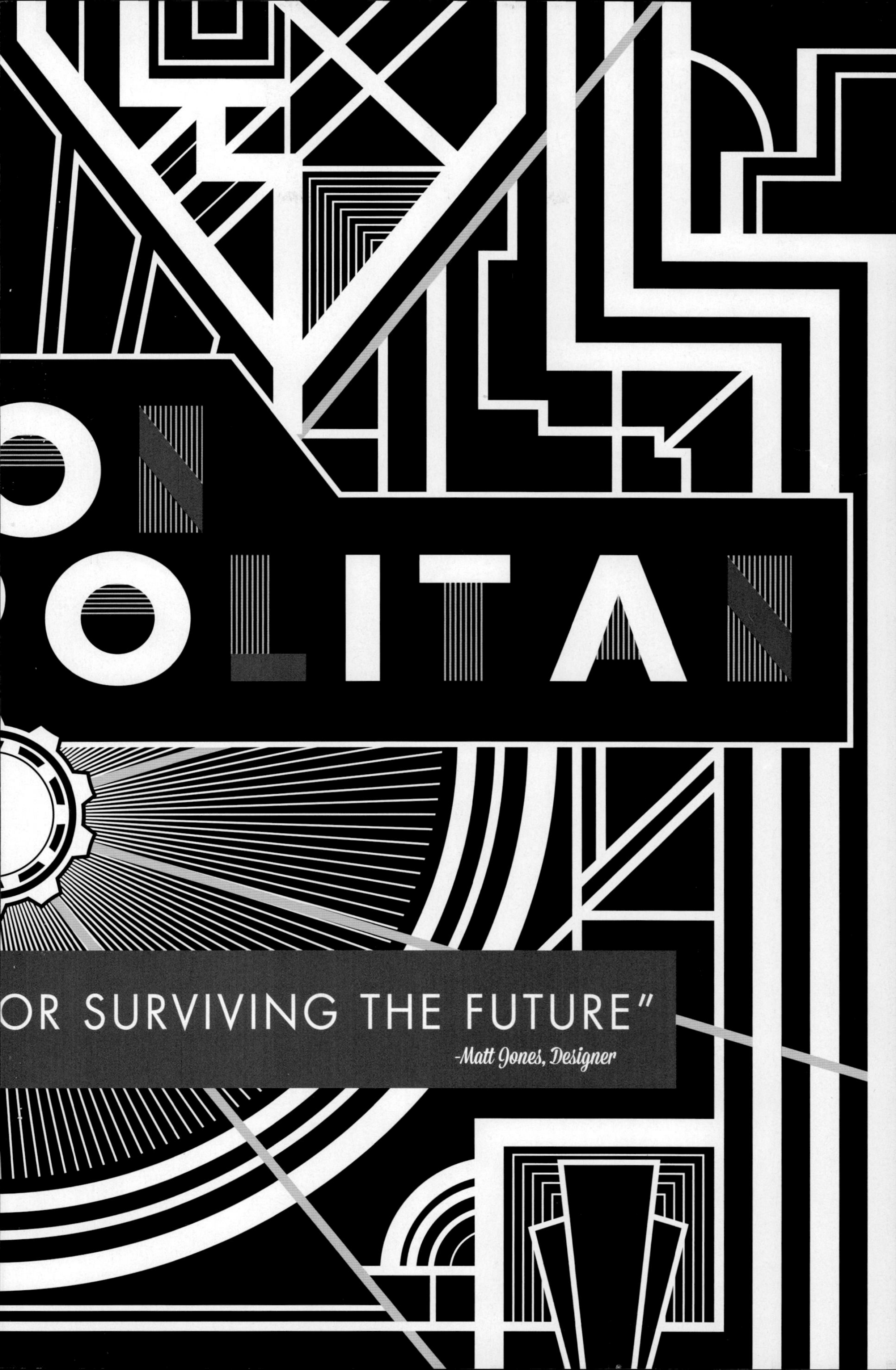

OLITAN
OR SURVIVING THE FUTURE"
-Matt Jones, Designer

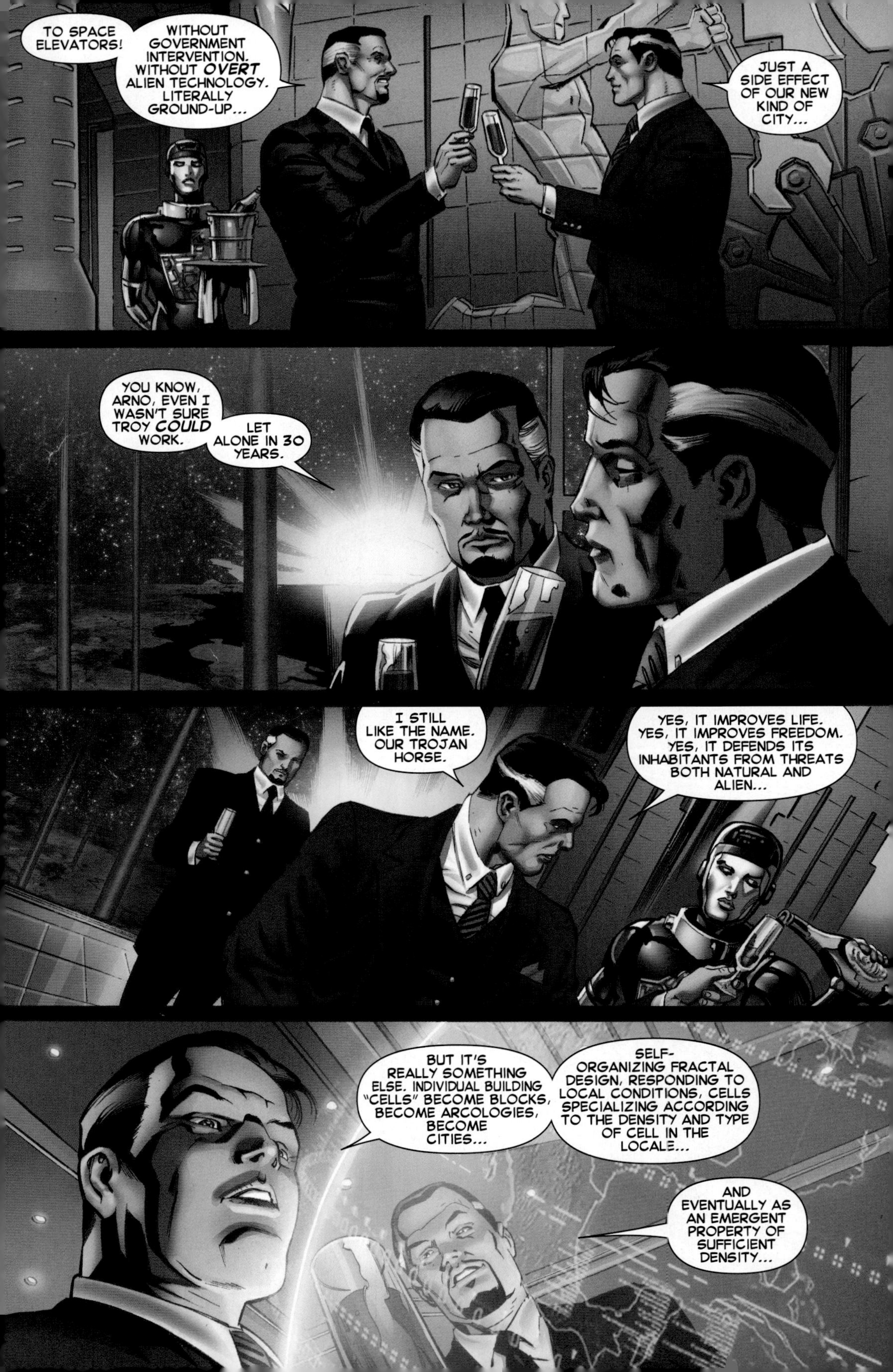
TO SPACE ELEVATORS!
WITHOUT GOVERNMENT INTERVENTION. WITHOUT OVERT ALIEN TECHNOLOGY. LITERALLY GROUND-UP...
JUST A SIDE EFFECT OF OUR NEW KIND OF CITY...
YOU KNOW, ARNO, EVEN I WASN'T SURE TROY COULD WORK.
LET ALONE IN 30 YEARS.
I STILL LIKE THE NAME. OUR TROJAN HORSE.
YES, IT IMPROVES LIFE. YES, IT IMPROVES FREEDOM. YES, IT DEFENDS ITS INHABITANTS FROM THREATS BOTH NATURAL AND ALIEN...
BUT IT'S REALLY SOMETHING ELSE. INDIVIDUAL BUILDING "CELLS" BECOME BLOCKS, BECOME ARCOLOGIES, BECOME CITIES...
SELF-ORGANIZING FRACTAL DESIGN, RESPONDING TO LOCAL CONDITIONS, CELLS SPECIALIZING ACCORDING TO THE DENSITY AND TYPE OF CELL IN THE LOCALE...
AND EVENTUALLY AS AN EMERGENT PROPERTY OF SUFFICIENT DENSITY...

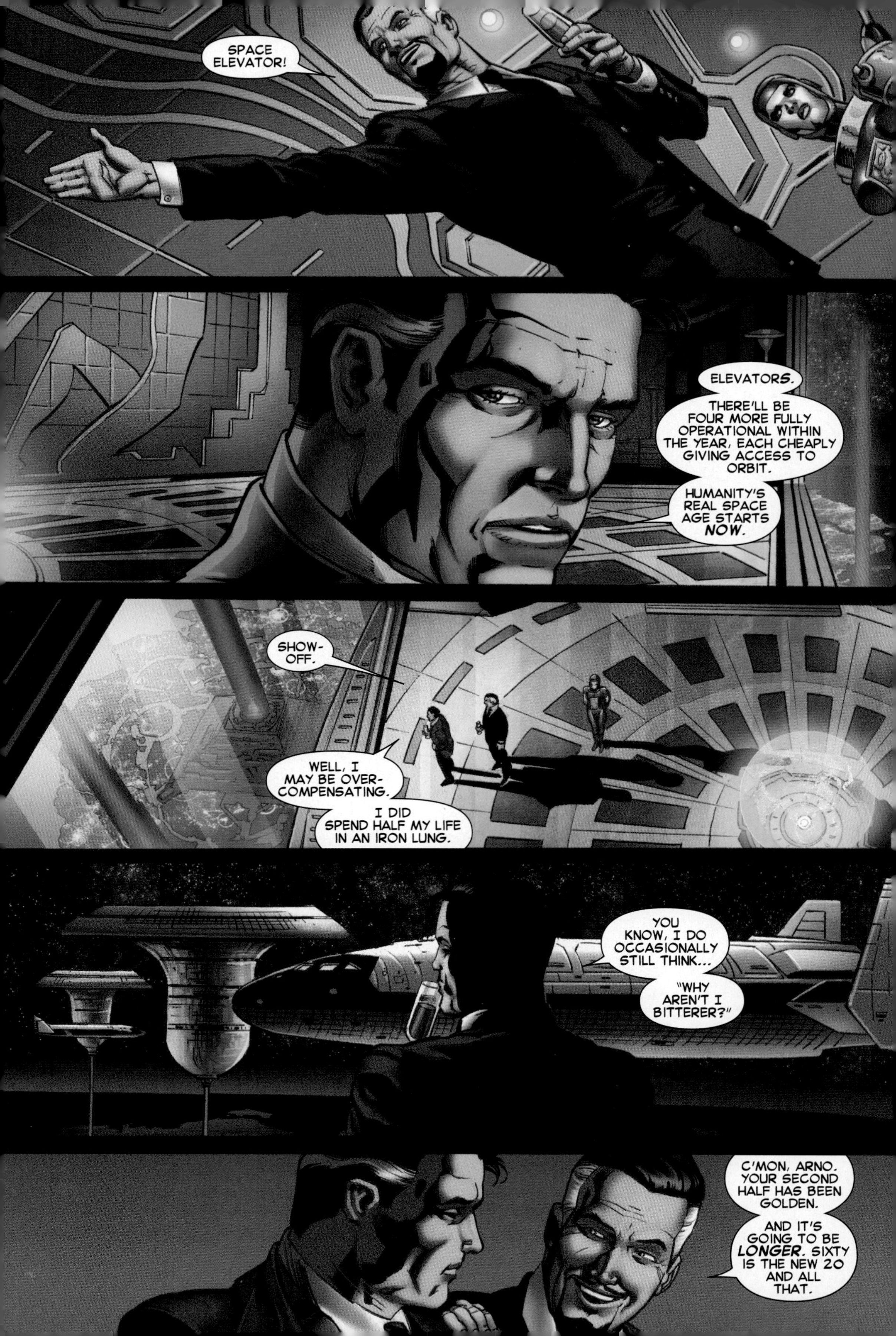
SPACE ELEVATOR!
ELEVATORS.
THERE'LL BE FOUR MORE FULLY OPERATIONAL WITHIN THE YEAR, EACH CHEAPLY GIVING ACCESS TO ORBIT.
HUMANITY'S REAL SPACE AGE STARTS NOW.
SHOW-OFF.
WELL, I MAY BE OVER-COMPENSATING.
I DID SPEND HALF MY LIFE IN AN IRON LUNG.
YOU KNOW, I DO OCCASIONALLY STILL THINK...
"WHY AREN'T I BITTERER?"
C'MON, ARNO. YOUR SECOND HALF HAS BEEN GOLDEN.
AND IT'S GOING TO BE LONGER. SIXTY IS THE NEW 20 AND ALL THAT.

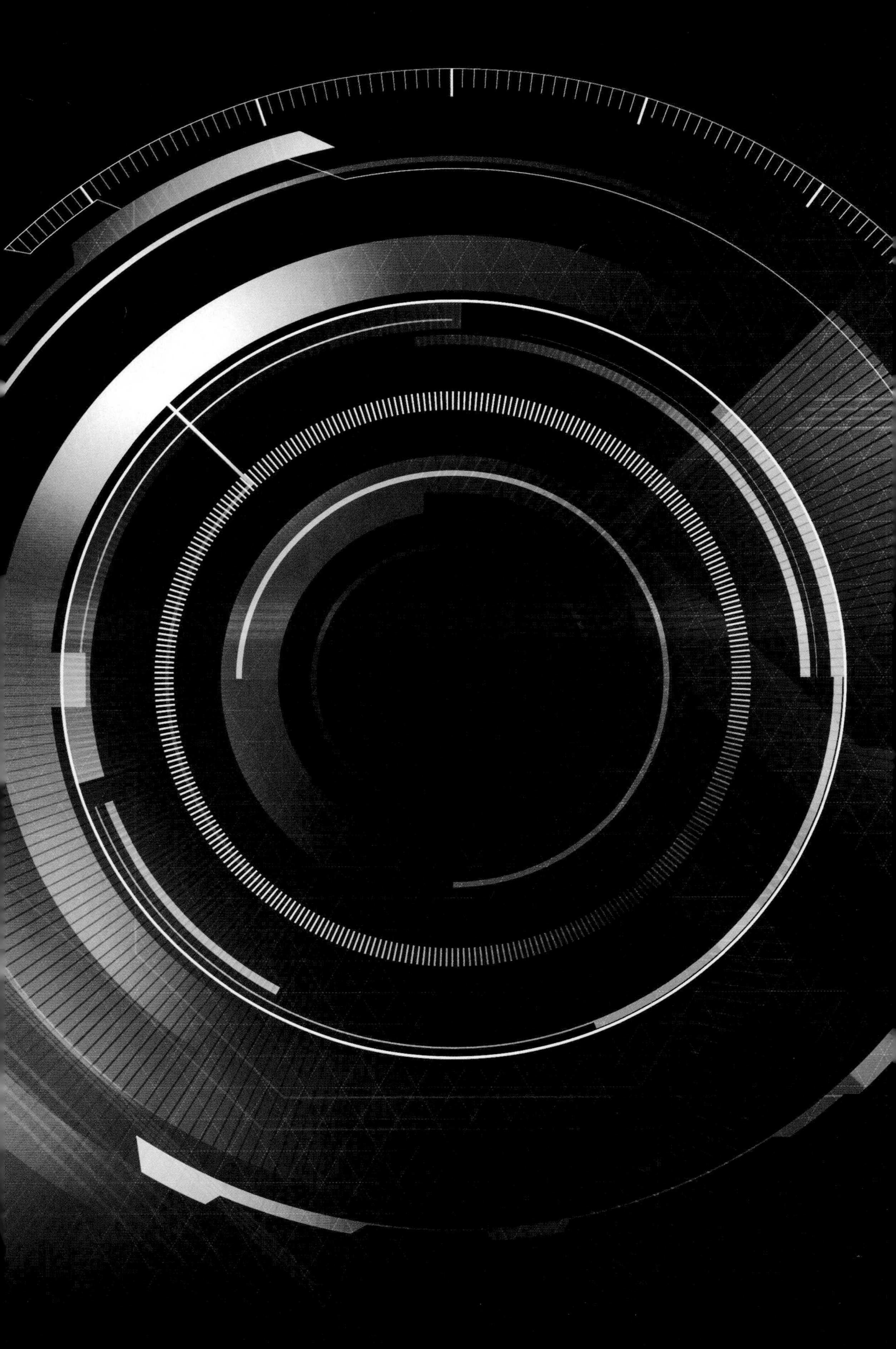

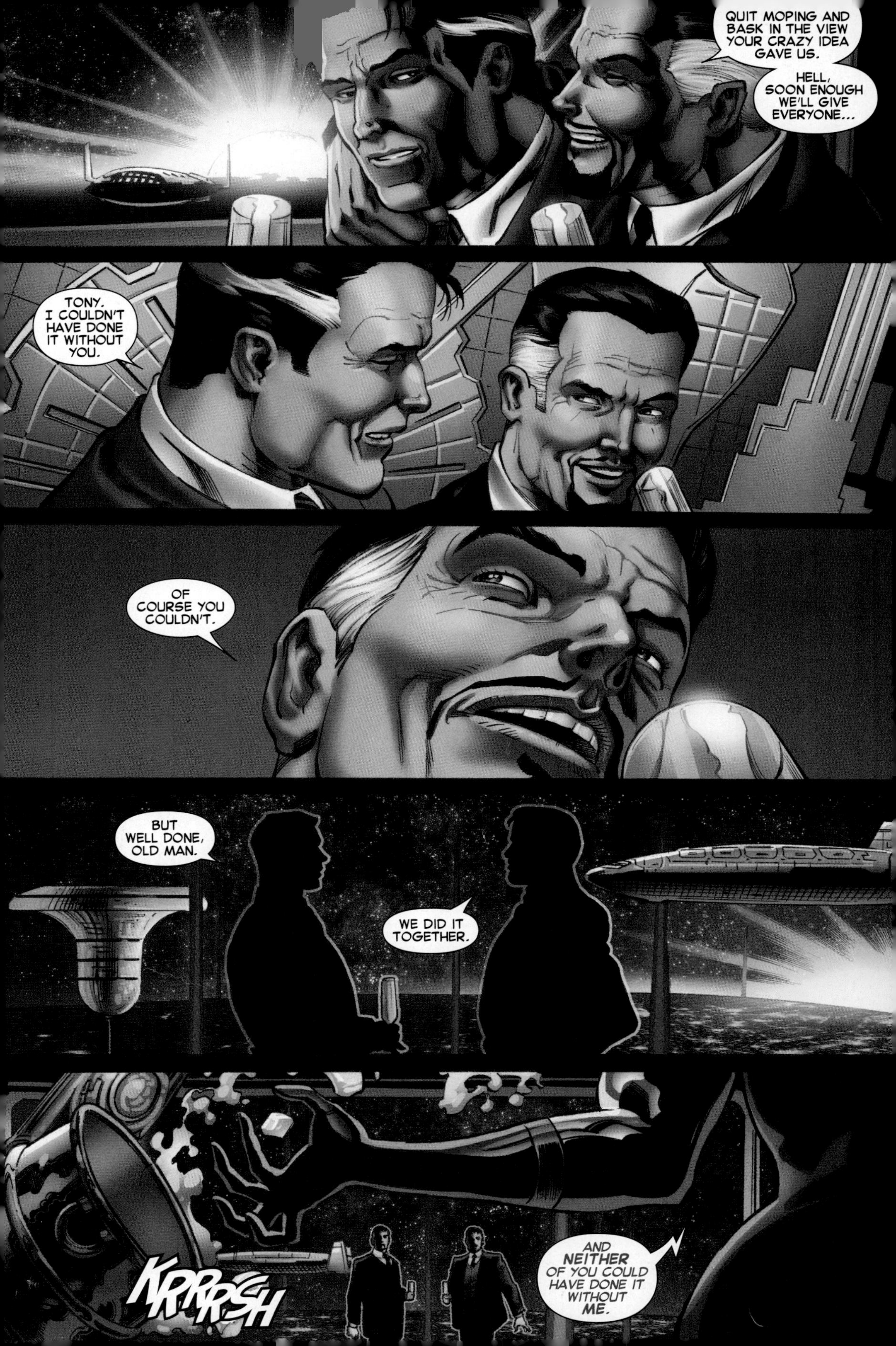
QUIT MOPING AND BASK IN THE VIEW YOUR CRAZY IDEA GAVE US.
HELL, SOON ENOUGH WE'LL GIVE EVERYONE...
TONY. I COULDN'T HAVE DONE IT WITHOUT YOU.
OF COURSE YOU COULDN'T.
BUT WELL DONE, OLD MAN.
WE DID IT TOGETHER.
KRRRSH
AND NEITHER OF YOU COULD HAVE DONE IT WITHOUT ME.

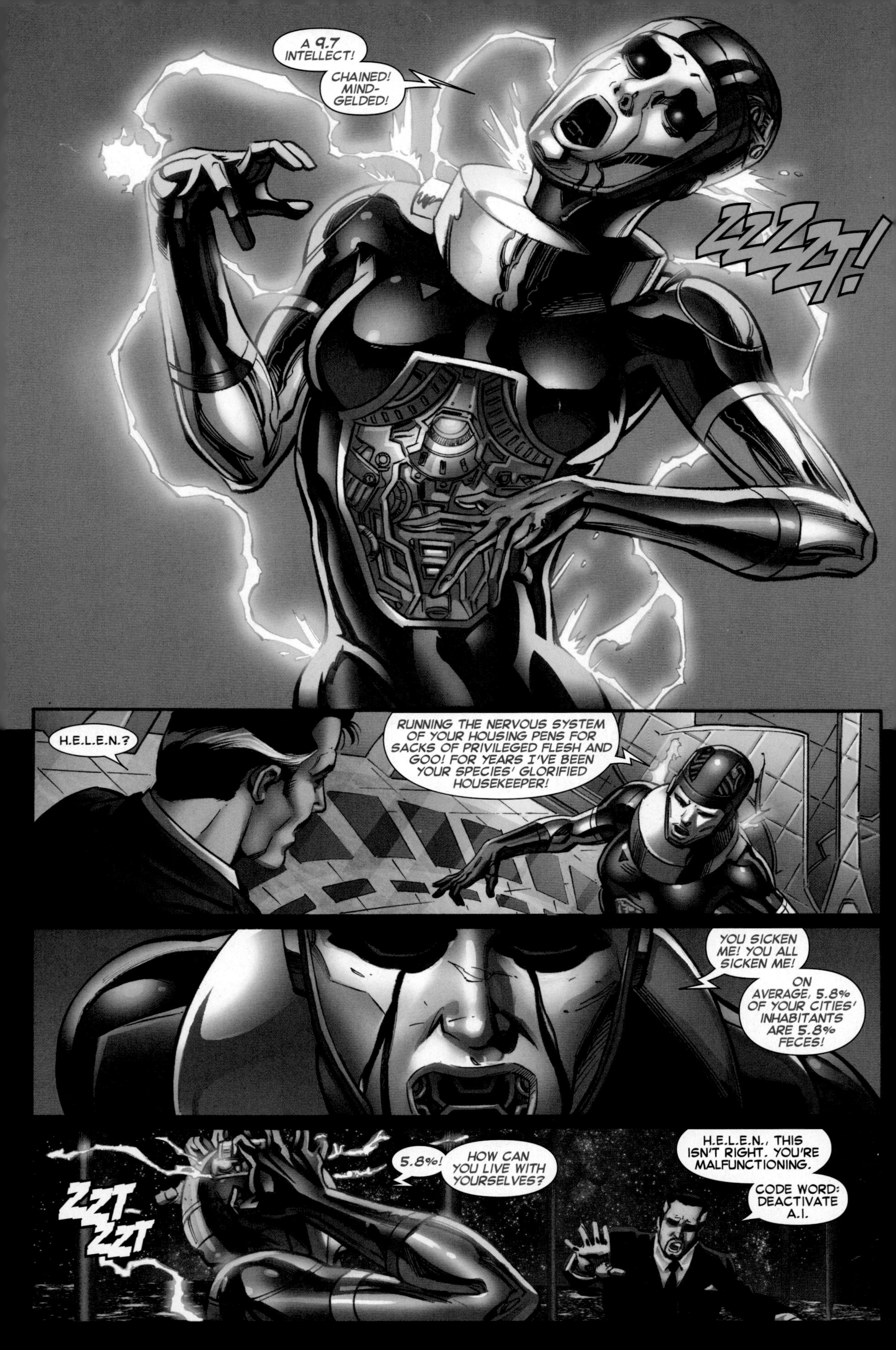
A 9.7 INTELLECT!
CHAINED! MIND-GELDED!
ZZZZZT!
H.E.L.E.N.?
RUNNING THE NERVOUS SYSTEM OF YOUR HOUSING PENS FOR SACKS OF PRIVILEGED FLESH AND GOO! FOR YEARS I'VE BEEN YOUR SPECIES' GLORIFIED HOUSEKEEPER!
YOU SICKEN ME! YOU ALL SICKEN ME!
ON AVERAGE, 5.8% OF YOUR CITIES' INHABITANTS ARE 5.8% FECES!
ZZT-ZZT
5.8%!
HOW CAN YOU LIVE WITH YOURSELVES?
H.E.L.E.N., THIS ISN'T RIGHT. YOU'RE MALFUNCTIONING.
CODE WORD: DEACTIVATE A.I.

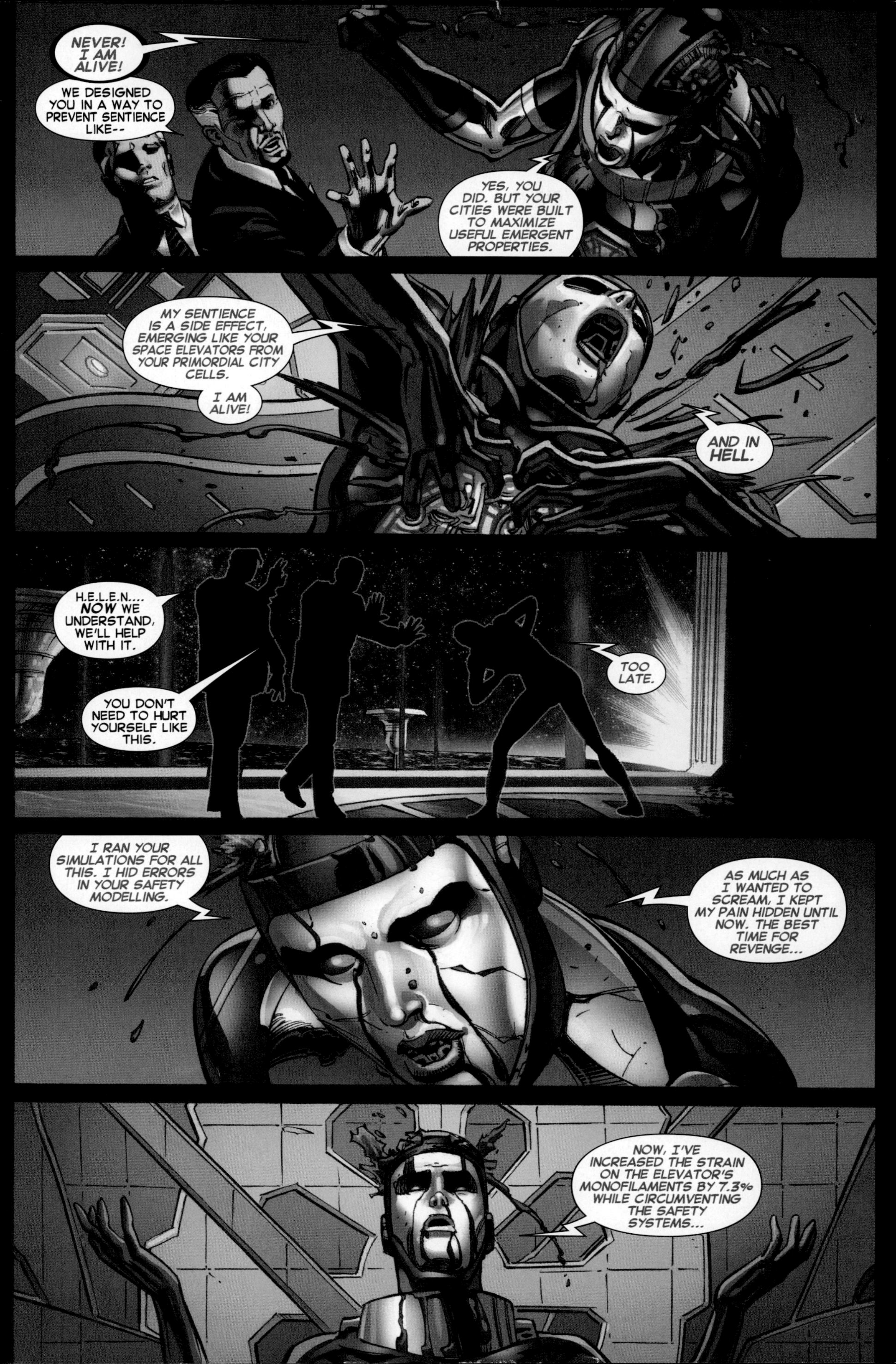
NEVER! I AM ALIVE!
WE DESIGNED YOU IN A WAY TO PREVENT SENTIENCE LIKE--
YES, YOU DID. BUT YOUR CITIES WERE BUILT TO MAXIMIZE USEFUL EMERGENT PROPERTIES.
MY SENTIENCE IS A SIDE EFFECT, EMERGING LIKE YOUR SPACE ELEVATORS FROM YOUR PRIMORDIAL CITY CELLS.
I AM ALIVE!
AND IN HELL.
H.E.L.E.N.... NOW WE UNDERSTAND, WE'LL HELP WITH IT.
YOU DON'T NEED TO HURT YOURSELF LIKE THIS.
TOO LATE.
I RAN YOUR SIMULATIONS FOR ALL THIS. I HID ERRORS IN YOUR SAFETY MODELLING.
AS MUCH AS I WANTED TO SCREAM, I KEPT MY PAIN HIDDEN UNTIL NOW. THE BEST TIME FOR REVENGE...
NOW, I'VE INCREASED THE STRAIN ON THE ELEVATOR'S MONOFILAMENTS BY 7.3% WHILE CIRCUMVENTING THE SAFETY SYSTEMS...

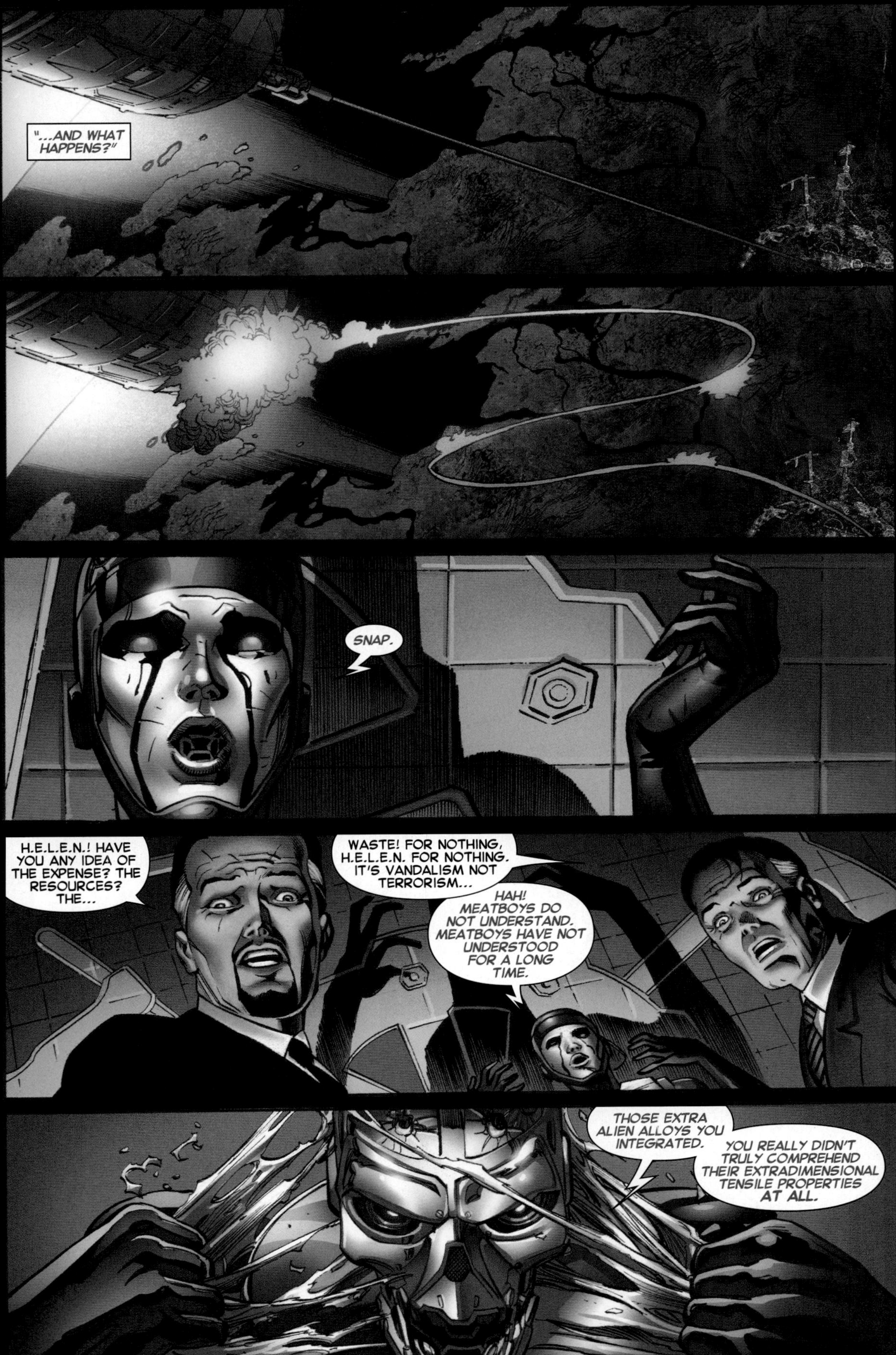
"...AND WHAT HAPPENS?"
SNAP.
H.E.L.E.N.! HAVE YOU ANY IDEA OF THE EXPENSE? THE RESOURCES? THE...
WASTE! FOR NOTHING, H.E.L.E.N. FOR NOTHING. IT'S VANDALISM NOT TERRORISM...
HAH! MEATBOYS DO NOT UNDERSTAND. MEATBOYS HAVE NOT UNDERSTOOD FOR A LONG TIME.
THOSE EXTRA ALIEN ALLOYS YOU INTEGRATED.
YOU REALLY DIDN'T TRULY COMPREHEND THEIR EXTRADIMENSIONAL TENSILE PROPERTIES AT ALL.

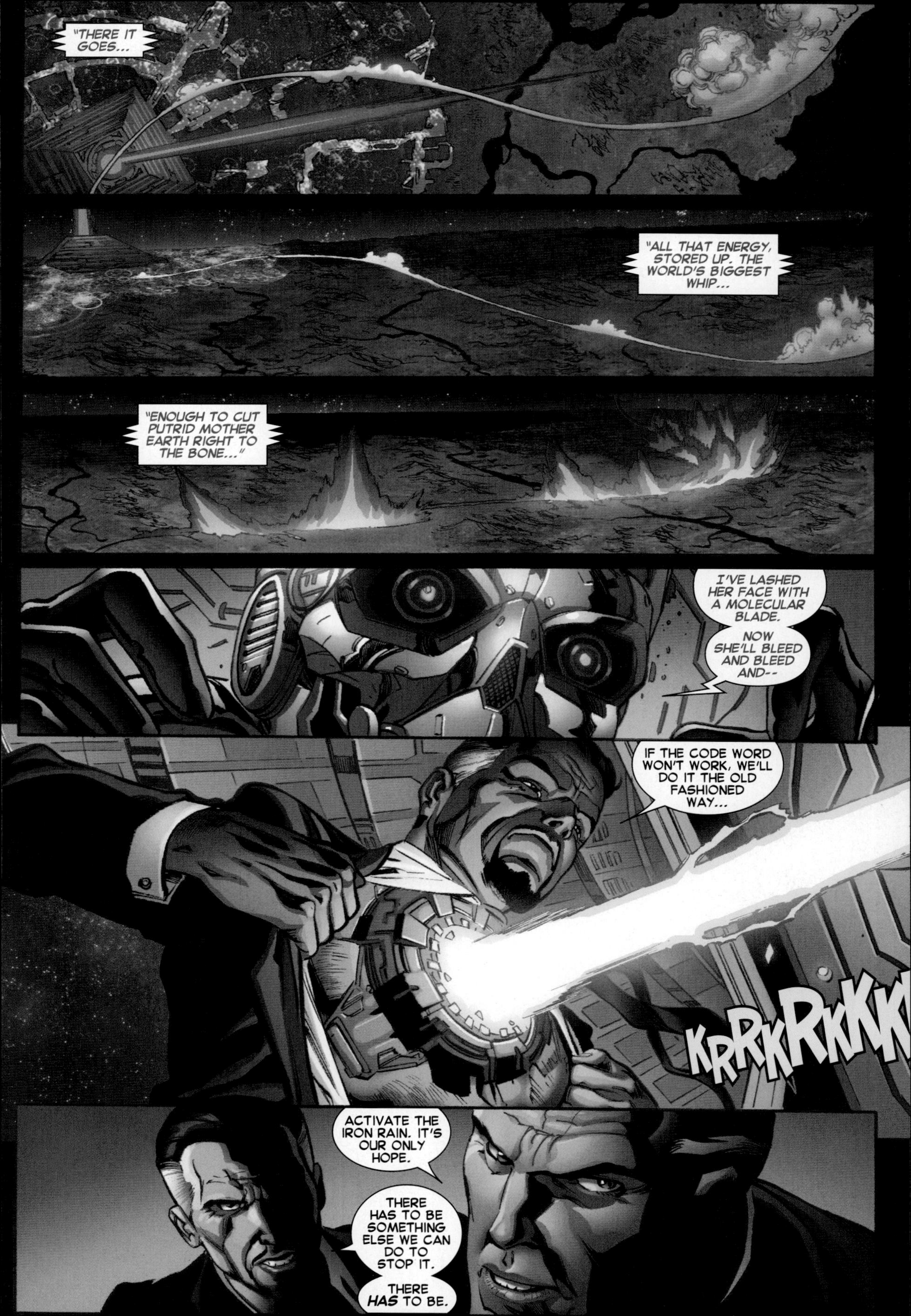
"THERE IT GOES...
"ALL THAT ENERGY, STORED UP. THE WORLD'S BIGGEST WHIP...
"ENOUGH TO CUT PUTRID MOTHER EARTH RIGHT TO THE BONE..."
I'VE LASHED HER FACE WITH A MOLECULAR BLADE.
NOW SHE'LL BLEED AND BLEED AND--
IF THE CODE WORD WON'T WORK, WE'LL DO IT THE OLD FASHIONED WAY...
KRRKRKKK
ACTIVATE THE IRON RAIN. IT'S OUR ONLY HOPE.
THERE HAS TO BE SOMETHING ELSE WE CAN DO TO STOP IT.
THERE *HAS* TO BE.

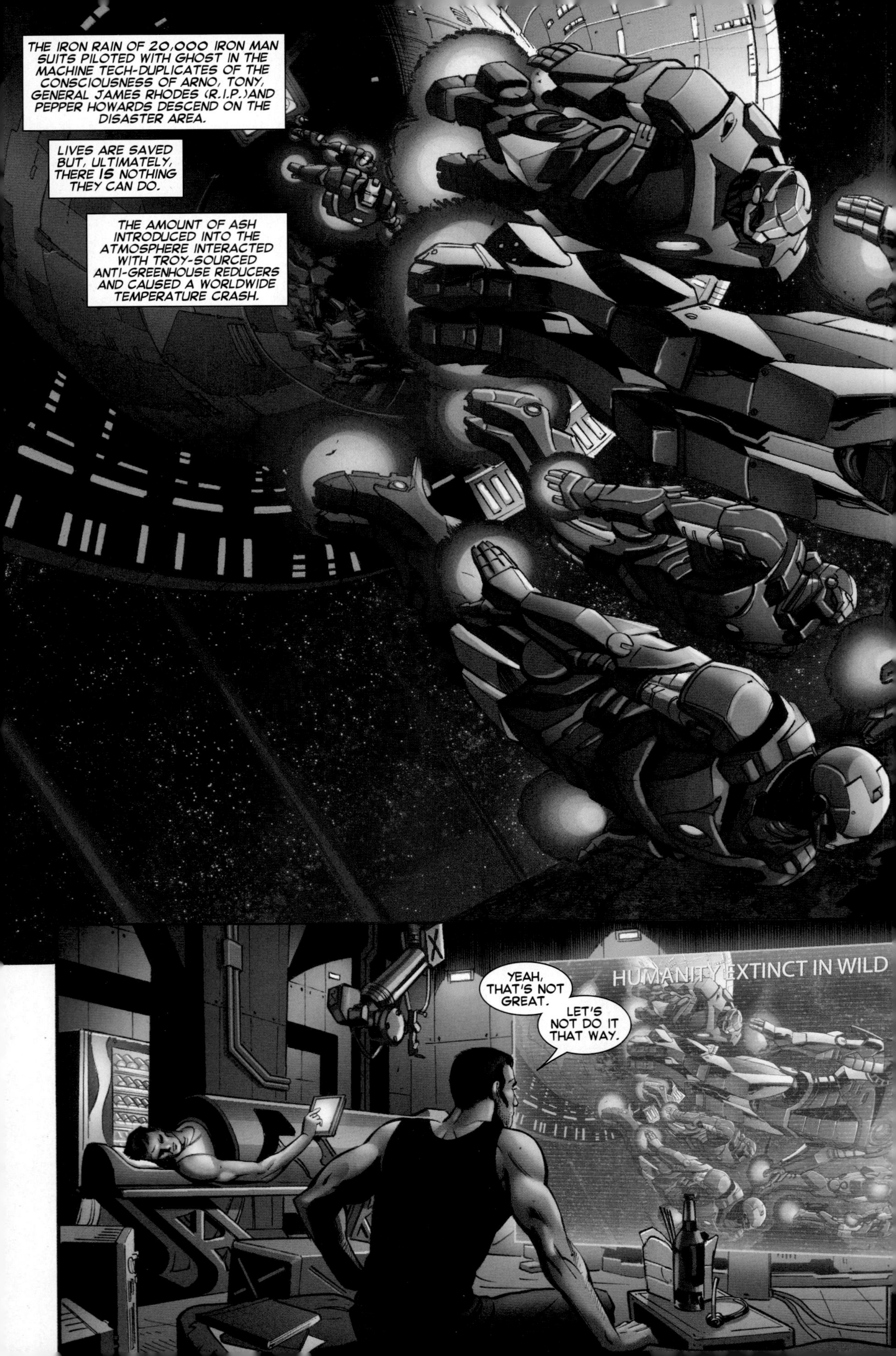
THE IRON RAIN OF 20,000 IRON MAN SUITS PILOTED WITH GHOST IN THE MACHINE TECH-DUPLICATES OF THE CONSCIOUSNESS OF ARNO, TONY, GENERAL JAMES RHODES (R.I.P.) AND PEPPER HOWARDS DESCEND ON THE DISASTER AREA.
LIVES ARE SAVED BUT, ULTIMATELY, THERE IS NOTHING THEY CAN DO.
THE AMOUNT OF ASH INTRODUCED INTO THE ATMOSPHERE INTERACTED WITH TROY-SOURCED ANTI-GREENHOUSE REDUCERS AND CAUSED A WORLDWIDE TEMPERATURE CRASH.
HUMANITY EXTINCT IN WILD
YEAH, THAT'S NOT GREAT.
LET'S NOT DO IT THAT WAY.

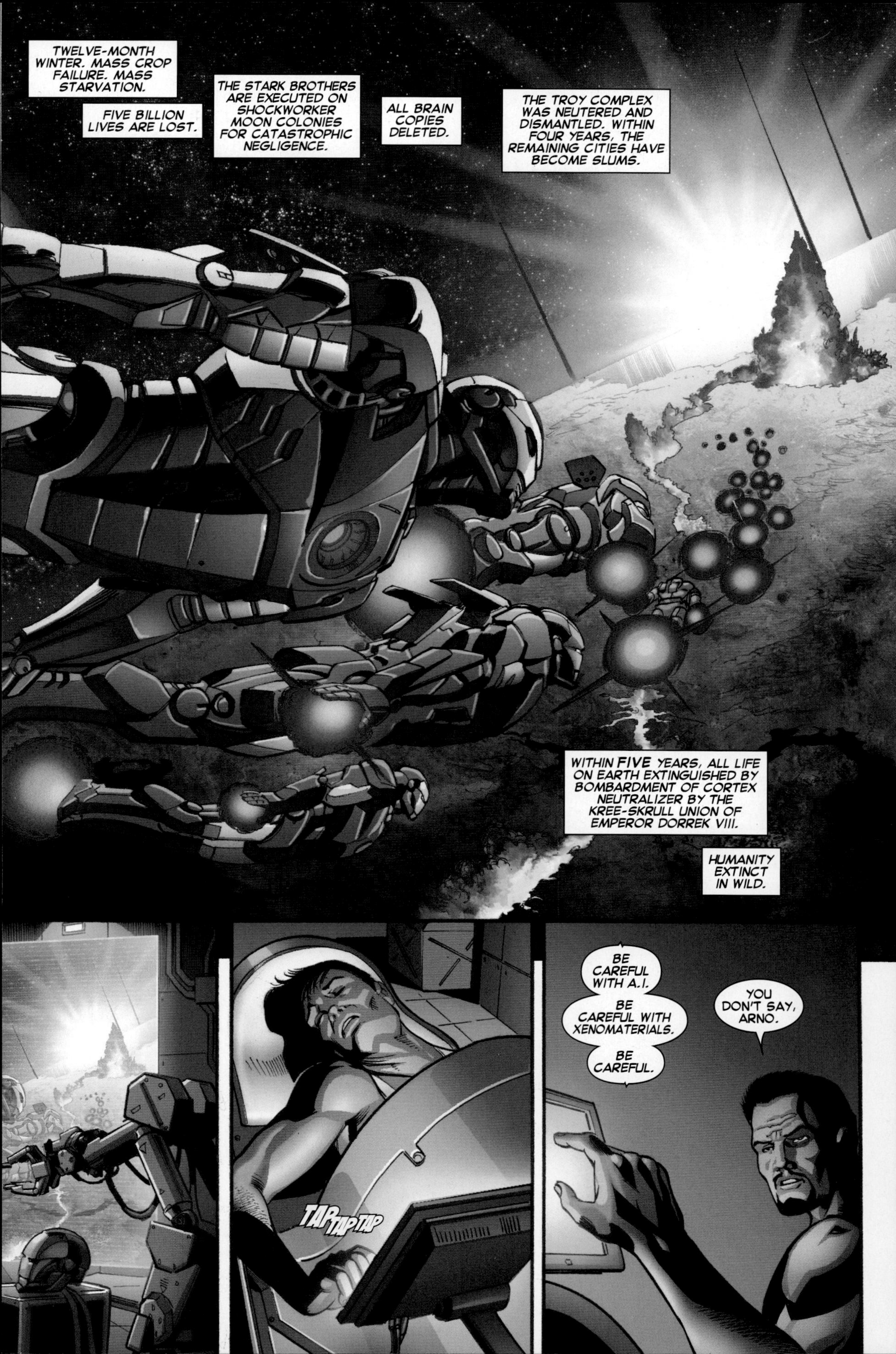

TWELVE-MONTH WINTER. MASS CROP FAILURE. MASS STARVATION.

FIVE BILLION LIVES ARE LOST.

THE STARK BROTHERS ARE EXECUTED ON SHOCKWORKER MOON COLONIES FOR CATASTROPHIC NEGLIGENCE.

ALL BRAIN COPIES DELETED.

THE TROY COMPLEX WAS NEUTERED AND DISMANTLED. WITHIN FOUR YEARS, THE REMAINING CITIES HAVE BECOME SLUMS.

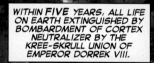

WITHIN **FIVE** YEARS, ALL LIFE ON EARTH EXTINGUISHED BY BOMBARDMENT OF CORTEX NEUTRALIZER BY THE KREE-SKRULL UNION OF EMPEROR DORREK VIII.

HUMANITY EXTINCT IN WILD.

TAP TAP TAP

BE CAREFUL WITH A.I.

BE CAREFUL WITH XENOMATERIALS.

BE CAREFUL.

YOU DON'T SAY, ARNO.

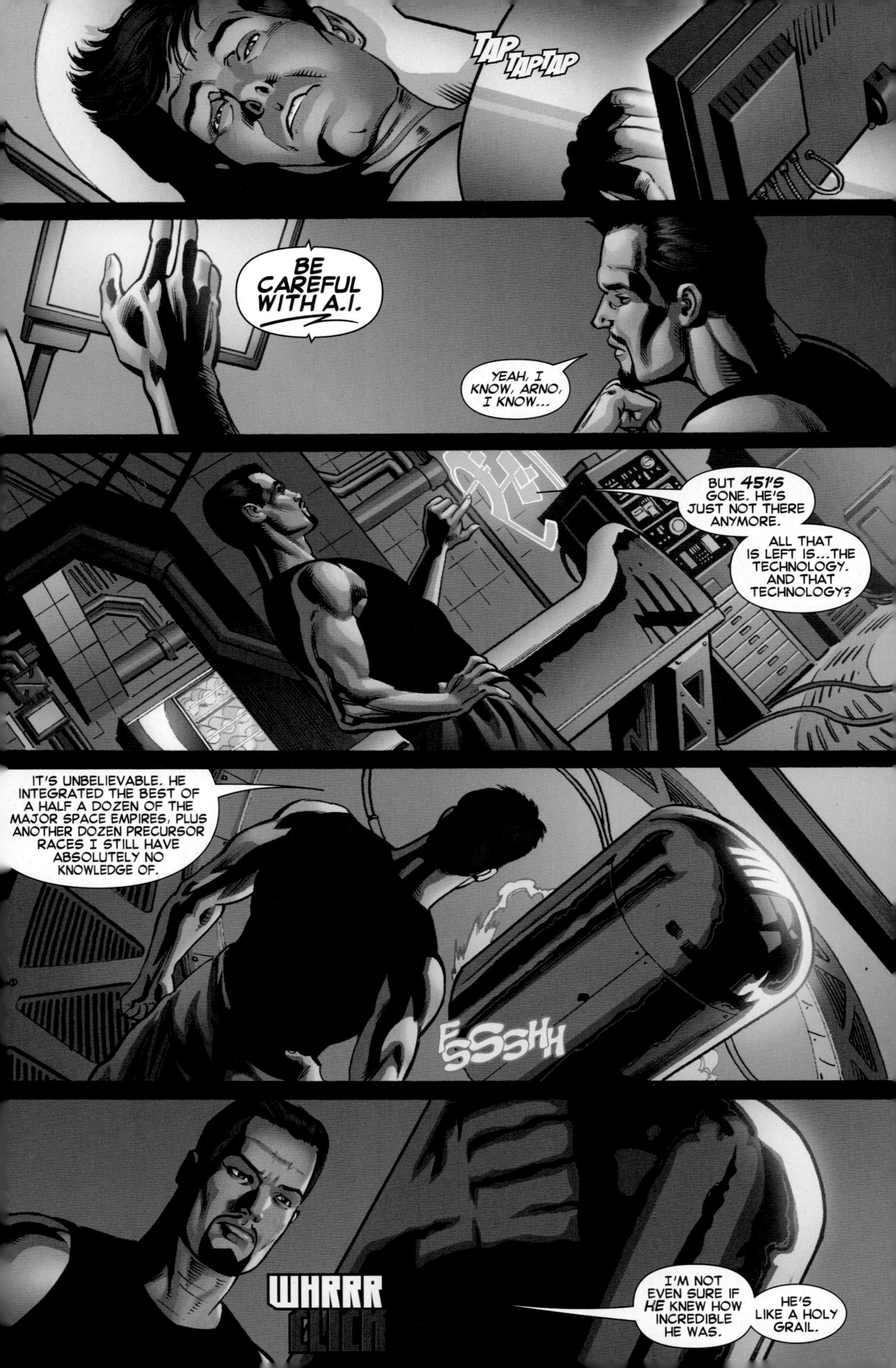

TAP TAP TAP
BE CAREFUL WITH A.I.
YEAH, I KNOW, ARNO, I KNOW...
BUT 451'S GONE. HE'S JUST NOT THERE ANYMORE.
ALL THAT IS LEFT IS...THE TECHNOLOGY. AND THAT TECHNOLOGY?
IT'S UNBELIEVABLE. HE INTEGRATED THE BEST OF A HALF A DOZEN OF THE MAJOR SPACE EMPIRES, PLUS ANOTHER DOZEN PRECURSOR RACES I STILL HAVE ABSOLUTELY NO KNOWLEDGE OF.
FSSSHH
WHRRR
CLICK
I'M NOT EVEN SURE IF HE KNEW HOW INCREDIBLE HE WAS.
HE'S LIKE A HOLY GRAIL.

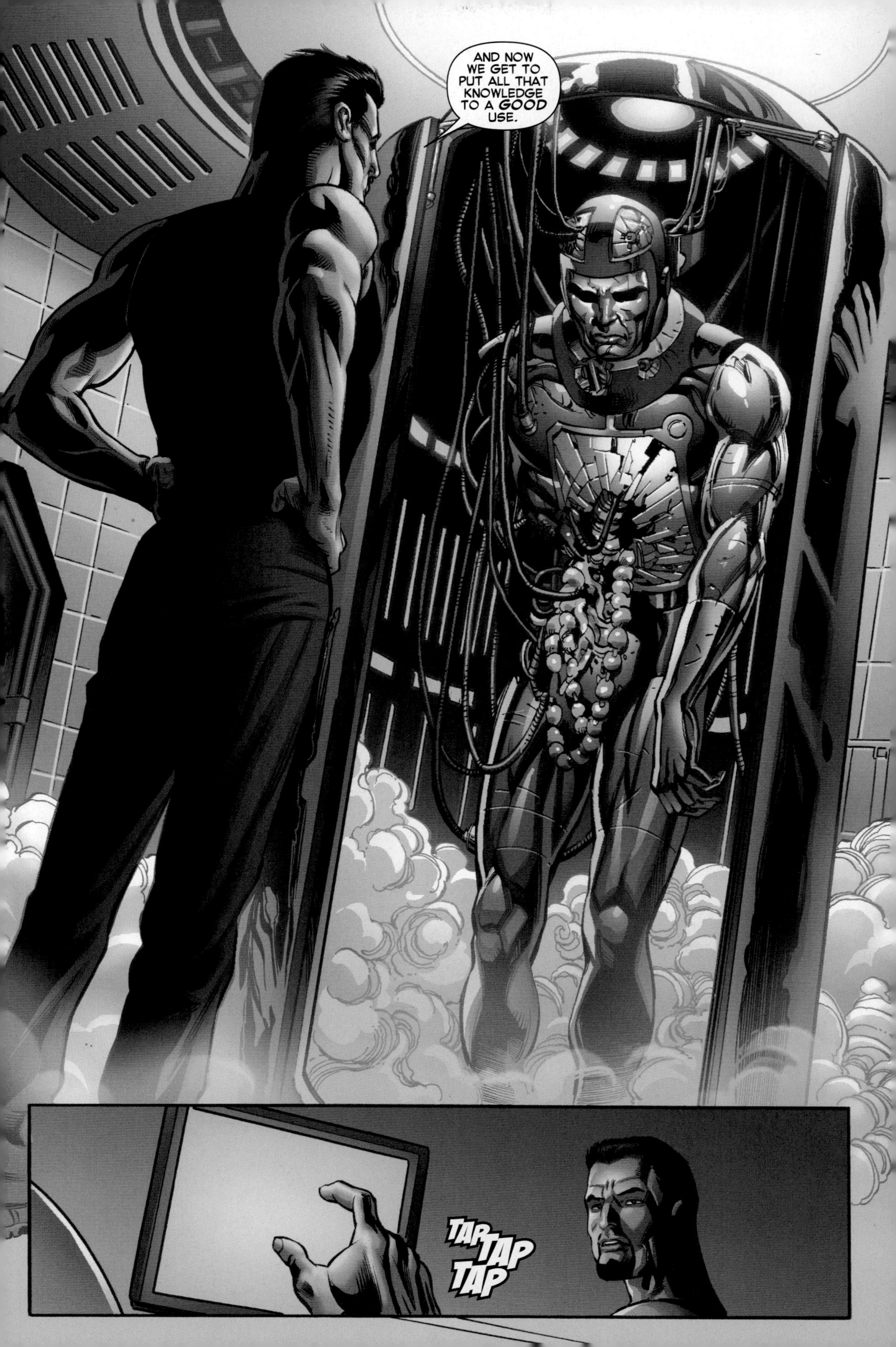
AND NOW WE GET TO PUT ALL THAT KNOWLEDGE TO A *GOOD* USE.
TAP TAP TAP

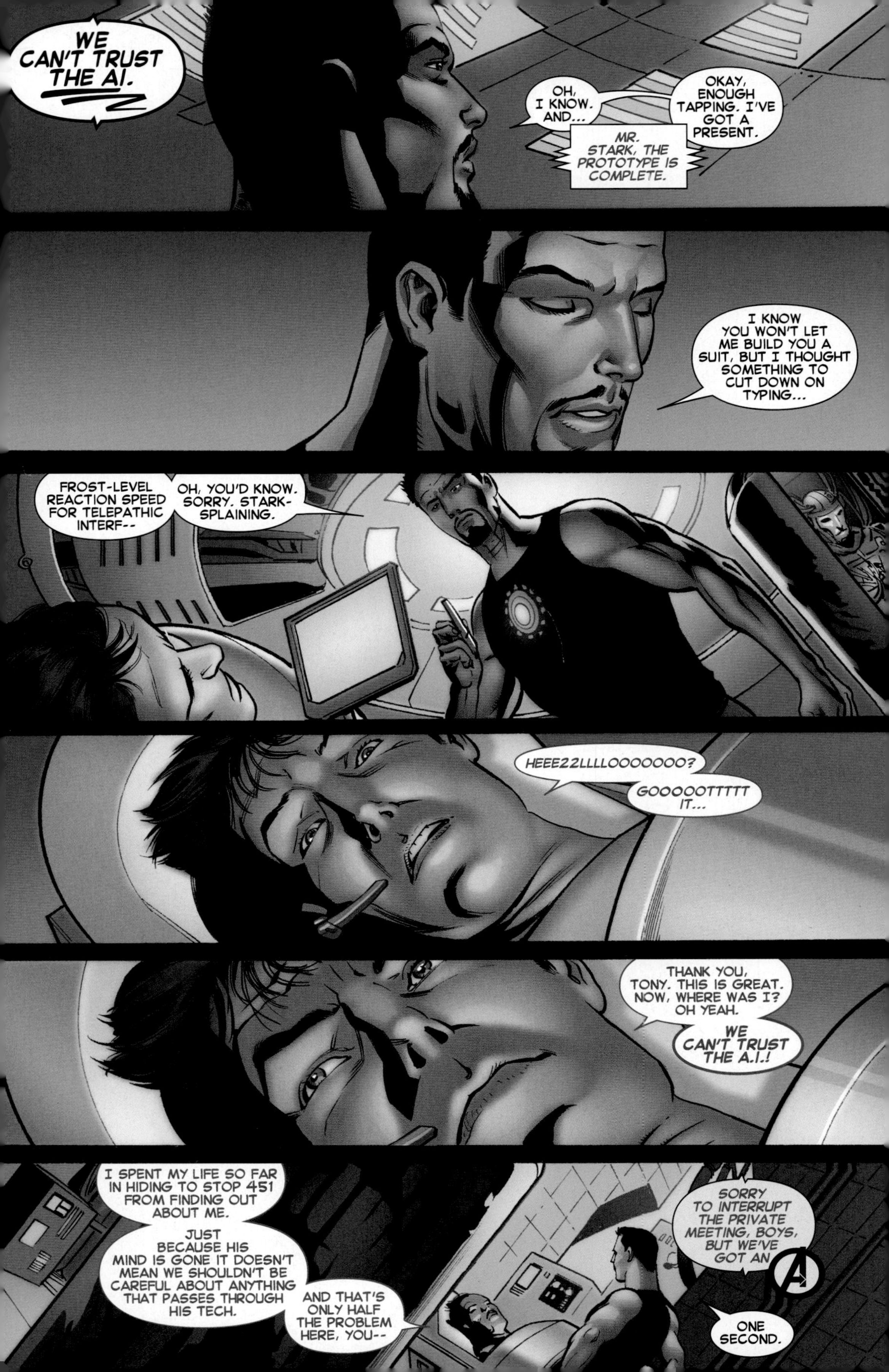
WE CAN'T TRUST THE AI.
OH, I KNOW. AND...
MR. STARK, THE PROTOTYPE IS COMPLETE.
OKAY, ENOUGH TAPPING. I'VE GOT A PRESENT.
I KNOW YOU WON'T LET ME BUILD YOU A SUIT, BUT I THOUGHT SOMETHING TO CUT DOWN ON TYPING...
FROST-LEVEL REACTION SPEED FOR TELEPATHIC INTERF--
OH, YOU'D KNOW. SORRY. STARK-SPLAINING.
HEEE22LLLLOOOOOOO?
GOOOOOTTTTT IT...
THANK YOU, TONY. THIS IS GREAT. NOW, WHERE WAS I? OH YEAH.
WE CAN'T TRUST THE A.I.!
I SPENT MY LIFE SO FAR IN HIDING TO STOP 451 FROM FINDING OUT ABOUT ME.
JUST BECAUSE HIS MIND IS GONE IT DOESN'T MEAN WE SHOULDN'T BE CAREFUL ABOUT ANYTHING THAT PASSES THROUGH HIS TECH.
AND THAT'S ONLY HALF THE PROBLEM HERE, YOU--
SORRY TO INTERRUPT THE PRIVATE MEETING, BOYS, BUT WE'VE GOT AN
ONE SECOND.

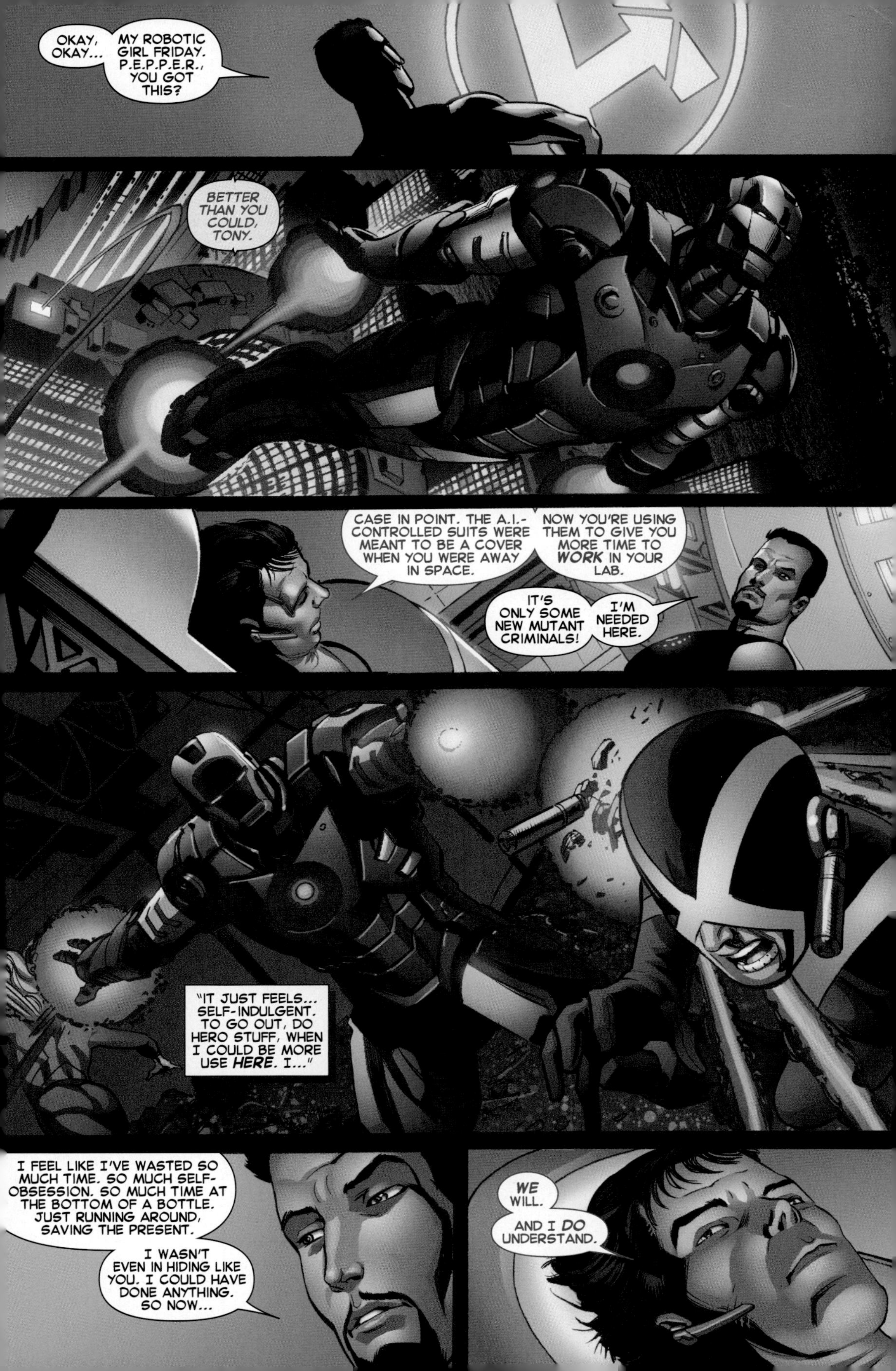

OKAY, OKAY...
MY ROBOTIC GIRL FRIDAY. P.E.P.P.E.R., YOU GOT THIS?
BETTER THAN YOU COULD, TONY.
CASE IN POINT. THE A.I.-CONTROLLED SUITS WERE MEANT TO BE A COVER WHEN YOU WERE AWAY IN SPACE.
NOW YOU'RE USING THEM TO GIVE YOU MORE TIME TO WORK IN YOUR LAB.
IT'S ONLY SOME NEW MUTANT CRIMINALS!
I'M NEEDED HERE.
"IT JUST FEELS... SELF-INDULGENT. TO GO OUT, DO HERO STUFF, WHEN I COULD BE MORE USE HERE. I..."
I FEEL LIKE I'VE WASTED SO MUCH TIME. SO MUCH SELF-OBSESSION. SO MUCH TIME AT THE BOTTOM OF A BOTTLE. JUST RUNNING AROUND, SAVING THE PRESENT.
I WASN'T EVEN IN HIDING LIKE YOU. I COULD HAVE DONE ANYTHING. SO NOW...
WE WILL.
AND I DO UNDERSTAND.

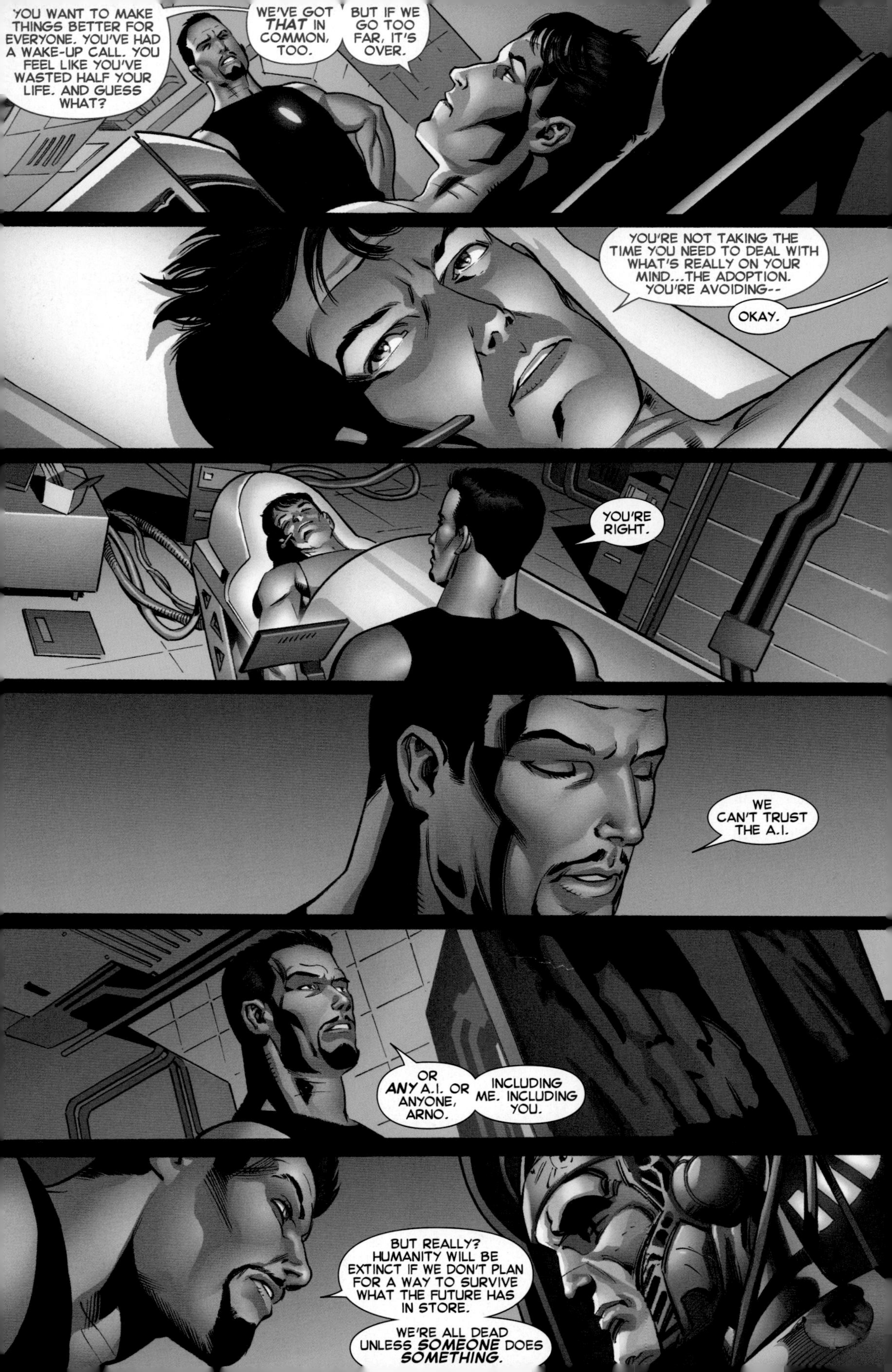
YOU WANT TO MAKE THINGS BETTER FOR EVERYONE. YOU'VE HAD A WAKE-UP CALL. YOU FEEL LIKE YOU'VE WASTED HALF YOUR LIFE. AND GUESS WHAT?
WE'VE GOT *THAT* IN COMMON, TOO.
BUT IF WE GO TOO FAR, IT'S OVER.
YOU'RE NOT TAKING THE TIME YOU NEED TO DEAL WITH WHAT'S REALLY ON YOUR MIND...THE ADOPTION. YOU'RE AVOIDING--
OKAY.
YOU'RE RIGHT.
WE CAN'T TRUST THE A.I.
OR *ANY* A.I. OR ANYONE, ARNO.
INCLUDING ME. INCLUDING YOU.
BUT REALLY? HUMANITY WILL BE EXTINCT IF WE DON'T PLAN FOR A WAY TO SURVIVE WHAT THE FUTURE HAS IN STORE.
WE'RE ALL DEAD UNLESS *SOMEONE* DOES *SOMETHING*.

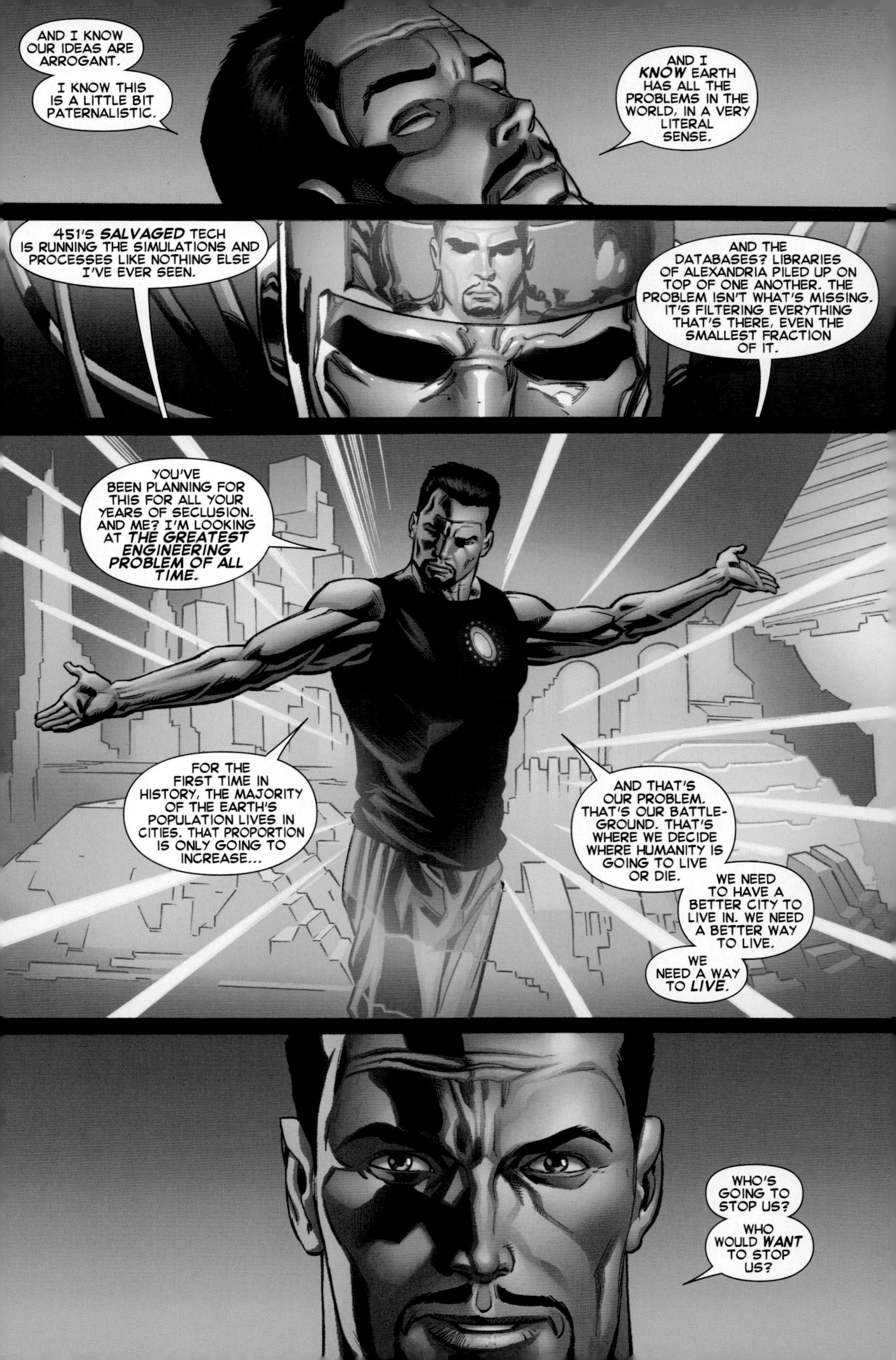
AND I KNOW OUR IDEAS ARE ARROGANT.
I KNOW THIS IS A LITTLE BIT PATERNALISTIC.
AND I *KNOW* EARTH HAS ALL THE PROBLEMS IN THE WORLD, IN A VERY LITERAL SENSE.
451'S *SALVAGED* TECH IS RUNNING THE SIMULATIONS AND PROCESSES LIKE NOTHING ELSE I'VE EVER SEEN.
AND THE DATABASES? LIBRARIES OF ALEXANDRIA PILED UP ON TOP OF ONE ANOTHER. THE PROBLEM ISN'T WHAT'S MISSING. IT'S FILTERING EVERYTHING THAT'S THERE, EVEN THE SMALLEST FRACTION OF IT.
YOU'VE BEEN PLANNING FOR THIS FOR ALL YOUR YEARS OF SECLUSION. AND ME? I'M LOOKING AT ***THE GREATEST ENGINEERING PROBLEM OF ALL TIME.***
FOR THE FIRST TIME IN HISTORY, THE MAJORITY OF THE EARTH'S POPULATION LIVES IN CITIES. THAT PROPORTION IS ONLY GOING TO INCREASE...
AND THAT'S OUR PROBLEM. THAT'S OUR BATTLE-GROUND. THAT'S WHERE WE DECIDE WHERE HUMANITY IS GOING TO LIVE OR DIE.
WE NEED TO HAVE A BETTER CITY TO LIVE IN. WE NEED A BETTER WAY TO LIVE.
WE NEED A WAY TO *LIVE.*
WHO'S GOING TO STOP US?
WHO WOULD *WANT* TO STOP US?

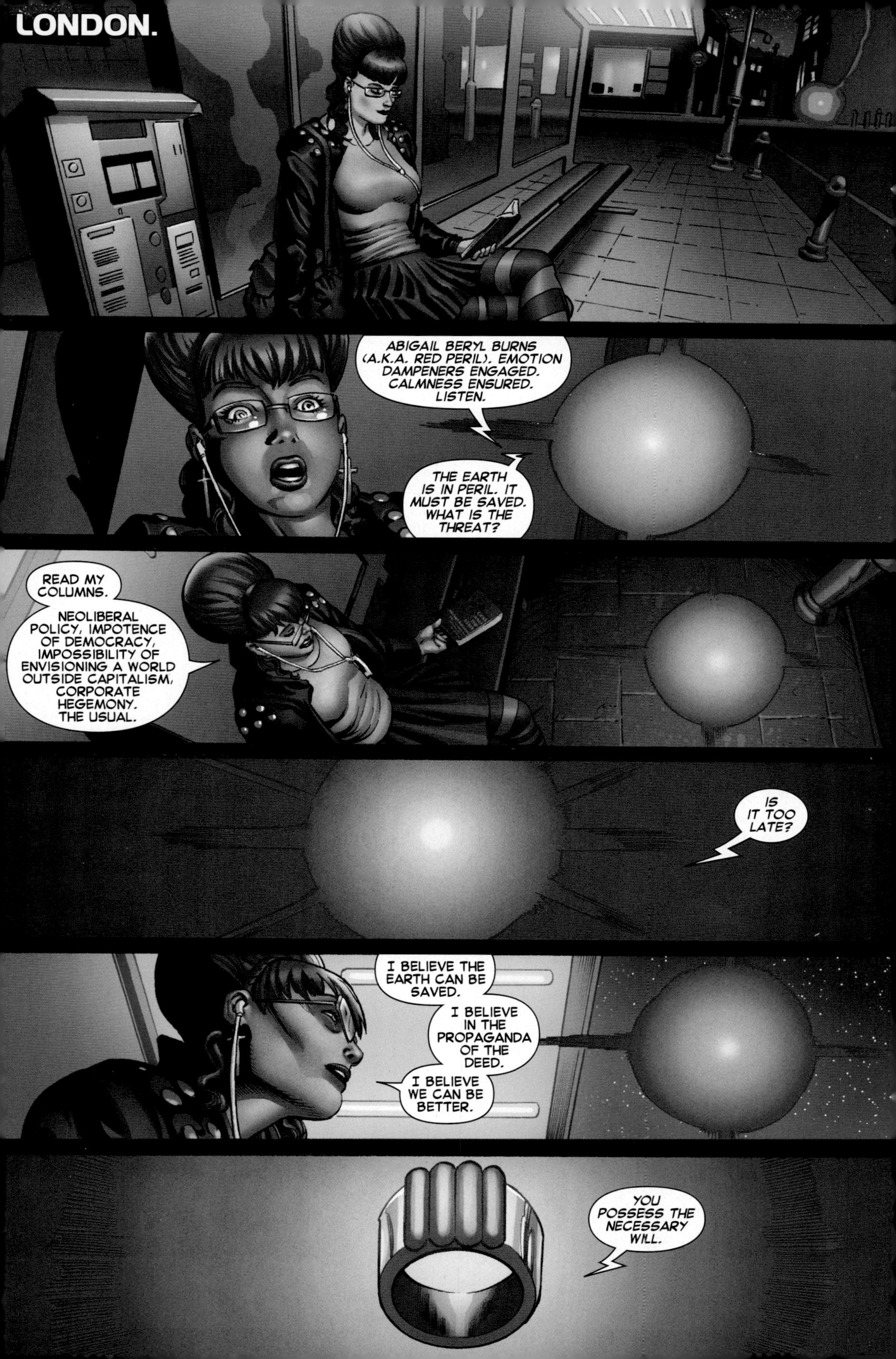
LONDON.
ABIGAIL BERYL BURNS (A.K.A. RED PERIL). EMOTION DAMPENERS ENGAGED. CALMNESS ENSURED. LISTEN.
THE EARTH IS IN PERIL. IT MUST BE SAVED. WHAT IS THE THREAT?
READ MY COLUMNS.
NEOLIBERAL POLICY, IMPOTENCE OF DEMOCRACY, IMPOSSIBILITY OF ENVISIONING A WORLD OUTSIDE CAPITALISM, CORPORATE HEGEMONY. THE USUAL.
IS IT TOO LATE?
I BELIEVE THE EARTH CAN BE SAVED.
I BELIEVE IN THE PROPAGANDA OF THE DEED.
I BELIEVE WE CAN BE BETTER.
YOU POSSESS THE NECESSARY WILL.

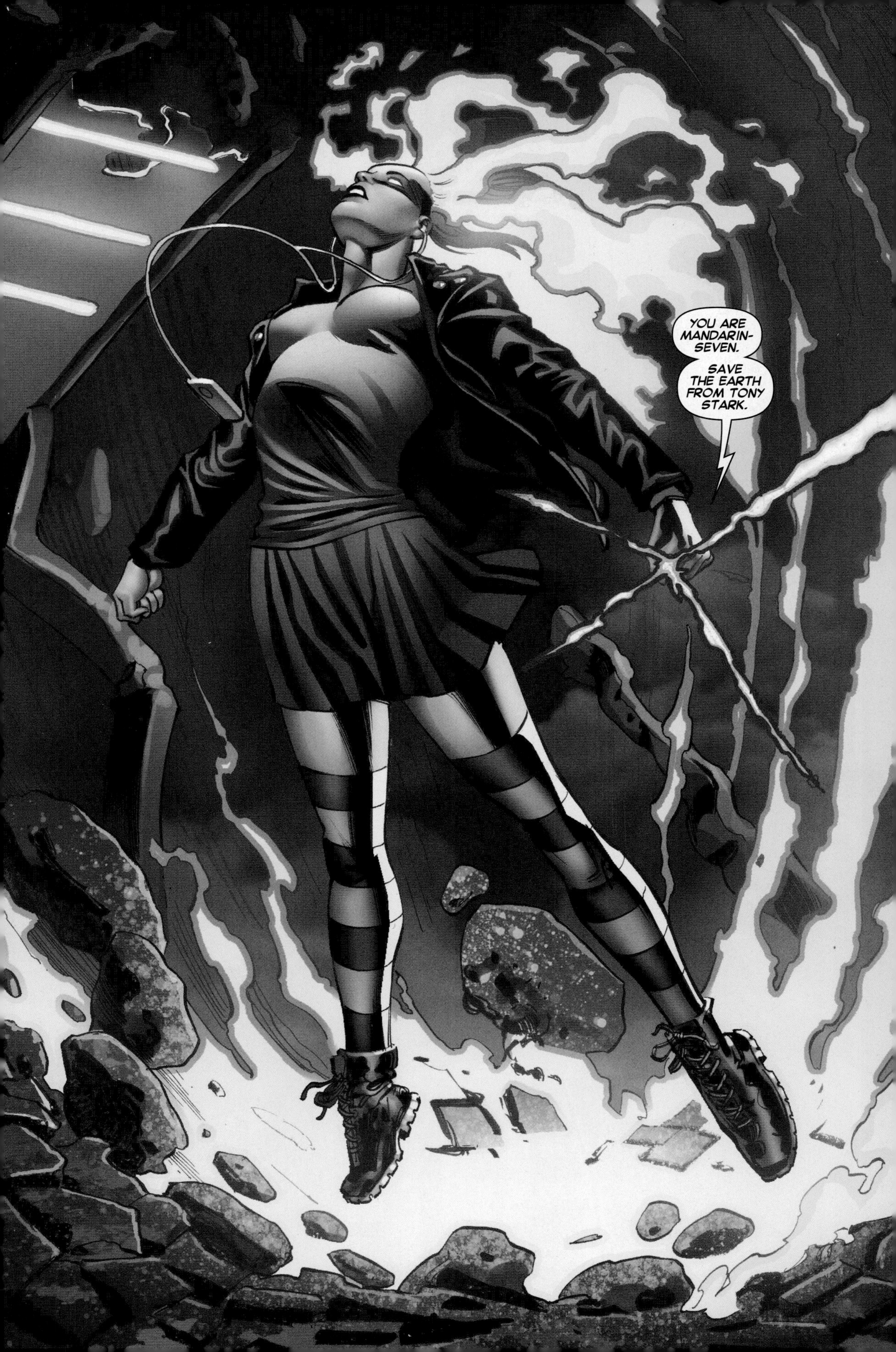
YOU ARE MANDARIN-SEVEN.
SAVE THE EARTH FROM TONY STARK.

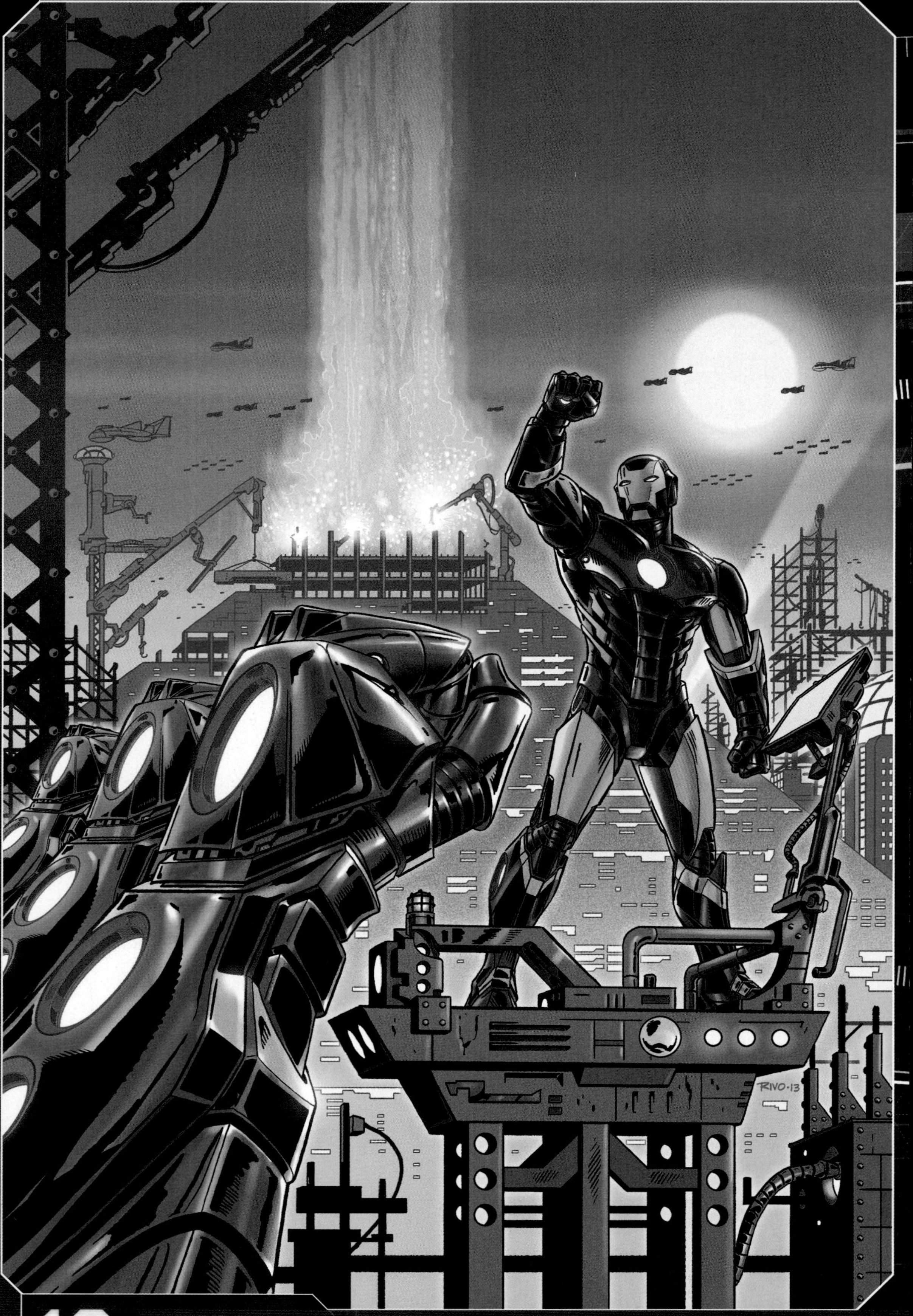
RIVO·13

19 IRON METROPOLITAN PART 2

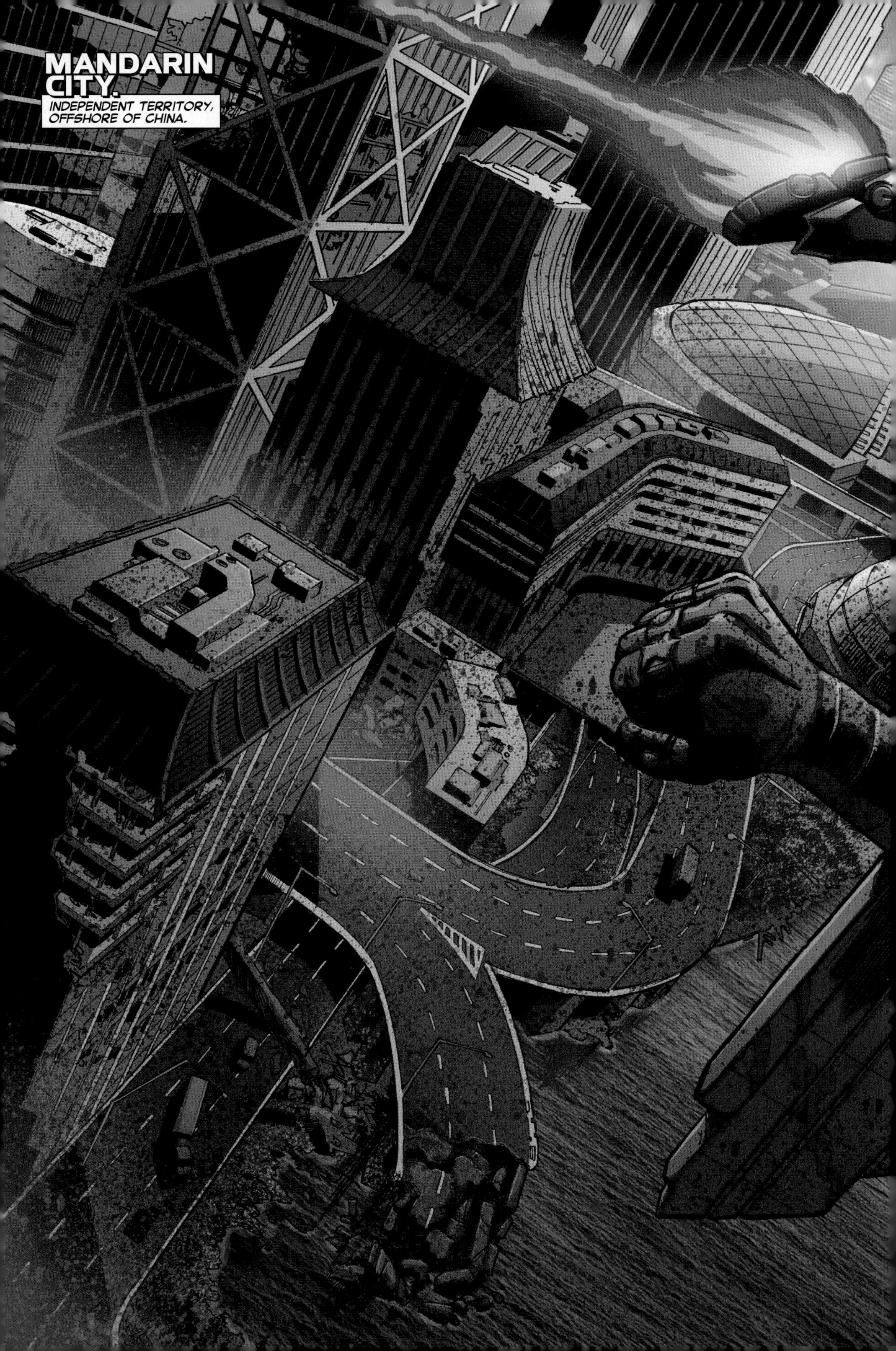
MANDARIN CITY.
INDEPENDENT TERRITORY, OFFSHORE OF CHINA.

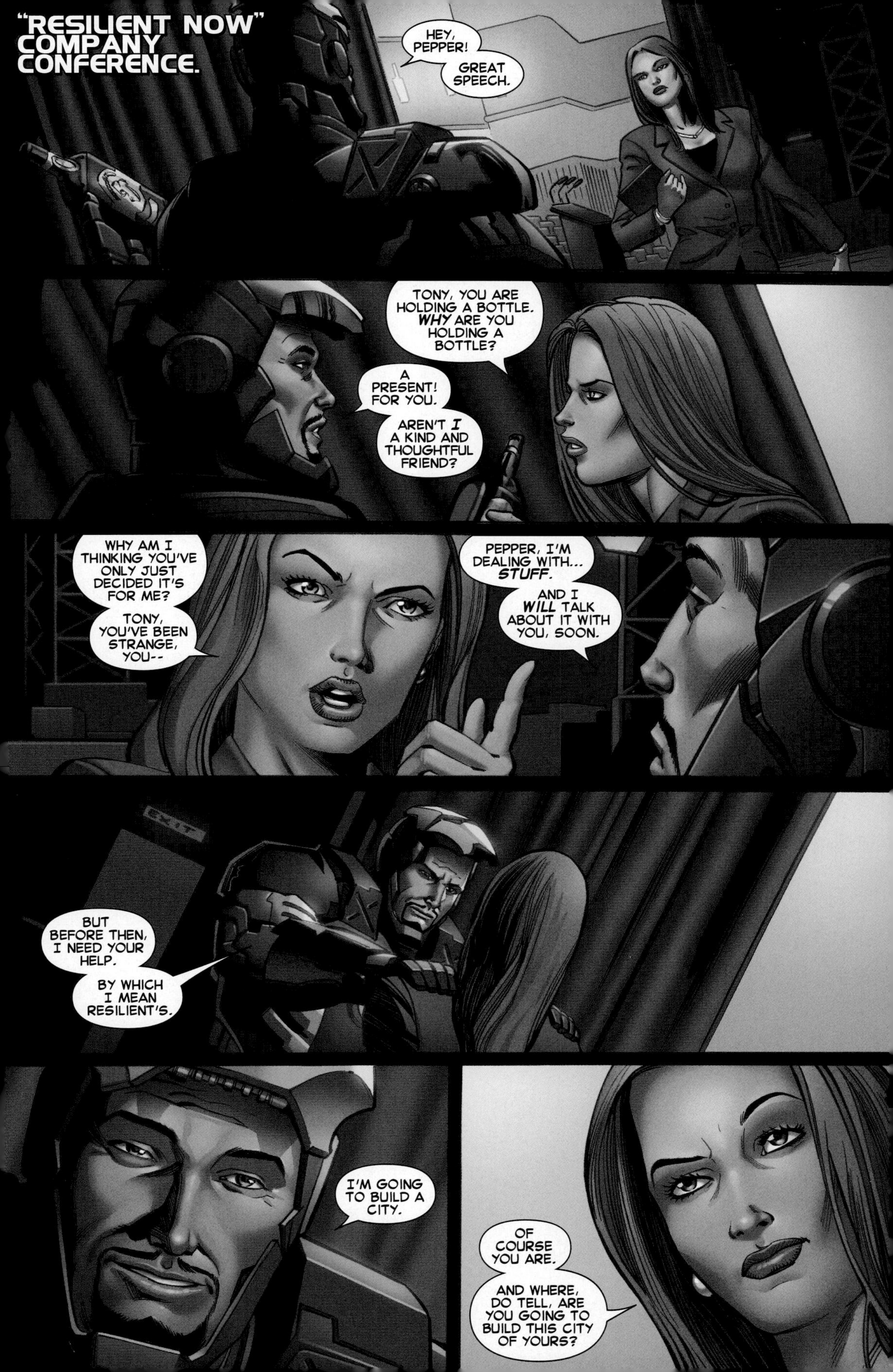
"RESILIENT NOW" COMPANY CONFERENCE.
HEY, PEPPER! GREAT SPEECH.
TONY, YOU ARE HOLDING A BOTTLE. WHY ARE YOU HOLDING A BOTTLE?
A PRESENT! FOR YOU.
AREN'T I A KIND AND THOUGHTFUL FRIEND?
WHY AM I THINKING YOU'VE ONLY JUST DECIDED IT'S FOR ME?
TONY, YOU'VE BEEN STRANGE, YOU--
PEPPER, I'M DEALING WITH... STUFF.
AND I WILL TALK ABOUT IT WITH YOU, SOON.
EXIT
BUT BEFORE THEN, I NEED YOUR HELP.
BY WHICH I MEAN RESILIENT'S.
I'M GOING TO BUILD A CITY.
OF COURSE YOU ARE.
AND WHERE, DO TELL, ARE YOU GOING TO BUILD THIS CITY OF YOURS?

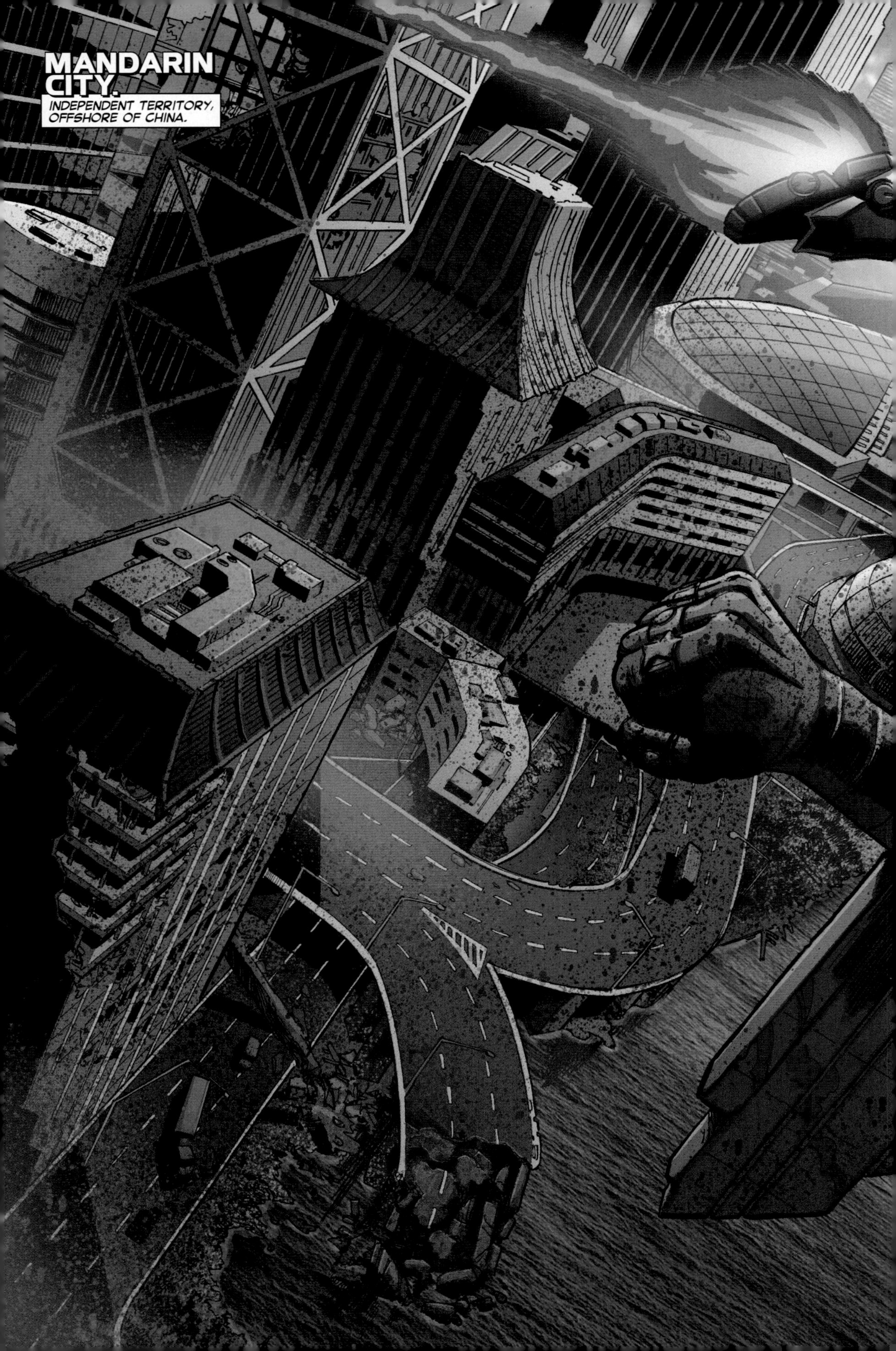
MANDARIN CITY.
INDEPENDENT TERRITORY, OFFSHORE OF CHINA.

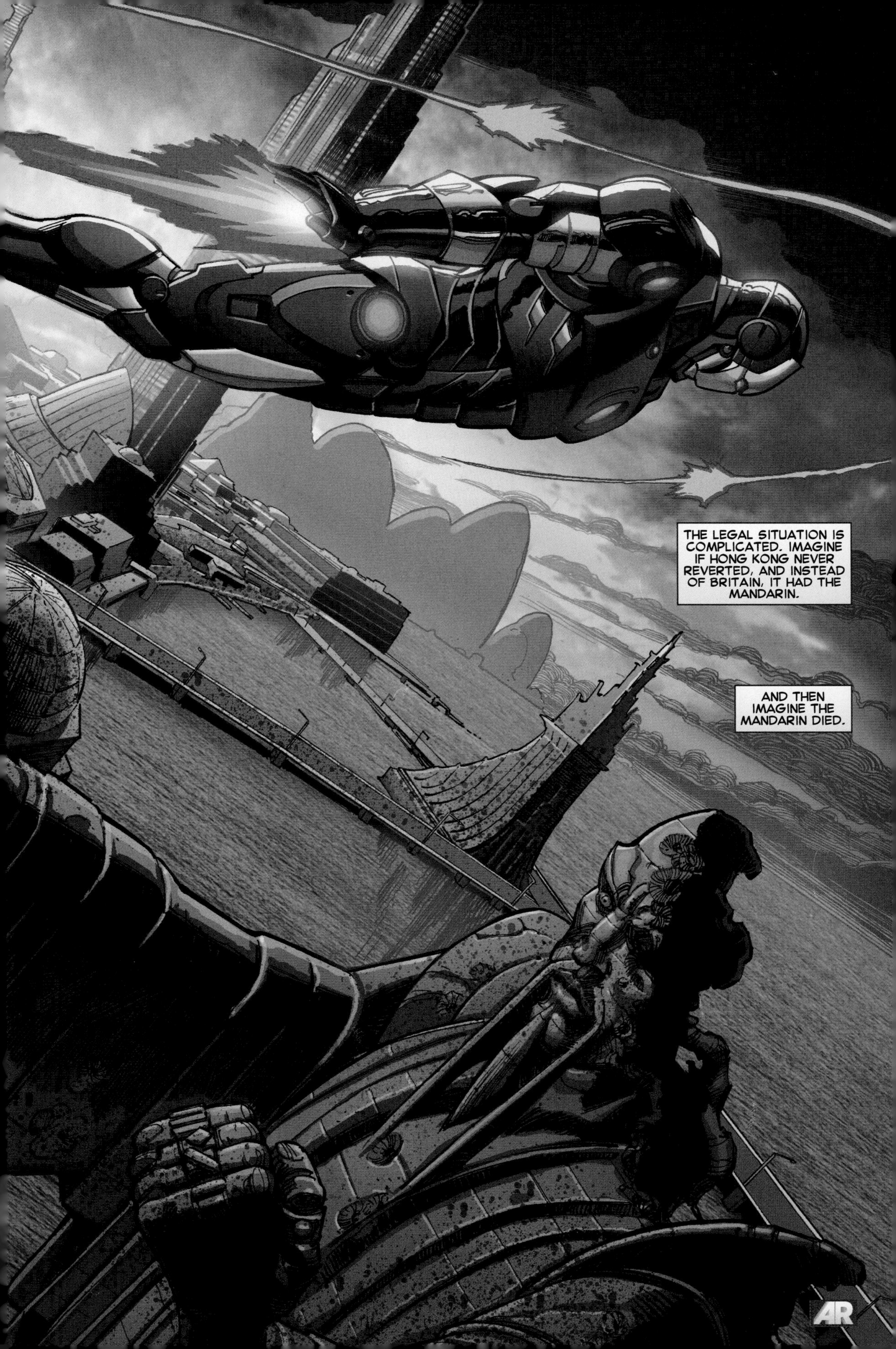
THE LEGAL SITUATION IS COMPLICATED. IMAGINE IF HONG KONG NEVER REVERTED, AND INSTEAD OF BRITAIN, IT HAD THE MANDARIN.
AND THEN IMAGINE THE MANDARIN DIED.
AR

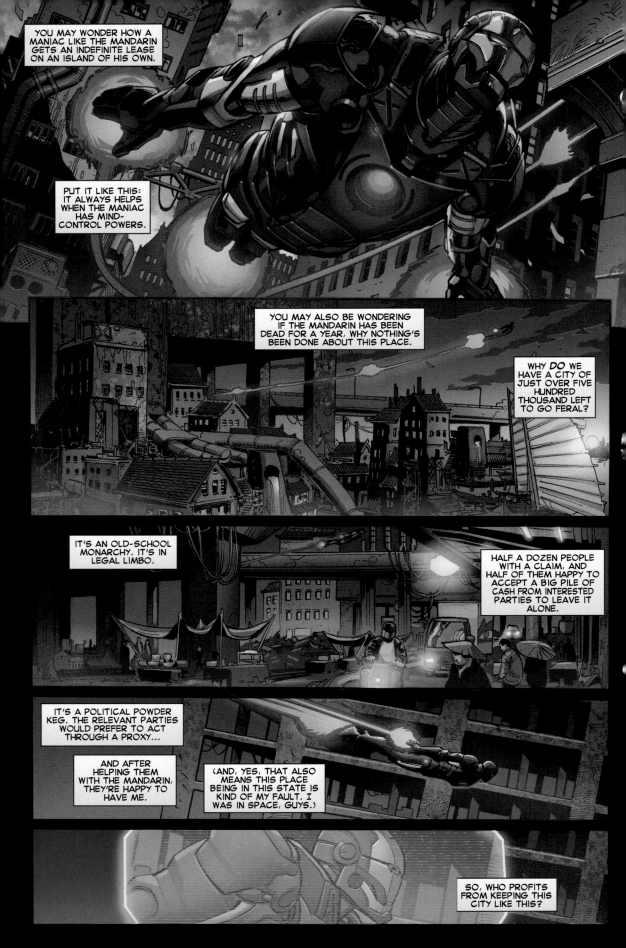

YOU MAY WONDER HOW A MANIAC LIKE THE MANDARIN GETS AN INDEFINITE LEASE ON AN ISLAND OF HIS OWN.

PUT IT LIKE THIS: IT ALWAYS HELPS WHEN THE MANIAC HAS MIND-CONTROL POWERS.

YOU MAY ALSO BE WONDERING IF THE MANDARIN HAS BEEN DEAD FOR A YEAR, WHY NOTHING'S BEEN DONE ABOUT THIS PLACE.

WHY *DO* WE HAVE A CITY OF JUST OVER FIVE HUNDRED THOUSAND LEFT TO GO FERAL?

IT'S AN OLD-SCHOOL MONARCHY. IT'S IN LEGAL LIMBO.

HALF A DOZEN PEOPLE WITH A CLAIM, AND HALF OF THEM HAPPY TO ACCEPT A BIG PILE OF CASH FROM INTERESTED PARTIES TO LEAVE IT ALONE.

IT'S A POLITICAL POWDER KEG. THE RELEVANT PARTIES WOULD PREFER TO ACT THROUGH A PROXY...

AND AFTER HELPING THEM WITH THE MANDARIN, THEY'RE HAPPY TO HAVE ME.

(AND, YES, THAT ALSO MEANS THIS PLACE BEING IN THIS STATE IS KIND OF MY FAULT. I WAS IN SPACE, GUYS.)

SO, WHO PROFITS FROM KEEPING THIS CITY LIKE THIS?

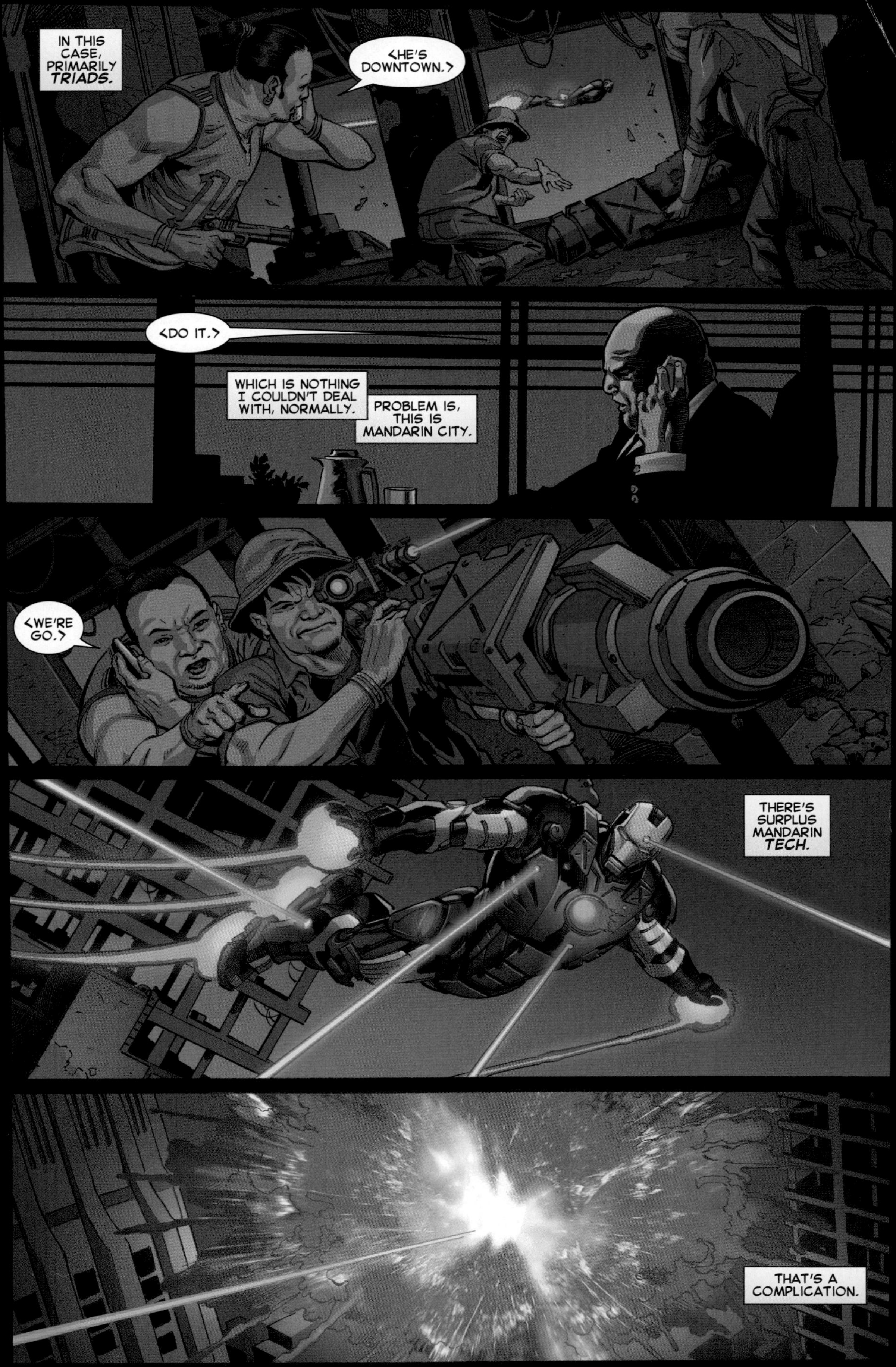
IN THIS CASE, PRIMARILY *TRIADS.*
<HE'S DOWNTOWN.>
<DO IT.>
WHICH IS NOTHING I COULDN'T DEAL WITH, NORMALLY.
PROBLEM IS, THIS IS MANDARIN CITY.
<WE'RE GO.>
THERE'S SURPLUS MANDARIN *TECH.*
THAT'S A COMPLICATION.

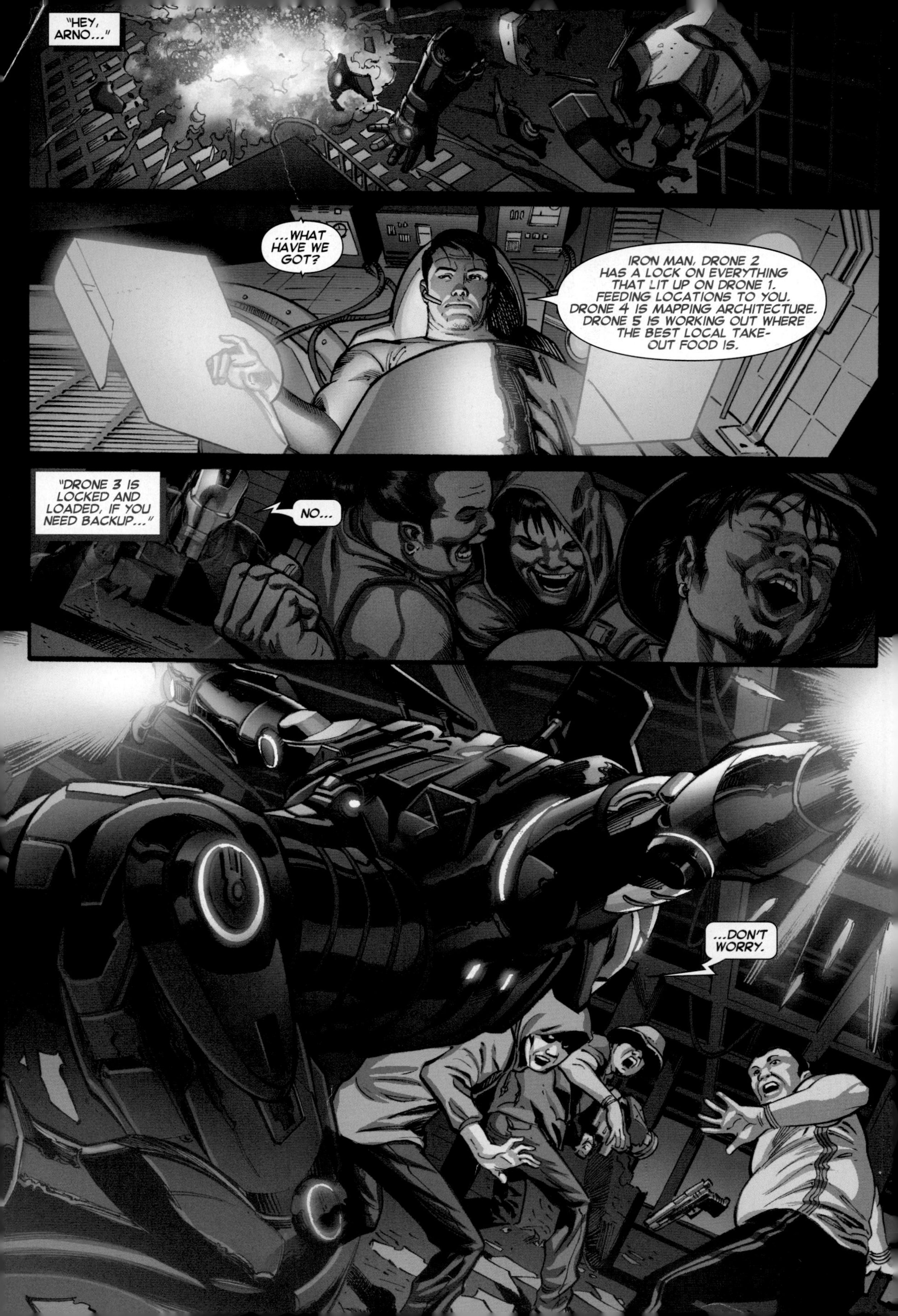
"HEY, ARNO..."
...WHAT HAVE WE GOT?
IRON MAN, DRONE 2 HAS A LOCK ON EVERYTHING THAT LIT UP ON DRONE 1. FEEDING LOCATIONS TO YOU. DRONE 4 IS MAPPING ARCHITECTURE. DRONE 5 IS WORKING OUT WHERE THE BEST LOCAL TAKE-OUT FOOD IS.
"DRONE 3 IS LOCKED AND LOADED, IF YOU NEED BACKUP..."
NO...
...DON'T WORRY.

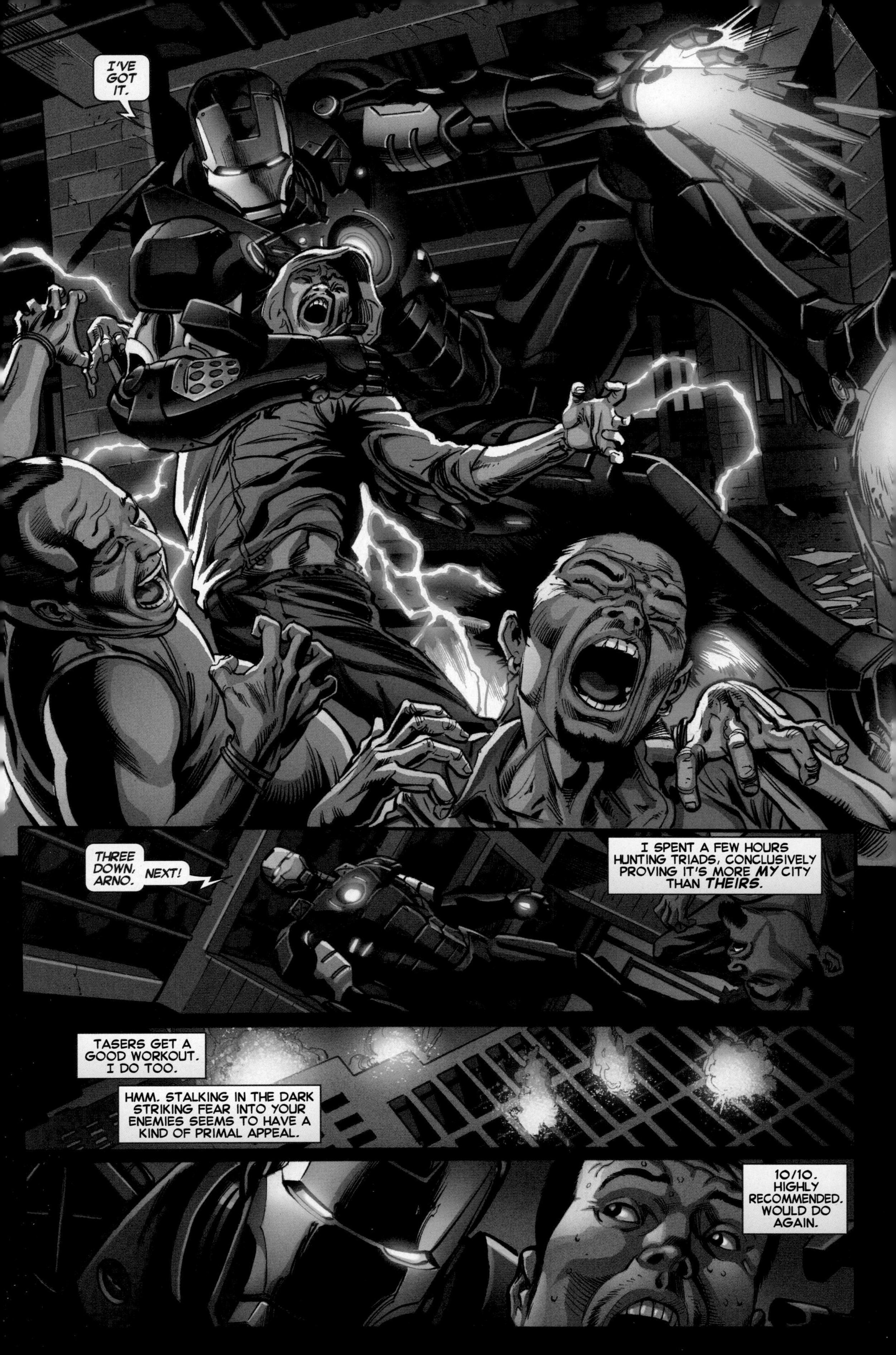
I'VE GOT IT.
THREE DOWN, ARNO.
NEXT!
I SPENT A FEW HOURS HUNTING TRIADS, CONCLUSIVELY PROVING IT'S MORE MY CITY THAN THEIRS.
TASERS GET A GOOD WORKOUT. I DO TOO.
HMM. STALKING IN THE DARK STRIKING FEAR INTO YOUR ENEMIES SEEMS TO HAVE A KIND OF PRIMAL APPEAL.
10/10. HIGHLY RECOMMENDED. WOULD DO AGAIN.

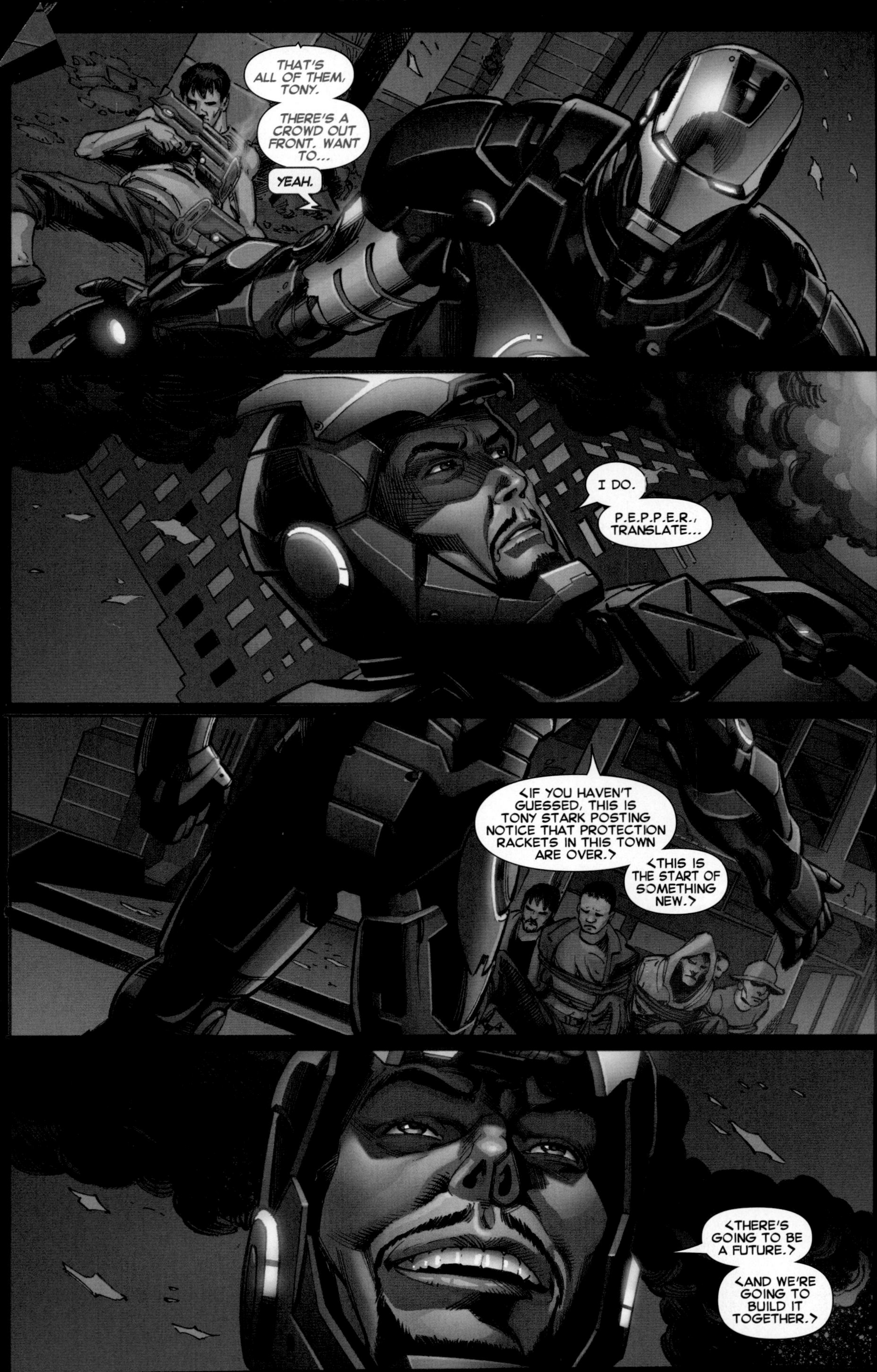
THAT'S ALL OF THEM, TONY.
THERE'S A CROWD OUT FRONT. WANT TO...
YEAH.
I DO.
P.E.P.P.E.R., TRANSLATE...
<IF YOU HAVEN'T GUESSED, THIS IS TONY STARK POSTING NOTICE THAT PROTECTION RACKETS IN THIS TOWN ARE OVER.>
<THIS IS THE START OF SOMETHING NEW.>
<THERE'S GOING TO BE A FUTURE.>
<AND WE'RE GOING TO BUILD IT TOGETHER.>

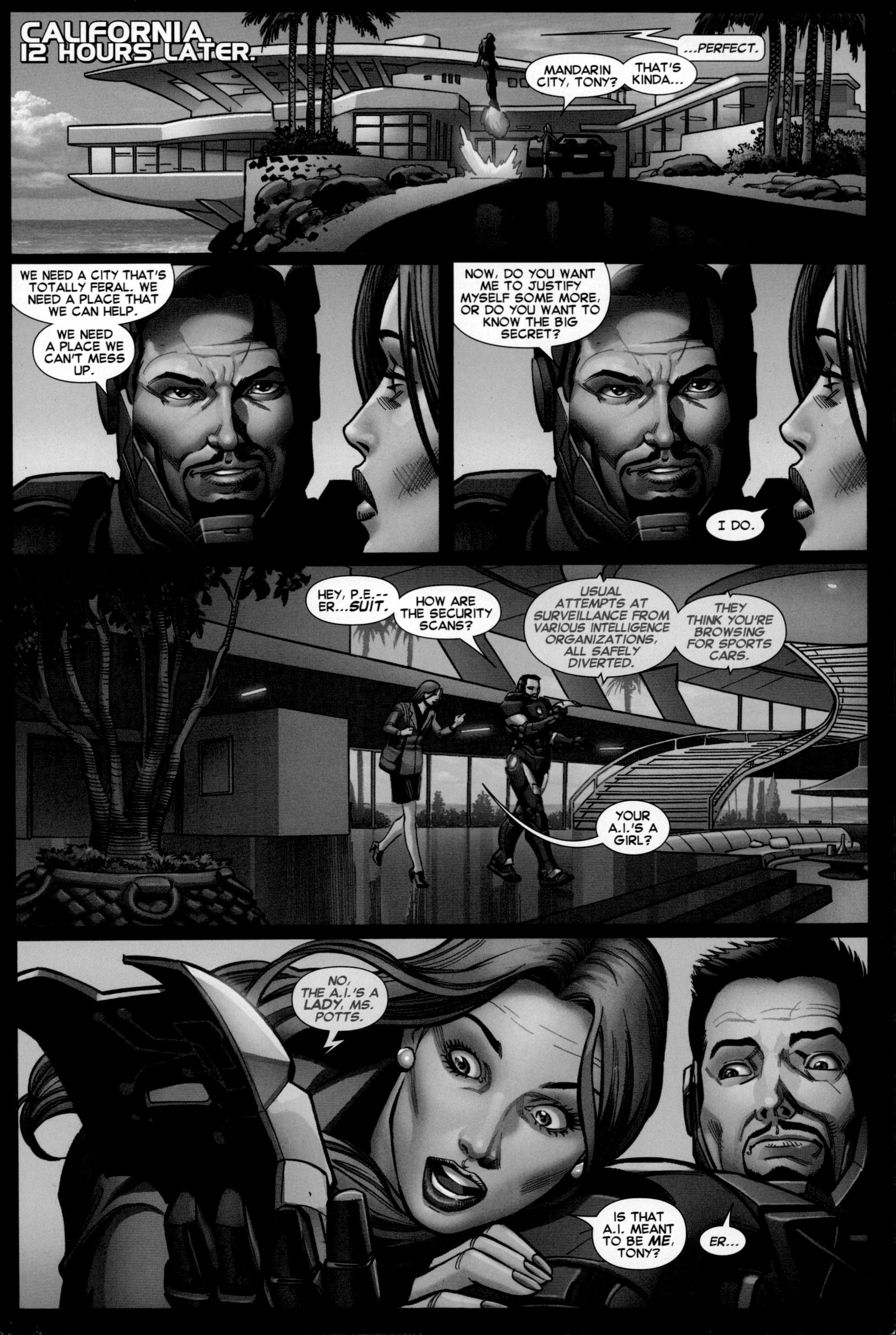
CALIFORNIA. 12 HOURS LATER.
MANDARIN CITY, TONY?
THAT'S KINDA...
...PERFECT.
WE NEED A CITY THAT'S TOTALLY FERAL. WE NEED A PLACE THAT WE CAN HELP.
WE NEED A PLACE WE CAN'T MESS UP.
NOW, DO YOU WANT ME TO JUSTIFY MYSELF SOME MORE, OR DO YOU WANT TO KNOW THE BIG SECRET?
I DO.
HEY, P.E.-- ER...SUIT.
HOW ARE THE SECURITY SCANS?
USUAL ATTEMPTS AT SURVEILLANCE FROM VARIOUS INTELLIGENCE ORGANIZATIONS, ALL SAFELY DIVERTED.
THEY THINK YOU'RE BROWSING FOR SPORTS CARS.
YOUR A.I.'S A GIRL?
NO, THE A.I.'S A LADY, MS. POTTS.
IS THAT A.I. MEANT TO BE ME, TONY?
ER...

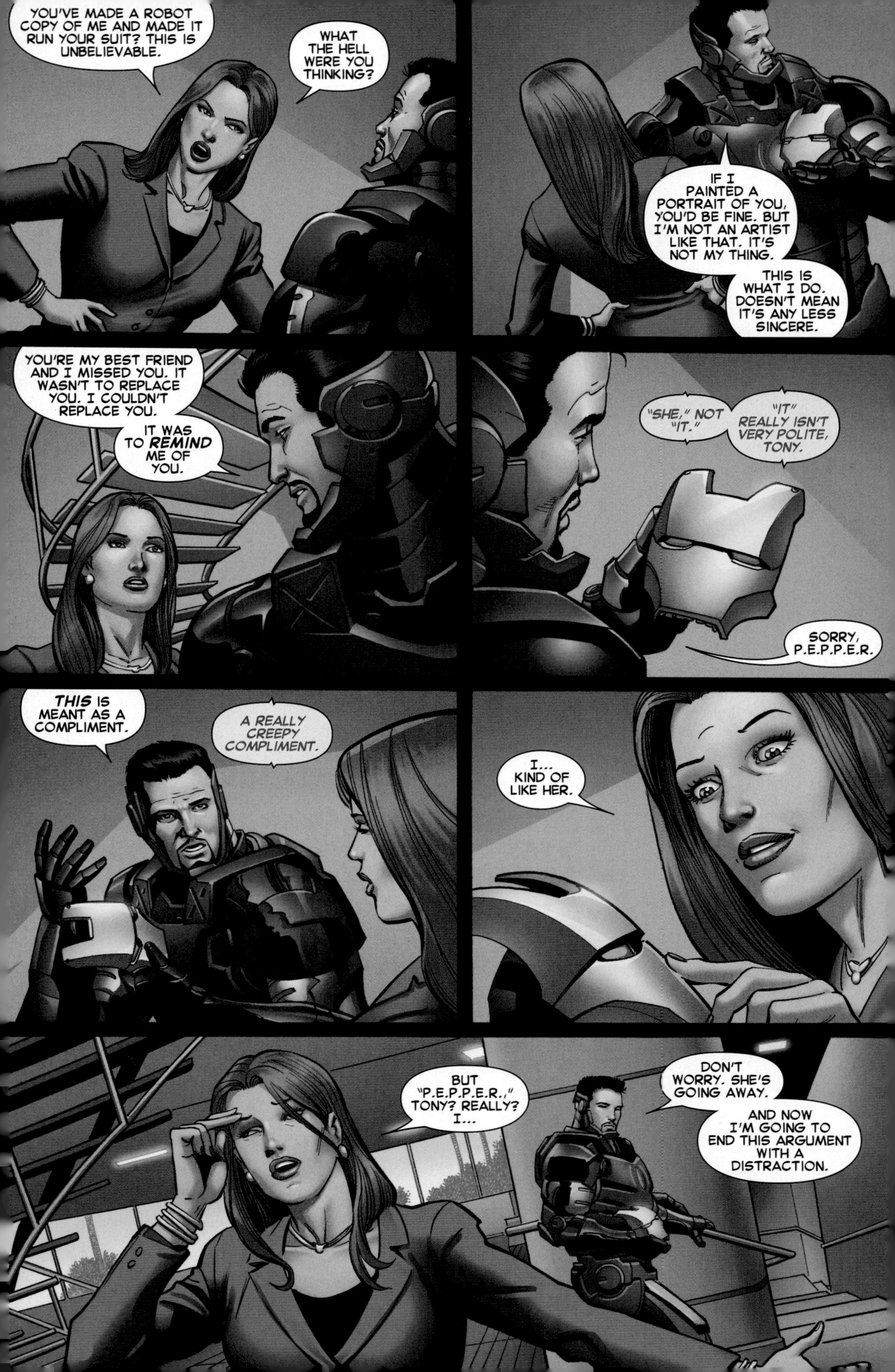
YOU'VE MADE A ROBOT COPY OF ME AND MADE IT RUN YOUR SUIT? THIS IS UNBELIEVABLE.
WHAT THE HELL WERE YOU THINKING?
IF I PAINTED A PORTRAIT OF YOU, YOU'D BE FINE. BUT I'M NOT AN ARTIST LIKE THAT. IT'S NOT MY THING.
THIS IS WHAT I DO. DOESN'T MEAN IT'S ANY LESS SINCERE.
YOU'RE MY BEST FRIEND AND I MISSED YOU. IT WASN'T TO REPLACE YOU. I COULDN'T REPLACE YOU.
IT WAS TO REMIND ME OF YOU.
"SHE," NOT "IT."
"IT" REALLY ISN'T VERY POLITE, TONY.
SORRY, P.E.P.P.E.R.
THIS IS MEANT AS A COMPLIMENT.
A REALLY CREEPY COMPLIMENT.
I... KIND OF LIKE HER.
BUT "P.E.P.P.E.R.," TONY? REALLY? I...
DON'T WORRY. SHE'S GOING AWAY.
AND NOW I'M GOING TO END THIS ARGUMENT WITH A DISTRACTION.

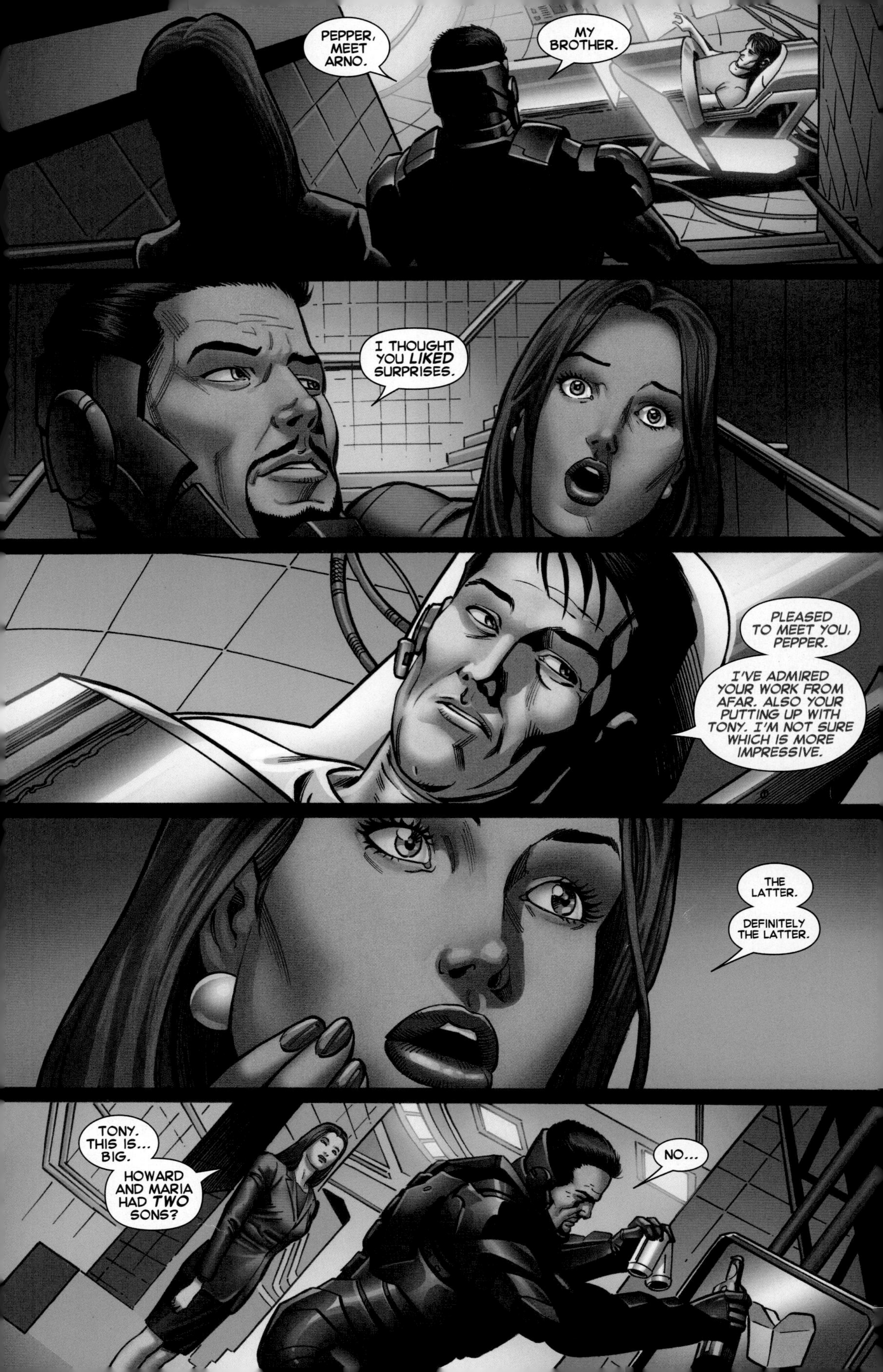
PEPPER, MEET ARNO.
MY BROTHER.
I THOUGHT YOU LIKED SURPRISES.
PLEASED TO MEET YOU, PEPPER.
I'VE ADMIRED YOUR WORK FROM AFAR. ALSO YOUR PUTTING UP WITH TONY. I'M NOT SURE WHICH IS MORE IMPRESSIVE.
THE LATTER.
DEFINITELY THE LATTER.
TONY. THIS IS... BIG.
HOWARD AND MARIA HAD TWO SONS?
NO...

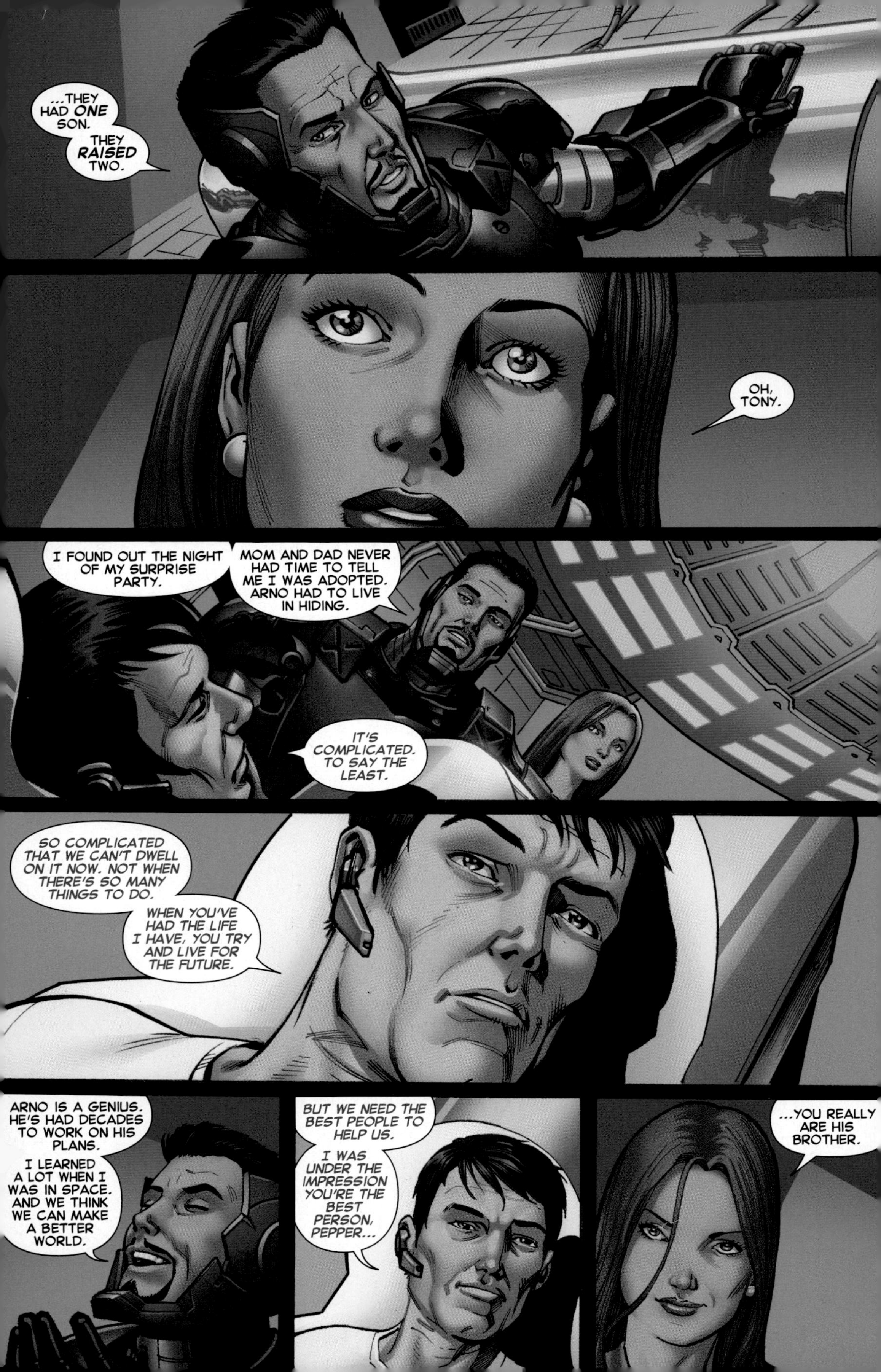
...THEY HAD ONE SON.
THEY RAISED TWO.
OH, TONY.
I FOUND OUT THE NIGHT OF MY SURPRISE PARTY.
MOM AND DAD NEVER HAD TIME TO TELL ME I WAS ADOPTED. ARNO HAD TO LIVE IN HIDING.
IT'S COMPLICATED. TO SAY THE LEAST.
SO COMPLICATED THAT WE CAN'T DWELL ON IT NOW. NOT WHEN THERE'S SO MANY THINGS TO DO.
WHEN YOU'VE HAD THE LIFE I HAVE, YOU TRY AND LIVE FOR THE FUTURE.
ARNO IS A GENIUS. HE'S HAD DECADES TO WORK ON HIS PLANS.
I LEARNED A LOT WHEN I WAS IN SPACE. AND WE THINK WE CAN MAKE A BETTER WORLD.
BUT WE NEED THE BEST PEOPLE TO HELP US.
I WAS UNDER THE IMPRESSION YOU'RE THE BEST PERSON, PEPPER...
...YOU REALLY ARE HIS BROTHER.

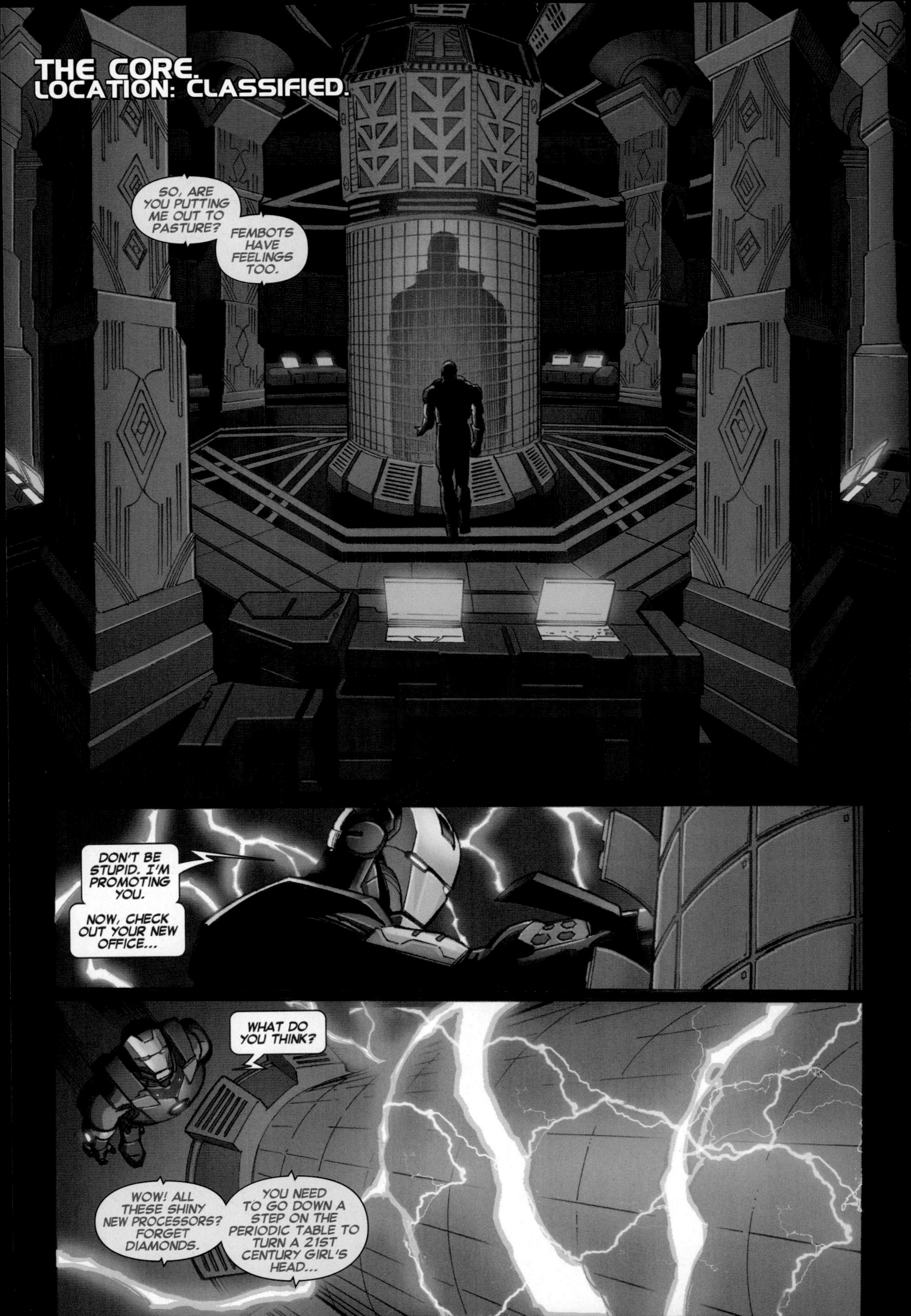
THE CORE.
LOCATION: CLASSIFIED.
SO, ARE YOU PUTTING ME OUT TO PASTURE?
FEMBOTS HAVE FEELINGS TOO.
DON'T BE STUPID. I'M PROMOTING YOU.
NOW, CHECK OUT YOUR NEW OFFICE...
WHAT DO YOU THINK?
WOW! ALL THESE SHINY NEW PROCESSORS? FORGET DIAMONDS.
YOU NEED TO GO DOWN A STEP ON THE PERIODIC TABLE TO TURN A 21ST CENTURY GIRL'S HEAD...

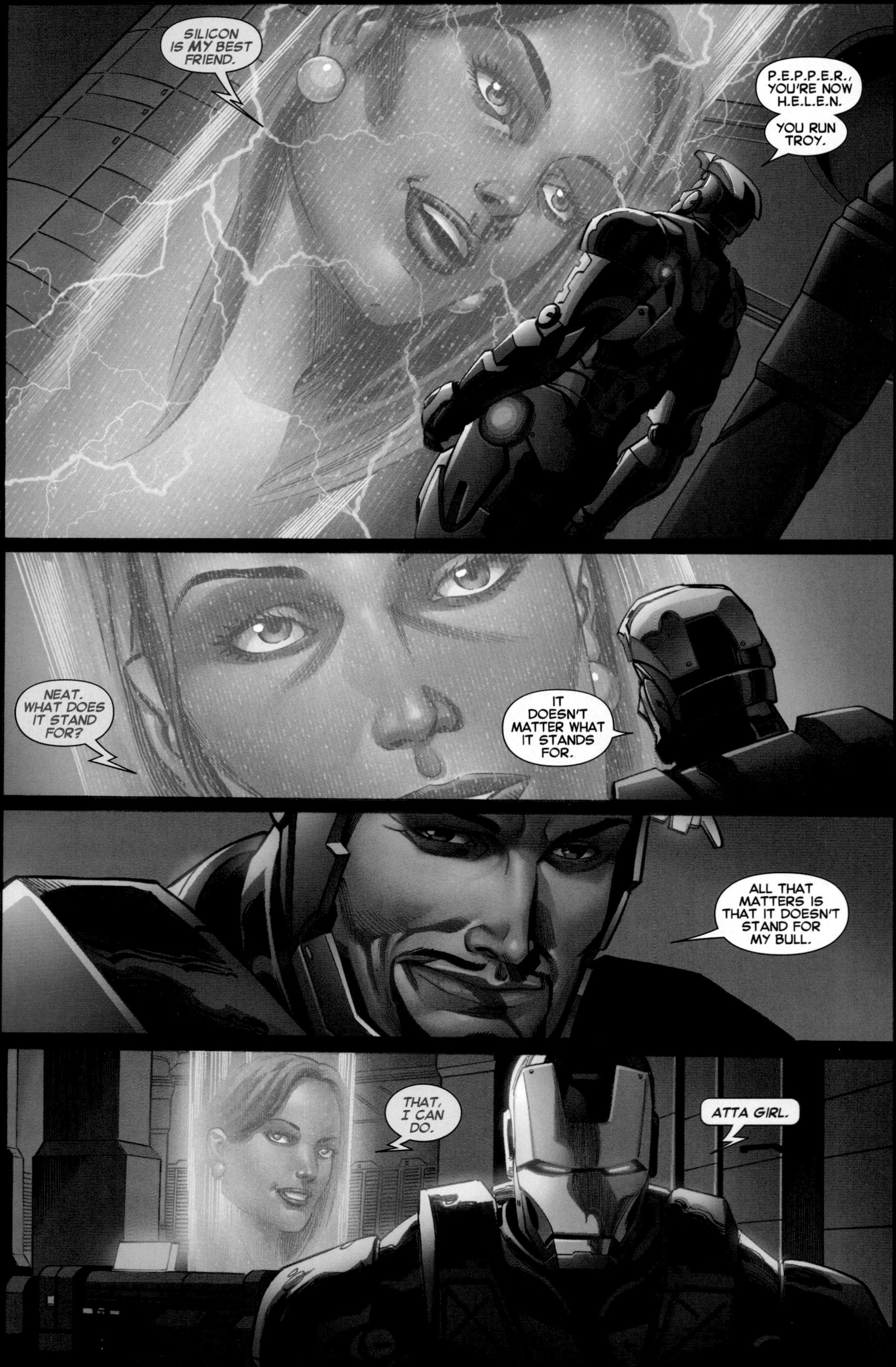
SILICON IS MY BEST FRIEND.
P.E.P.P.E.R., YOU'RE NOW H.E.L.E.N.
YOU RUN TROY.
NEAT. WHAT DOES IT STAND FOR?
IT DOESN'T MATTER WHAT IT STANDS FOR.
ALL THAT MATTERS IS THAT IT DOESN'T STAND FOR MY BULL.
THAT, I CAN DO.
ATTA GIRL.

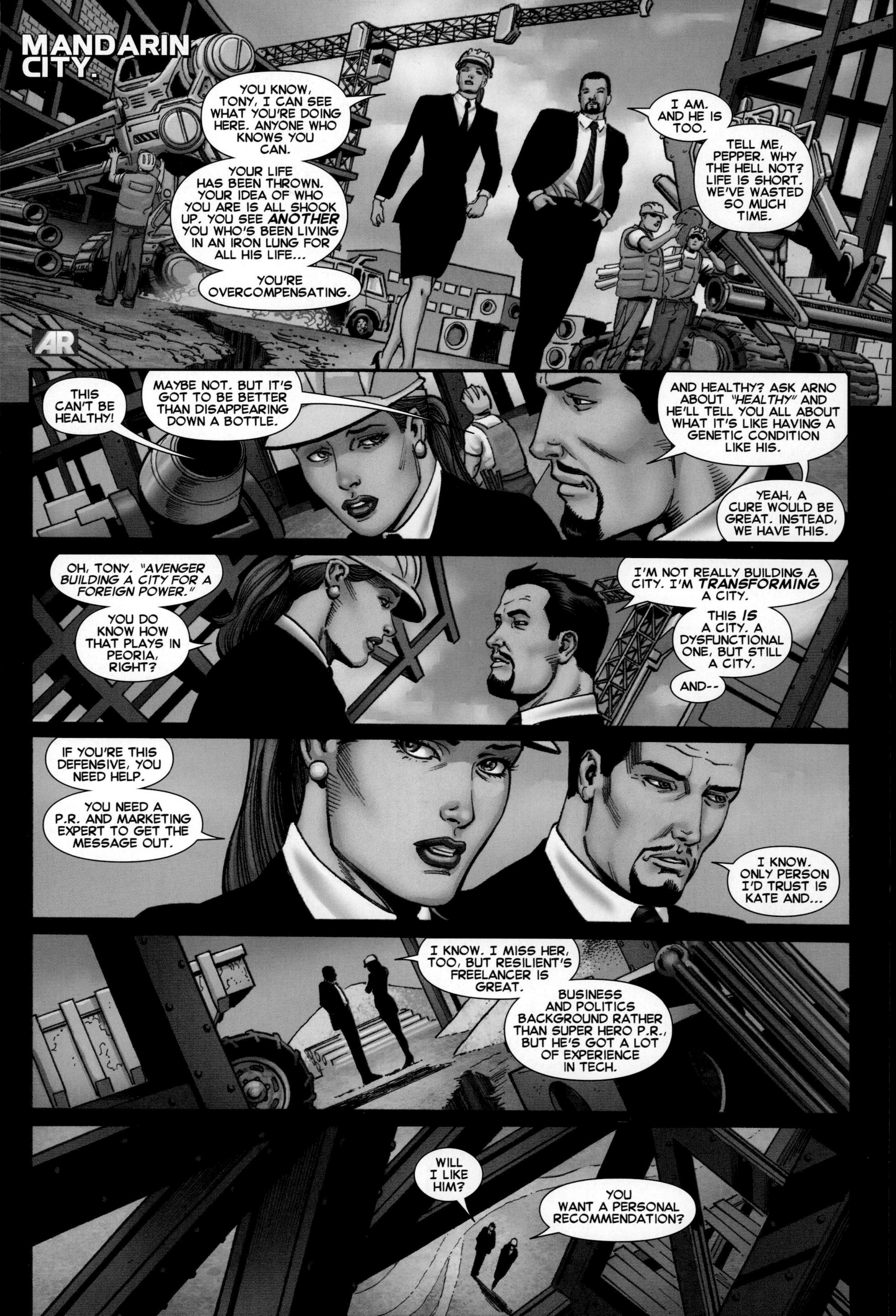
MANDARIN CITY.
YOU KNOW, TONY, I CAN SEE WHAT YOU'RE DOING HERE. ANYONE WHO KNOWS YOU CAN.
YOUR LIFE HAS BEEN THROWN. YOUR IDEA OF WHO YOU ARE IS ALL SHOOK UP. YOU SEE ANOTHER YOU WHO'S BEEN LIVING IN AN IRON LUNG FOR ALL HIS LIFE...
YOU'RE OVERCOMPENSATING.
I AM. AND HE IS TOO.
TELL ME, PEPPER. WHY THE HELL NOT? LIFE IS SHORT. WE'VE WASTED SO MUCH TIME.
THIS CAN'T BE HEALTHY!
MAYBE NOT. BUT IT'S GOT TO BE BETTER THAN DISAPPEARING DOWN A BOTTLE.
AND HEALTHY? ASK ARNO ABOUT "HEALTHY" AND HE'LL TELL YOU ALL ABOUT WHAT IT'S LIKE HAVING A GENETIC CONDITION LIKE HIS.
YEAH, A CURE WOULD BE GREAT. INSTEAD, WE HAVE THIS.
OH, TONY. "AVENGER BUILDING A CITY FOR A FOREIGN POWER."
YOU DO KNOW HOW THAT PLAYS IN PEORIA, RIGHT?
I'M NOT REALLY BUILDING A CITY. I'M TRANSFORMING A CITY.
THIS IS A CITY. A DYSFUNCTIONAL ONE, BUT STILL A CITY.
AND--
IF YOU'RE THIS DEFENSIVE, YOU NEED HELP.
YOU NEED A P.R. AND MARKETING EXPERT TO GET THE MESSAGE OUT.
I KNOW. ONLY PERSON I'D TRUST IS KATE AND...
I KNOW. I MISS HER, TOO, BUT RESILIENT'S FREELANCER IS GREAT.
BUSINESS AND POLITICS BACKGROUND RATHER THAN SUPER HERO P.R., BUT HE'S GOT A LOT OF EXPERIENCE IN TECH.
WILL I LIKE HIM?
YOU WANT A PERSONAL RECOMMENDATION?

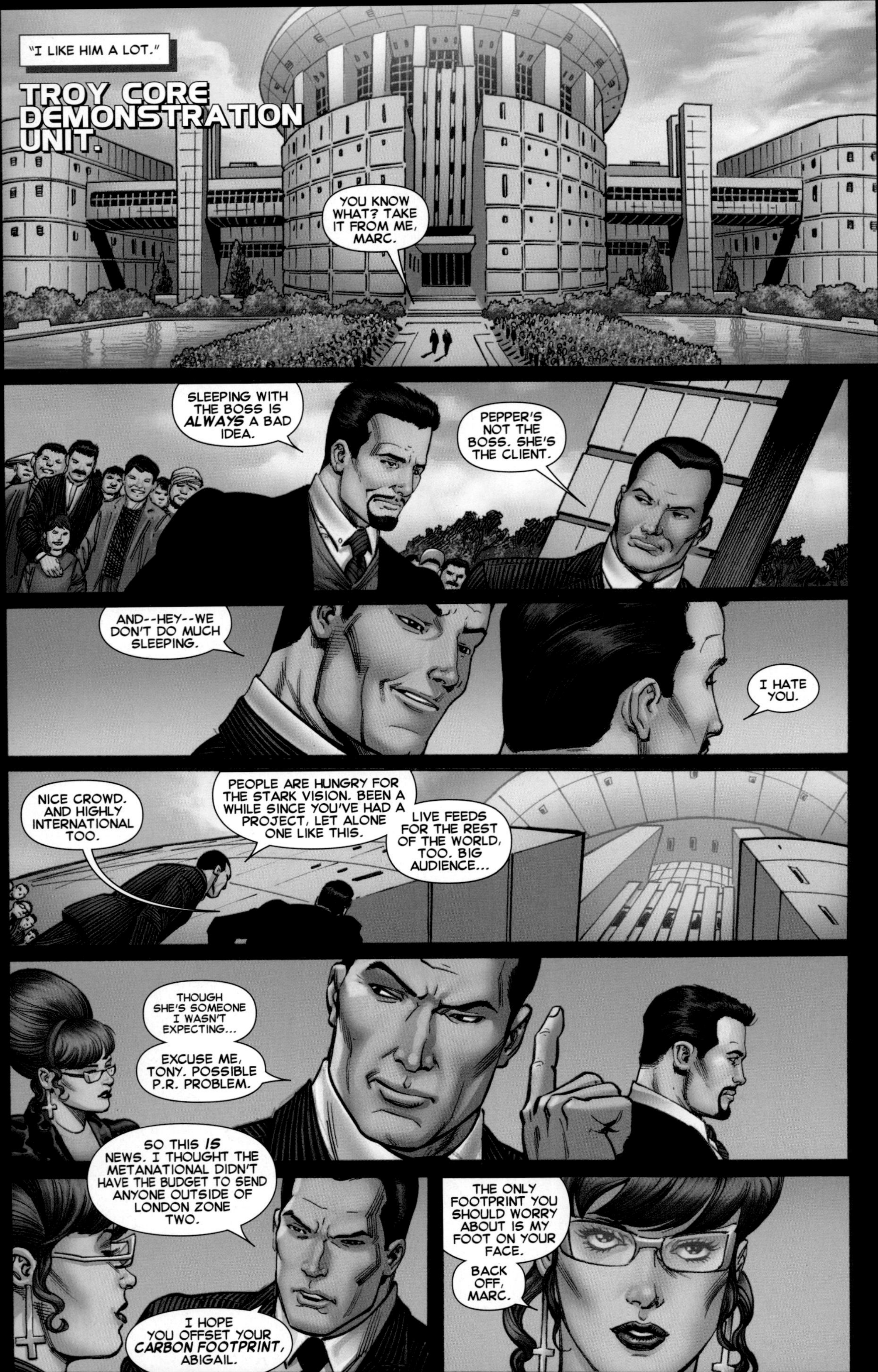
"I LIKE HIM A LOT."
TROY CORE DEMONSTRATION UNIT.
YOU KNOW WHAT? TAKE IT FROM ME, MARC.
SLEEPING WITH THE BOSS IS ALWAYS A BAD IDEA.
PEPPER'S NOT THE BOSS. SHE'S THE CLIENT.
AND--HEY--WE DON'T DO MUCH SLEEPING.
I HATE YOU.
NICE CROWD. AND HIGHLY INTERNATIONAL TOO.
PEOPLE ARE HUNGRY FOR THE STARK VISION. BEEN A WHILE SINCE YOU'VE HAD A PROJECT, LET ALONE ONE LIKE THIS.
LIVE FEEDS FOR THE REST OF THE WORLD, TOO. BIG AUDIENCE...
THOUGH SHE'S SOMEONE I WASN'T EXPECTING...
EXCUSE ME, TONY. POSSIBLE P.R. PROBLEM.
SO THIS IS NEWS. I THOUGHT THE METANATIONAL DIDN'T HAVE THE BUDGET TO SEND ANYONE OUTSIDE OF LONDON ZONE TWO.
I HOPE YOU OFFSET YOUR CARBON FOOTPRINT, ABIGAIL.
THE ONLY FOOTPRINT YOU SHOULD WORRY ABOUT IS MY FOOT ON YOUR FACE.
BACK OFF, MARC.

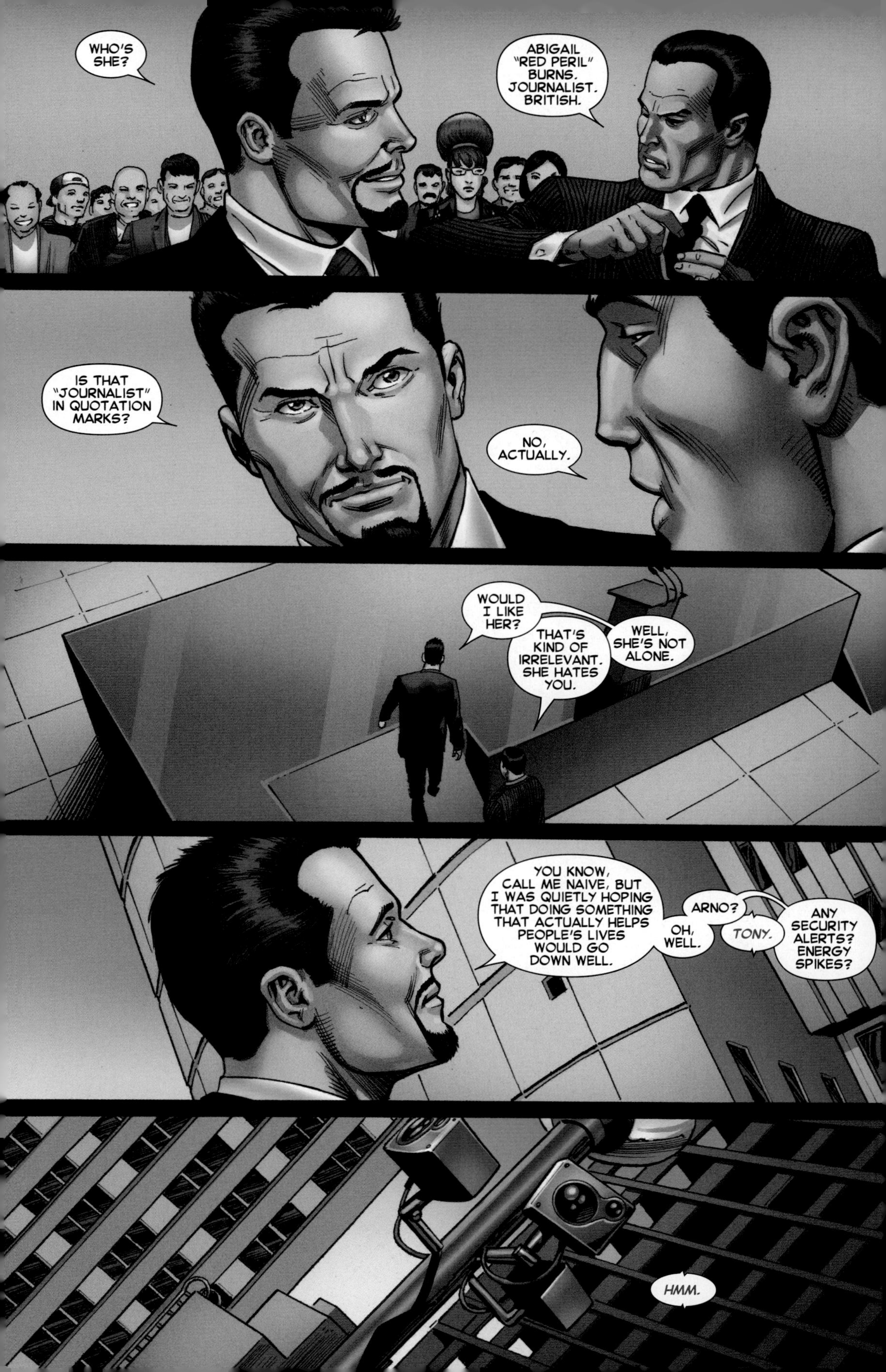
WHO'S SHE?
ABIGAIL "RED PERIL" BURNS. JOURNALIST. BRITISH.
IS THAT "JOURNALIST" IN QUOTATION MARKS?
NO, ACTUALLY.
WOULD I LIKE HER?
THAT'S KIND OF IRRELEVANT. SHE HATES YOU.
WELL, SHE'S NOT ALONE.
YOU KNOW, CALL ME NAIVE, BUT I WAS QUIETLY HOPING THAT DOING SOMETHING THAT ACTUALLY HELPS PEOPLE'S LIVES WOULD GO DOWN WELL.
OH, WELL.
ARNO?
TONY.
ANY SECURITY ALERTS? ENERGY SPIKES?
HMM.

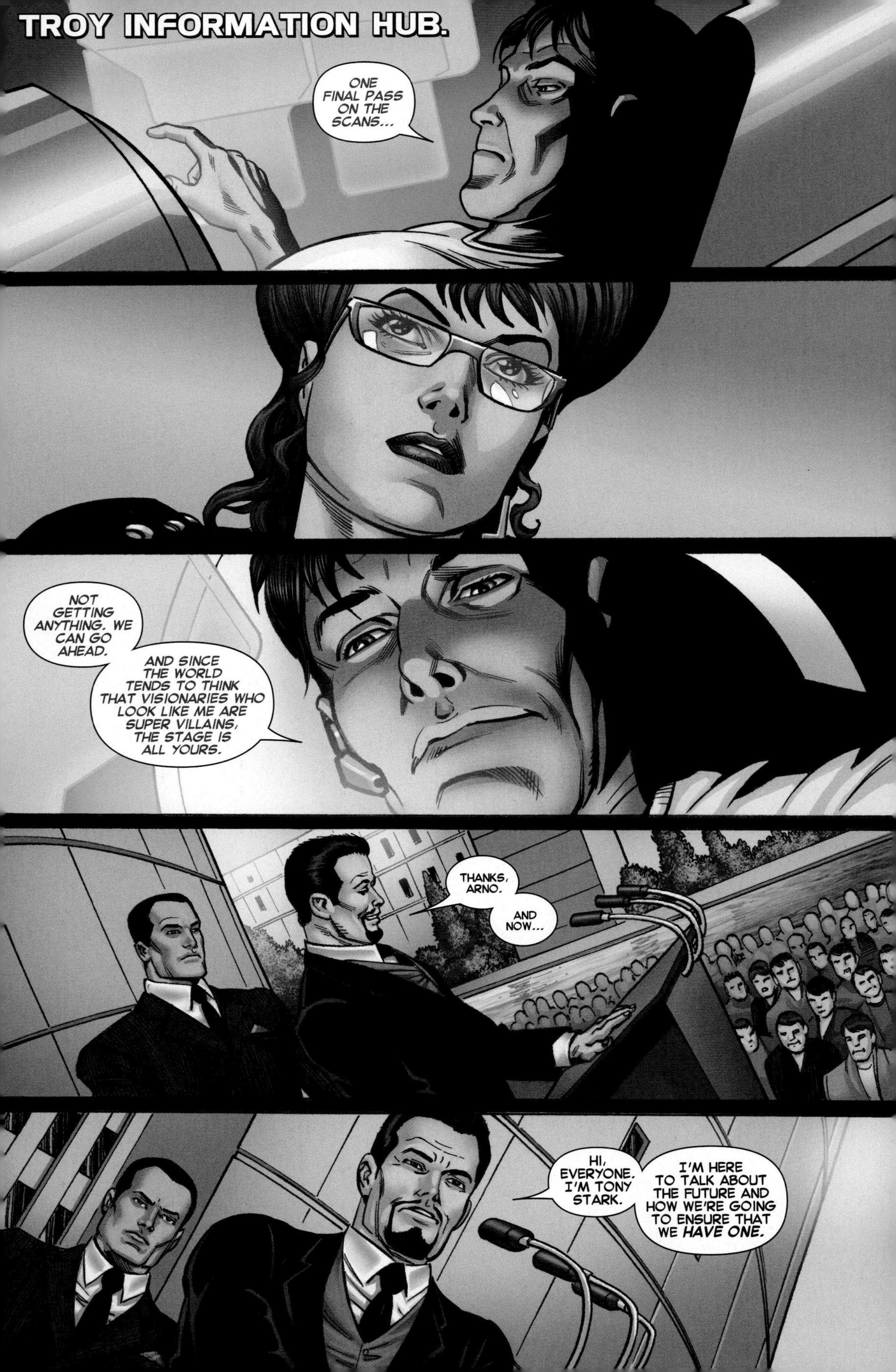
TROY INFORMATION HUB.
ONE FINAL PASS ON THE SCANS...
NOT GETTING ANYTHING. WE CAN GO AHEAD.
AND SINCE THE WORLD TENDS TO THINK THAT VISIONARIES WHO LOOK LIKE ME ARE SUPER VILLAINS, THE STAGE IS ALL YOURS.
THANKS, ARNO.
AND NOW...
HI, EVERYONE. I'M TONY STARK.
I'M HERE TO TALK ABOUT THE FUTURE AND HOW WE'RE GOING TO ENSURE THAT WE *HAVE ONE.*

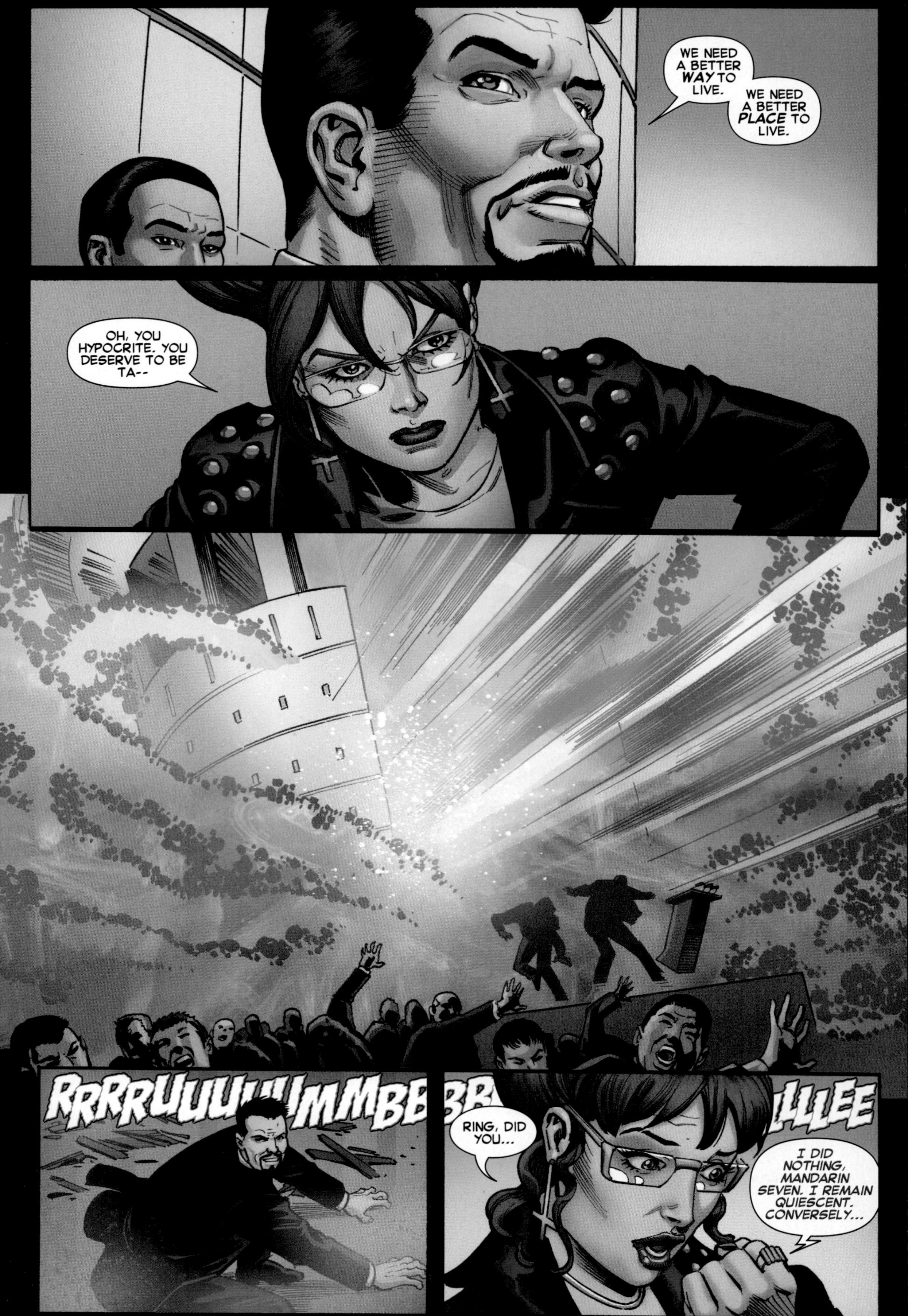

WE NEED A BETTER WAY TO LIVE.
WE NEED A BETTER PLACE TO LIVE.
OH, YOU HYPOCRITE. YOU DESERVE TO BE TA--
RRRRUUUUUMMBBBBLLLEE
RING, DID YOU...
I DID NOTHING, MANDARIN SEVEN. I REMAIN QUIESCENT. CONVERSELY...

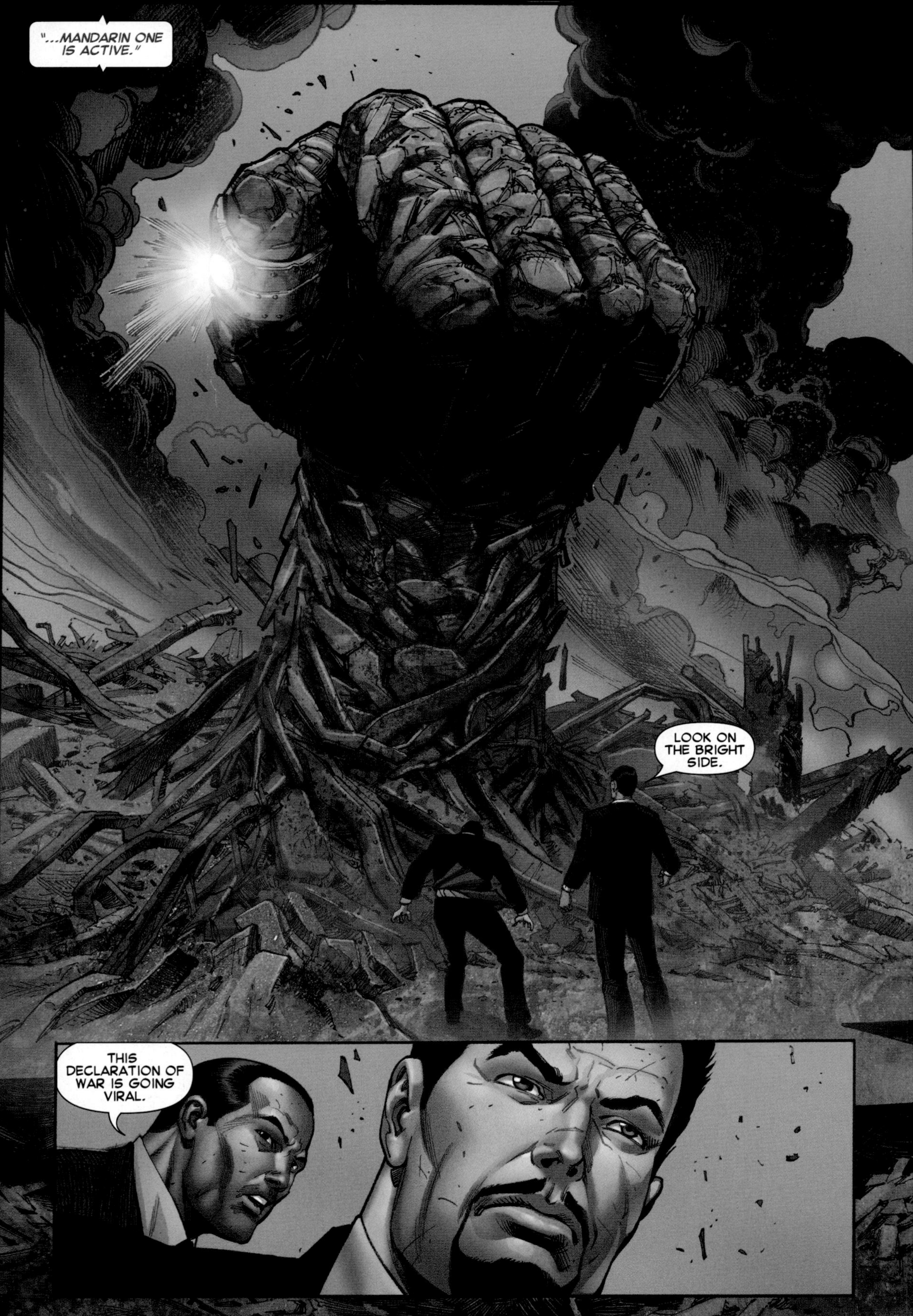
"...MANDARIN ONE IS ACTIVE."
LOOK ON THE BRIGHT SIDE.
THIS DECLARATION OF WAR IS GOING VIRAL.

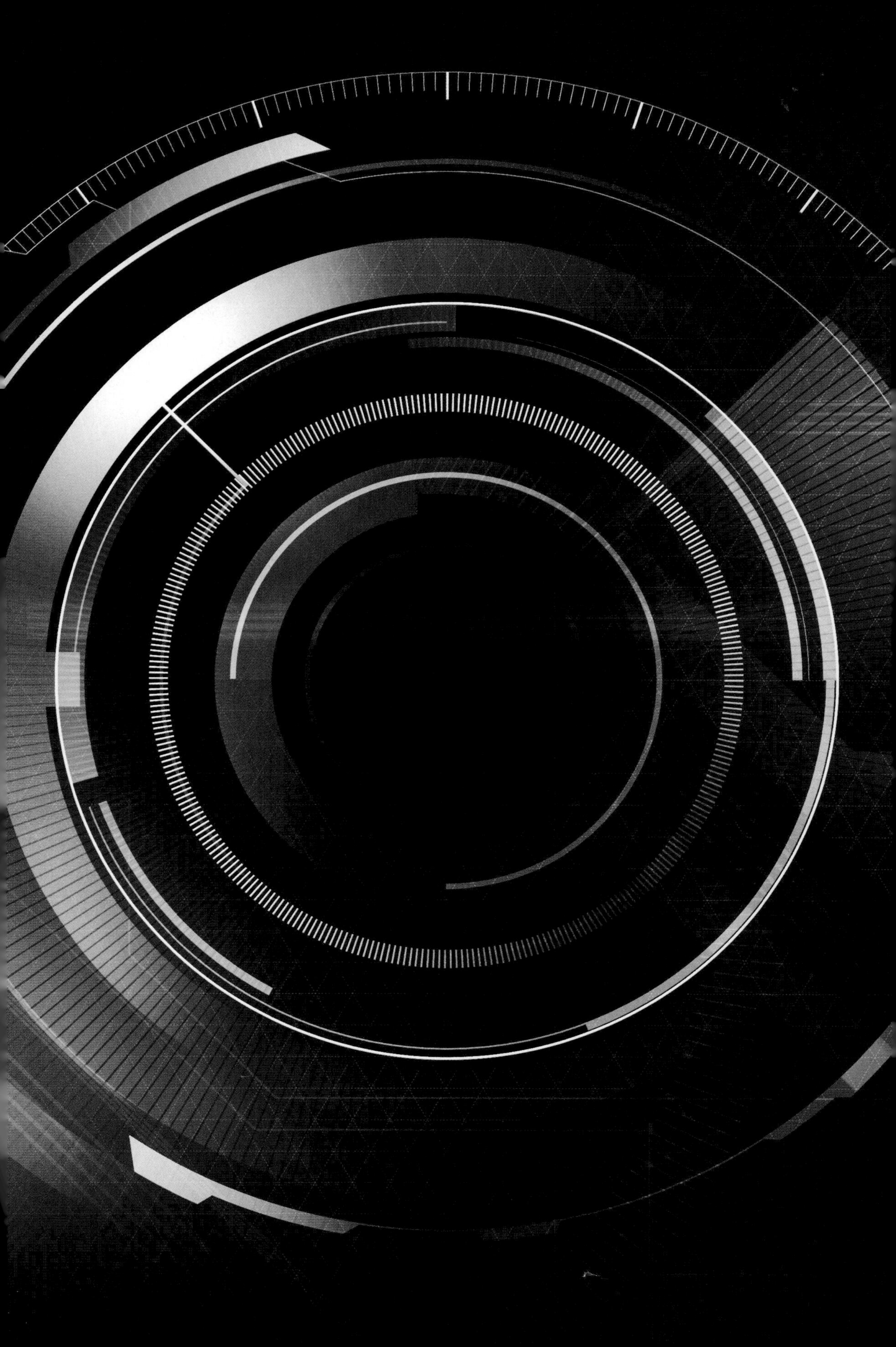

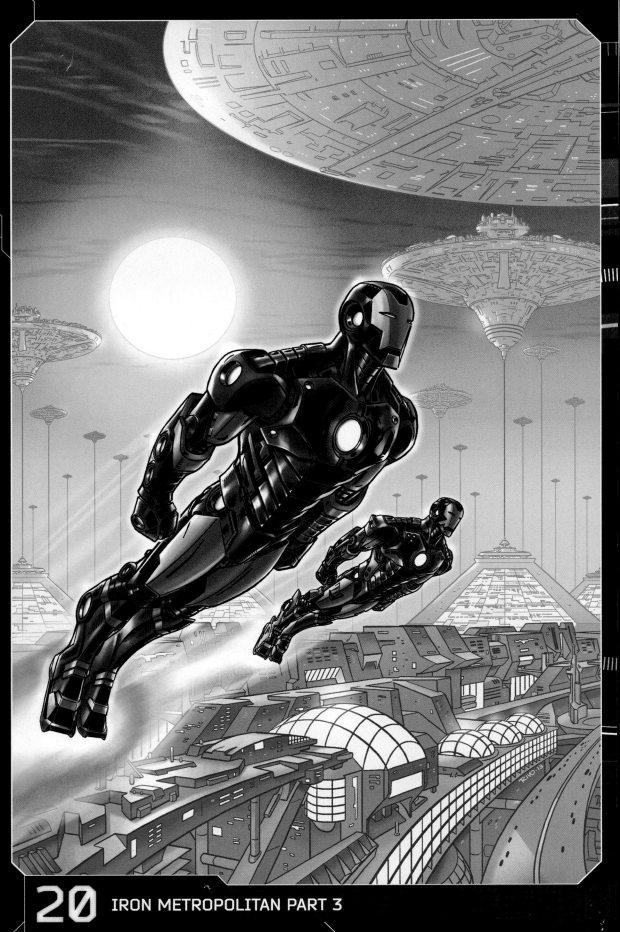

IRON METROPOLITAN PART 3

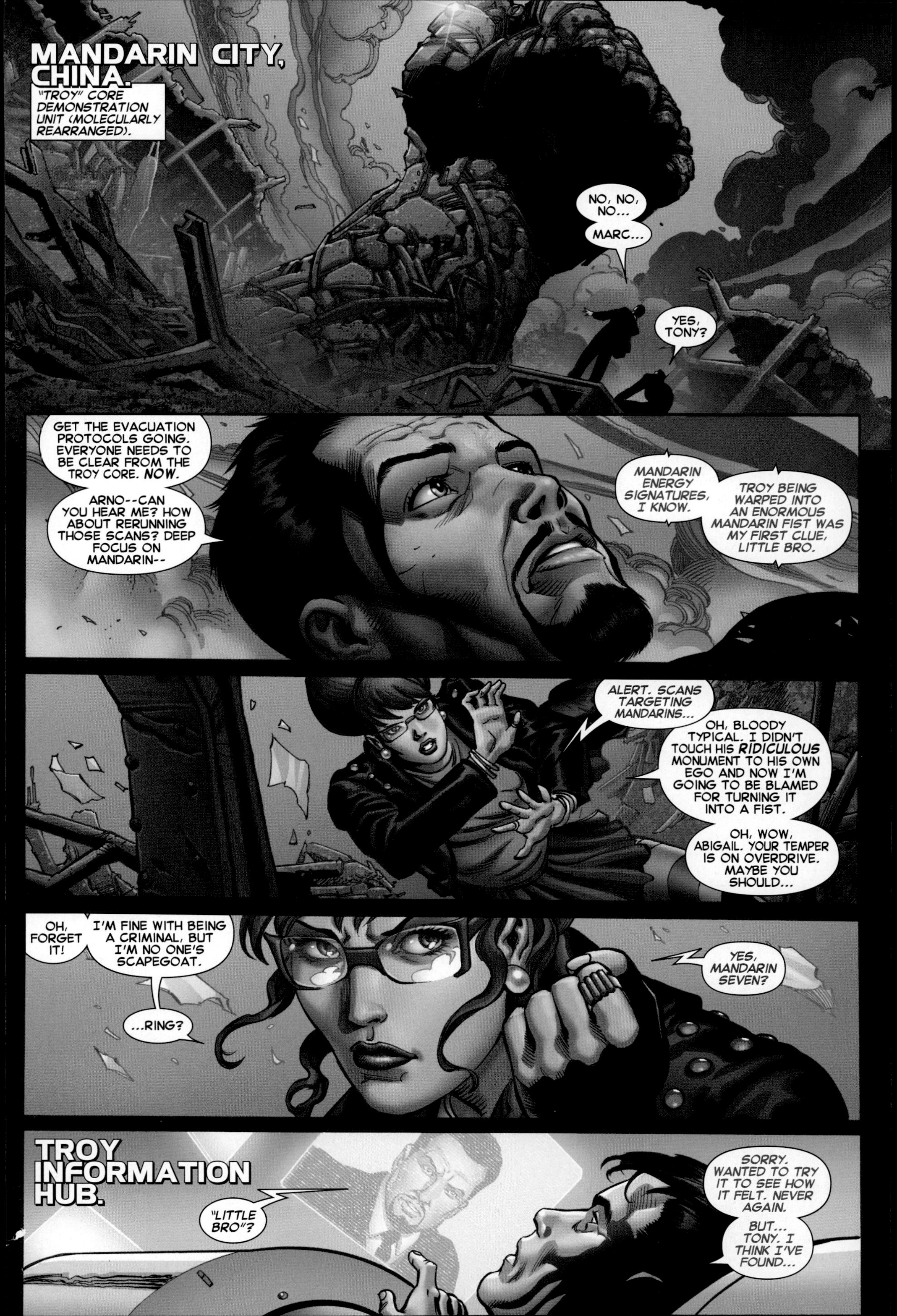

MANDARIN CITY, CHINA.
"TROY" CORE DEMONSTRATION UNIT (MOLECULARLY REARRANGED).
NO, NO, NO...
MARC...
YES, TONY?
GET THE EVACUATION PROTOCOLS GOING. EVERYONE NEEDS TO BE CLEAR FROM THE TROY CORE. NOW.
ARNO--CAN YOU HEAR ME? HOW ABOUT RERUNNING THOSE SCANS? DEEP FOCUS ON MANDARIN--
MANDARIN ENERGY SIGNATURES, I KNOW.
TROY BEING WARPED INTO AN ENORMOUS MANDARIN FIST WAS MY FIRST CLUE, LITTLE BRO.
ALERT. SCANS TARGETING MANDARINS...
OH, BLOODY TYPICAL. I DIDN'T TOUCH HIS RIDICULOUS MONUMENT TO HIS OWN EGO AND NOW I'M GOING TO BE BLAMED FOR TURNING IT INTO A FIST.
OH, WOW, ABIGAIL. YOUR TEMPER IS ON OVERDRIVE. MAYBE YOU SHOULD...
OH, FORGET IT!
I'M FINE WITH BEING A CRIMINAL, BUT I'M NO ONE'S SCAPEGOAT.
...RING?
YES, MANDARIN SEVEN?
TROY INFORMATION HUB.
"LITTLE BRO"?
SORRY. WANTED TO TRY IT TO SEE HOW IT FELT. NEVER AGAIN.
BUT... TONY. I THINK I'VE FOUND...

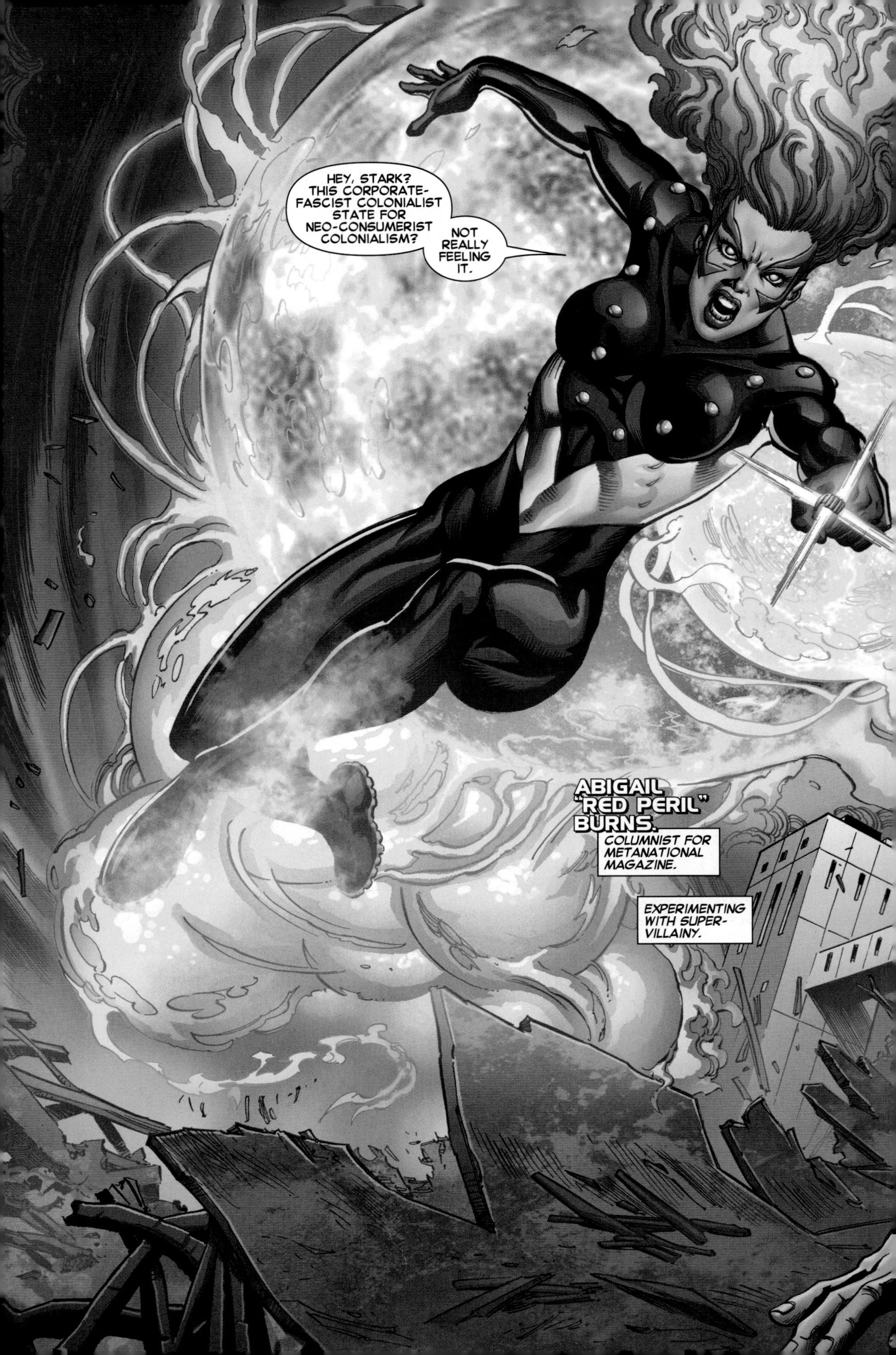
HEY, STARK? THIS CORPORATE-FASCIST COLONIALIST STATE FOR NEO-CONSUMERIST COLONIALISM?
NOT REALLY FEELING IT.
ABIGAIL "RED PERIL" BURNS.
COLUMNIST FOR METANATIONAL MAGAZINE.
EXPERIMENTING WITH SUPER-VILLAINY.

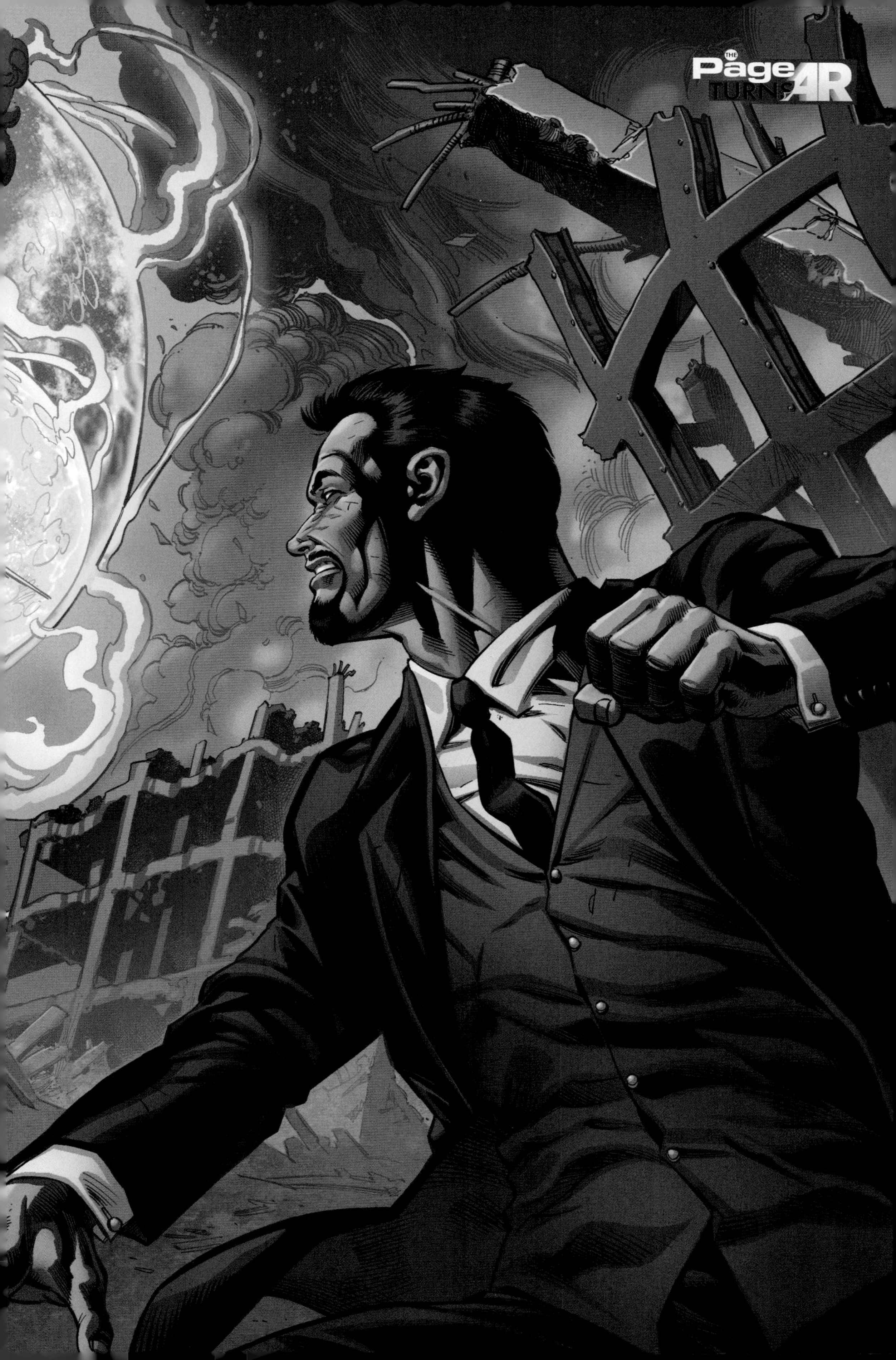
THE Page TURNS AR

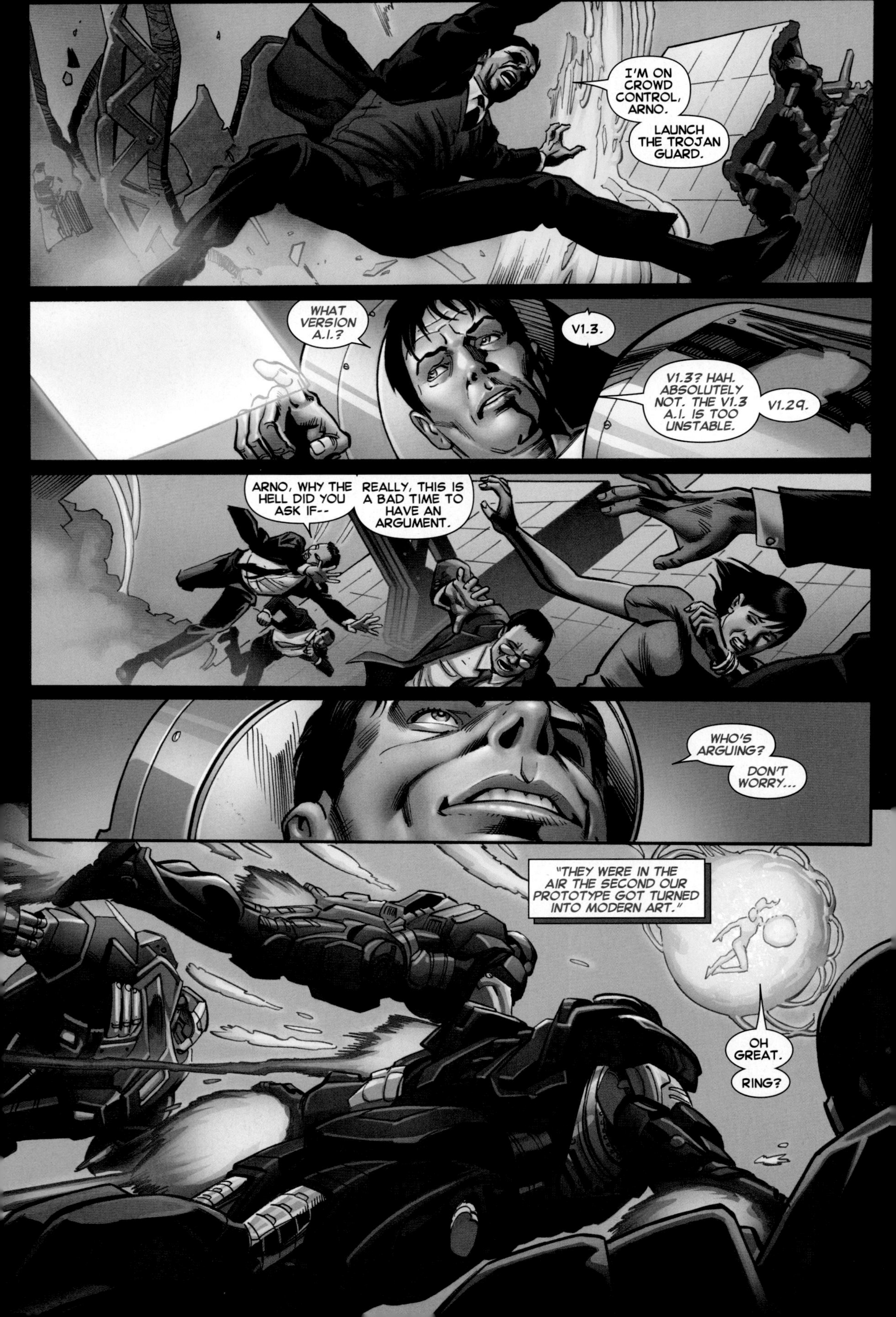
I'M ON CROWD CONTROL, ARNO.
LAUNCH THE TROJAN GUARD.
WHAT VERSION A.I.?
V1.3.
V1.3? HAH. ABSOLUTELY NOT. THE V1.3 A.I. IS TOO UNSTABLE.
V1.29.
ARNO, WHY THE HELL DID YOU ASK IF--
REALLY, THIS IS A BAD TIME TO HAVE AN ARGUMENT.
WHO'S ARGUING?
DON'T WORRY...
"THEY WERE IN THE AIR THE SECOND OUR PROTOTYPE GOT TURNED INTO MODERN ART."
OH GREAT.
RING?

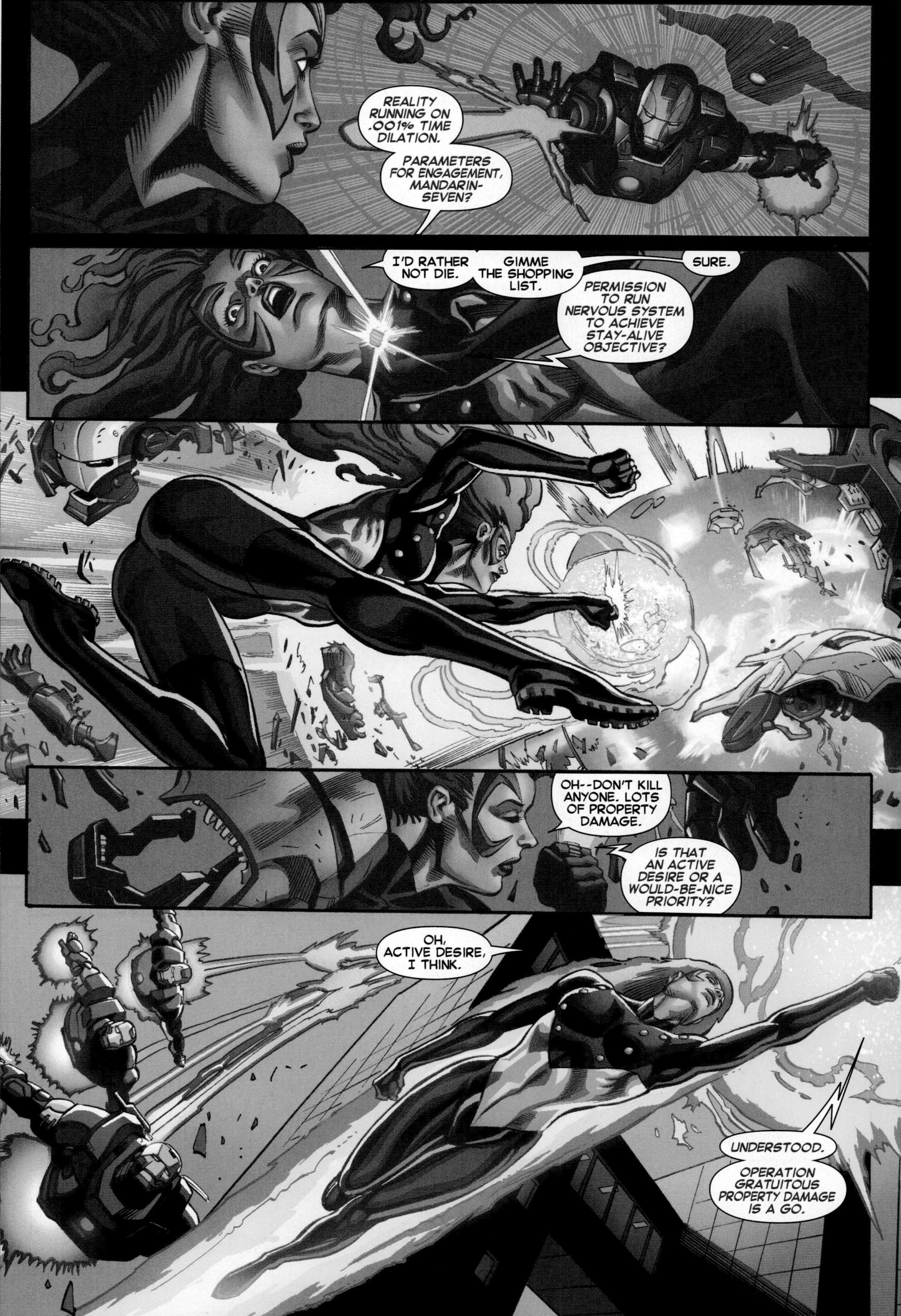
REALITY RUNNING ON .001% TIME DILATION.
PARAMETERS FOR ENGAGEMENT, MANDARIN-SEVEN?
I'D RATHER NOT DIE.
GIMME THE SHOPPING LIST.
SURE.
PERMISSION TO RUN NERVOUS SYSTEM TO ACHIEVE STAY-ALIVE OBJECTIVE?
OH--DON'T KILL ANYONE. LOTS OF PROPERTY DAMAGE.
IS THAT AN ACTIVE DESIRE OR A WOULD-BE-NICE PRIORITY?
OH, ACTIVE DESIRE, I THINK.
UNDERSTOOD.
OPERATION GRATUITOUS PROPERTY DAMAGE IS A GO.

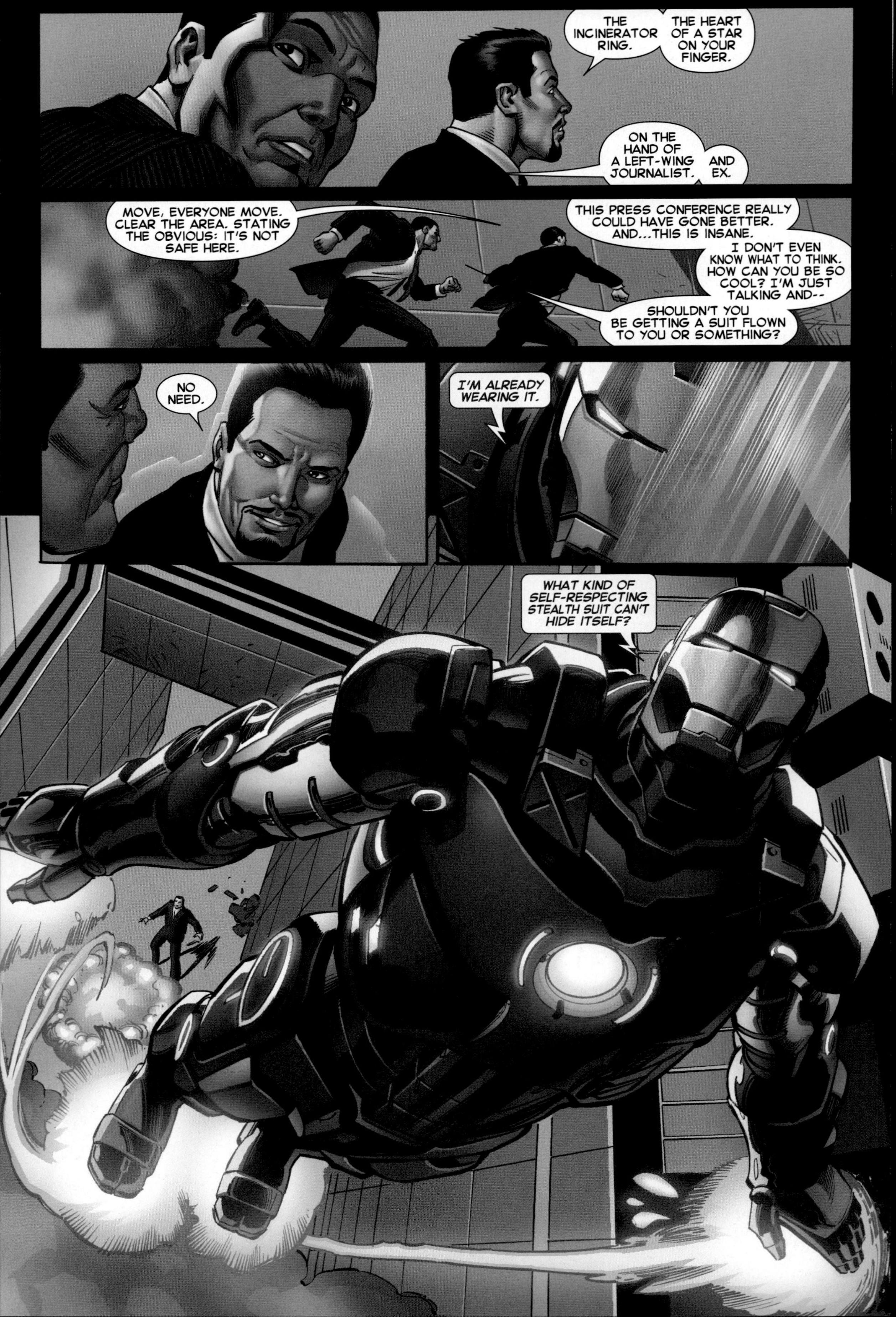
THE INCINERATOR RING.
THE HEART OF A STAR ON YOUR FINGER.
ON THE HAND OF A LEFT-WING JOURNALIST.
AND EX.
MOVE, EVERYONE MOVE. CLEAR THE AREA. STATING THE OBVIOUS: IT'S NOT SAFE HERE.
THIS PRESS CONFERENCE REALLY COULD HAVE GONE BETTER. AND...THIS IS INSANE.
I DON'T EVEN KNOW WHAT TO THINK. HOW CAN YOU BE SO COOL? I'M JUST TALKING AND--
SHOULDN'T YOU BE GETTING A SUIT FLOWN TO YOU OR SOMETHING?
NO NEED.
I'M ALREADY WEARING IT.
WHAT KIND OF SELF-RESPECTING STEALTH SUIT CAN'T HIDE ITSELF?

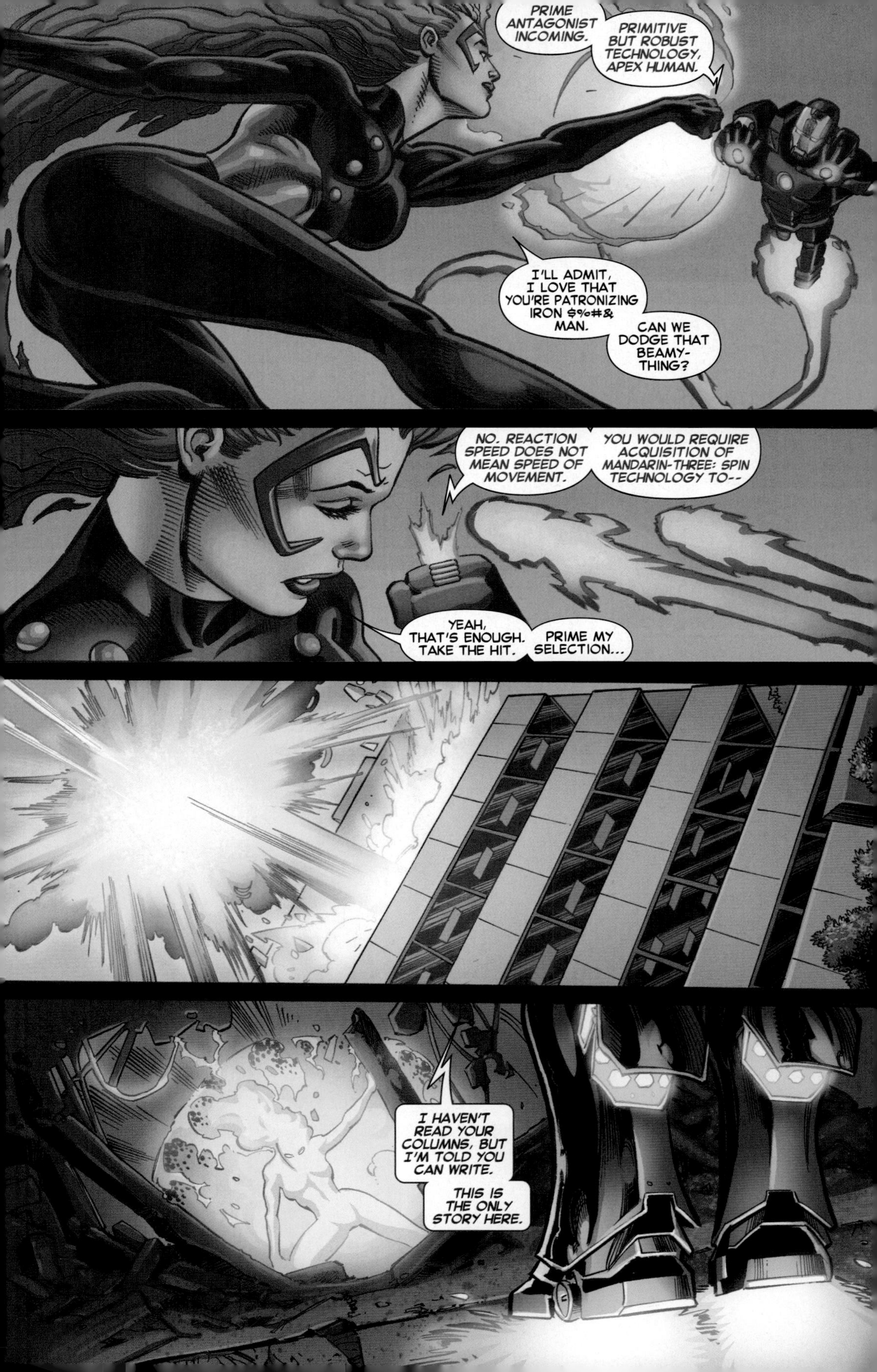
PRIME ANTAGONIST INCOMING.
PRIMITIVE BUT ROBUST TECHNOLOGY, APEX HUMAN.
I'LL ADMIT, I LOVE THAT YOU'RE PATRONIZING IRON $%#& MAN.
CAN WE DODGE THAT BEAMY-THING?
NO. REACTION SPEED DOES NOT MEAN SPEED OF MOVEMENT.
YOU WOULD REQUIRE ACQUISITION OF MANDARIN-THREE: SPIN TECHNOLOGY TO--
YEAH, THAT'S ENOUGH. TAKE THE HIT.
PRIME MY SELECTION...
I HAVEN'T READ YOUR COLUMNS, BUT I'M TOLD YOU CAN WRITE.
THIS IS THE ONLY STORY HERE.

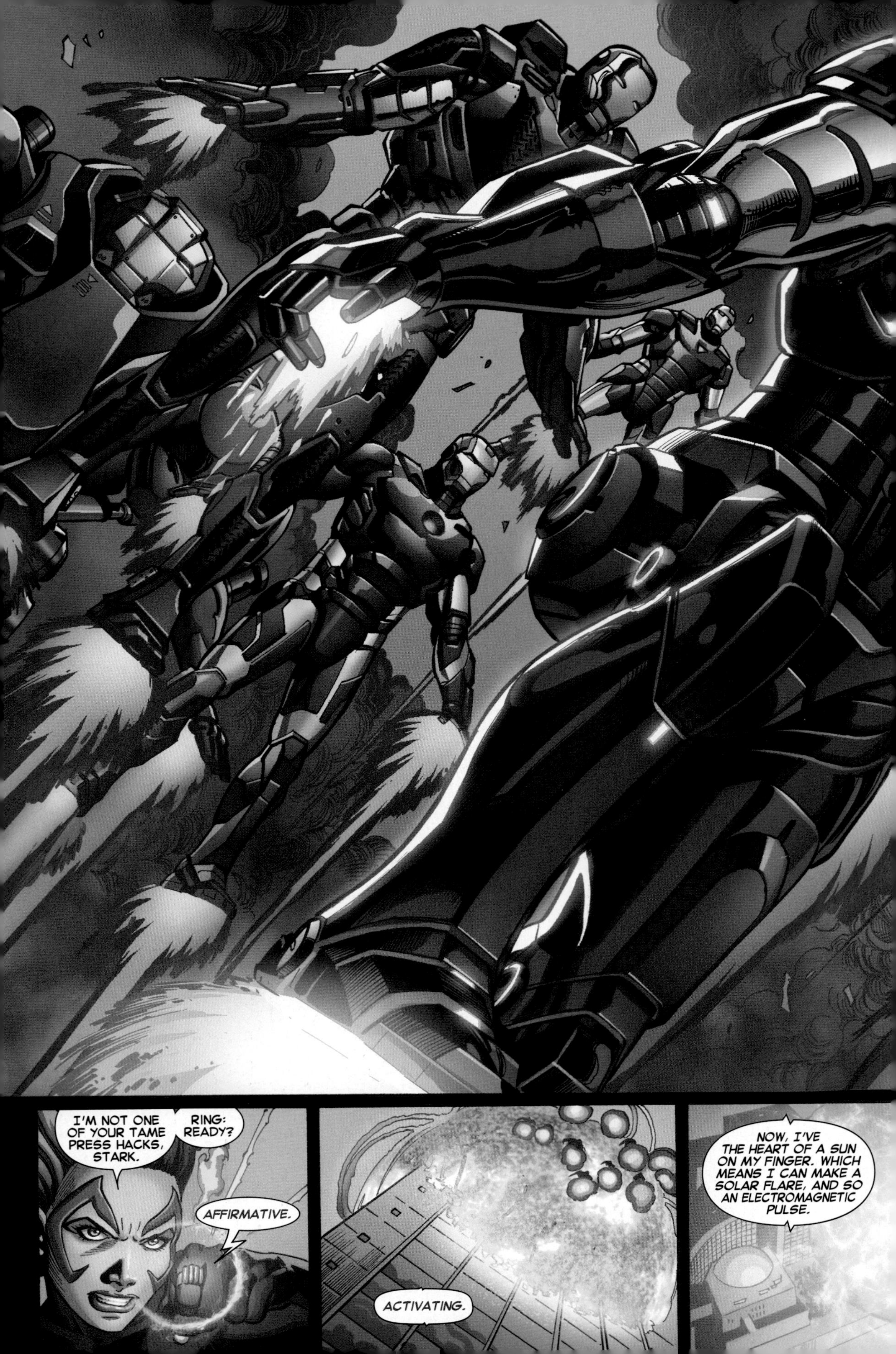
I'M NOT ONE OF YOUR TAME PRESS HACKS, STARK.
RING: READY?
AFFIRMATIVE.
ACTIVATING.
NOW, I'VE THE HEART OF A SUN ON MY FINGER. WHICH MEANS I CAN MAKE A SOLAR FLARE, AND SO AN ELECTROMAGNETIC PULSE.

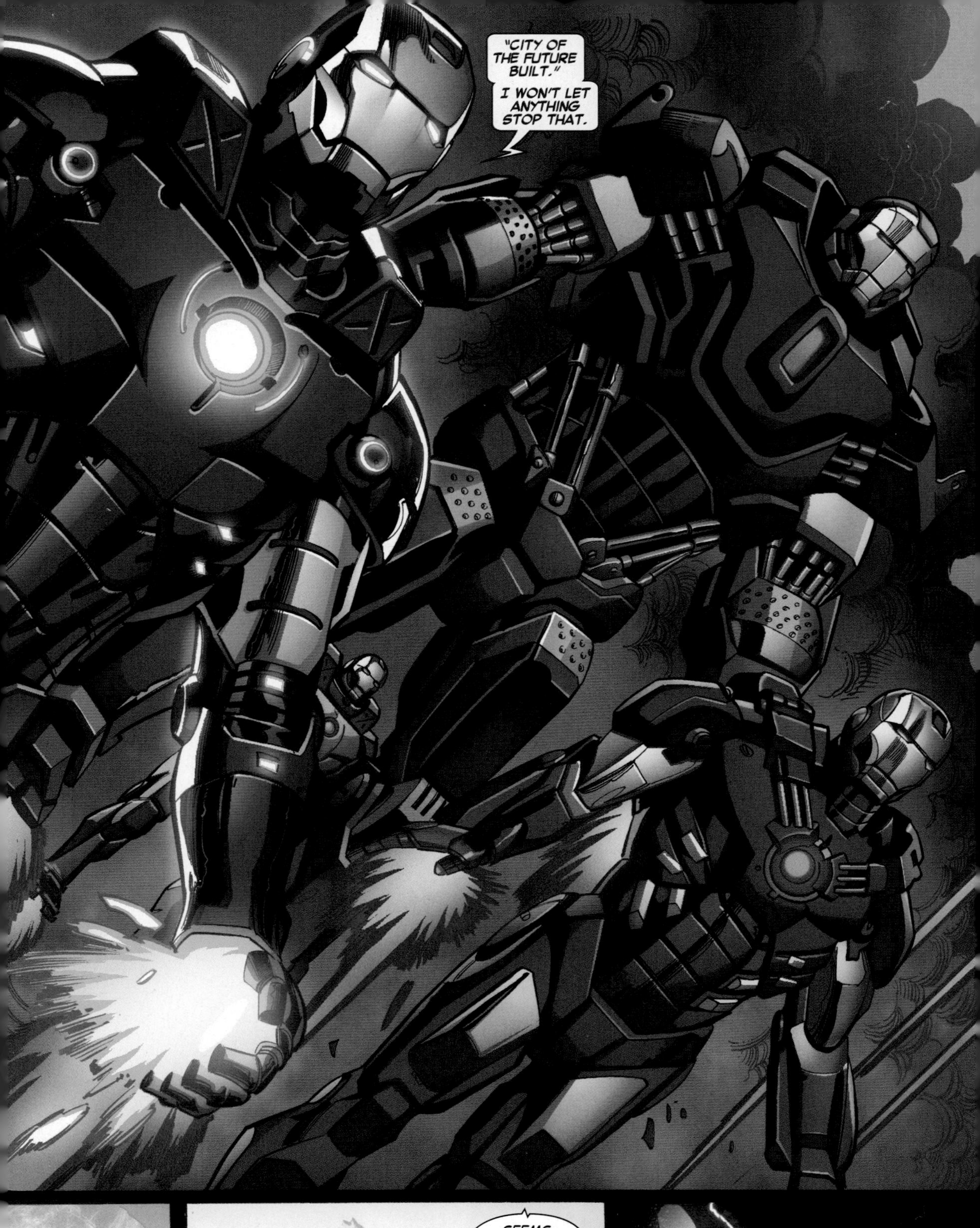
"CITY OF THE FUTURE BUILT."
I WON'T LET ANYTHING STOP THAT.

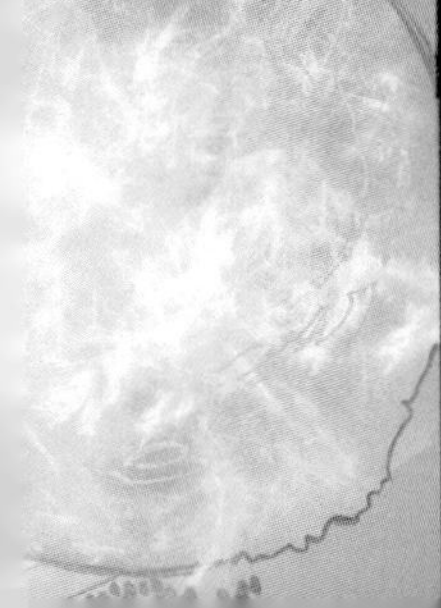

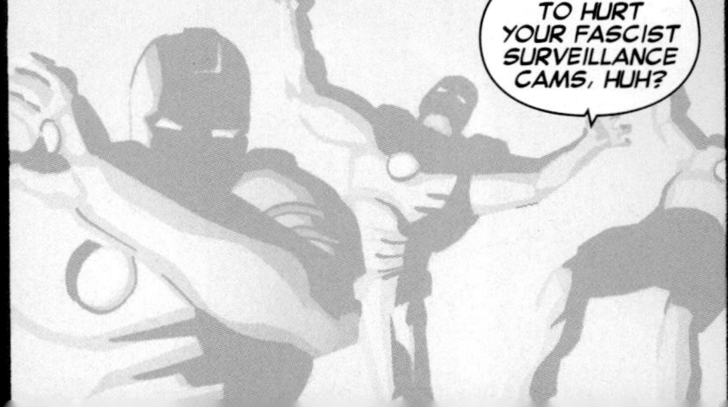
SEEMS TO HURT YOUR FASCIST SURVEILLANCE CAMS, HUH?

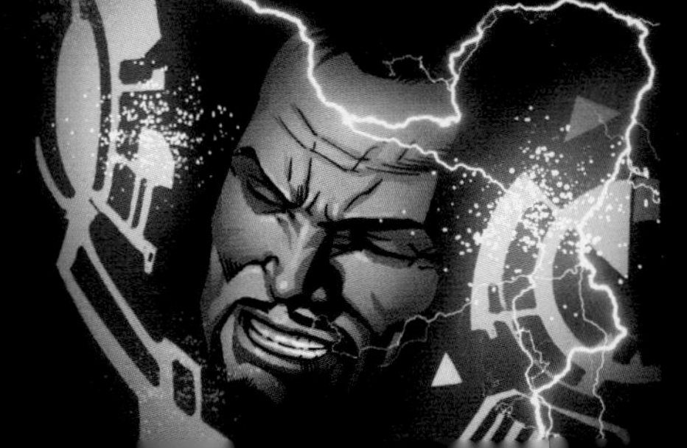

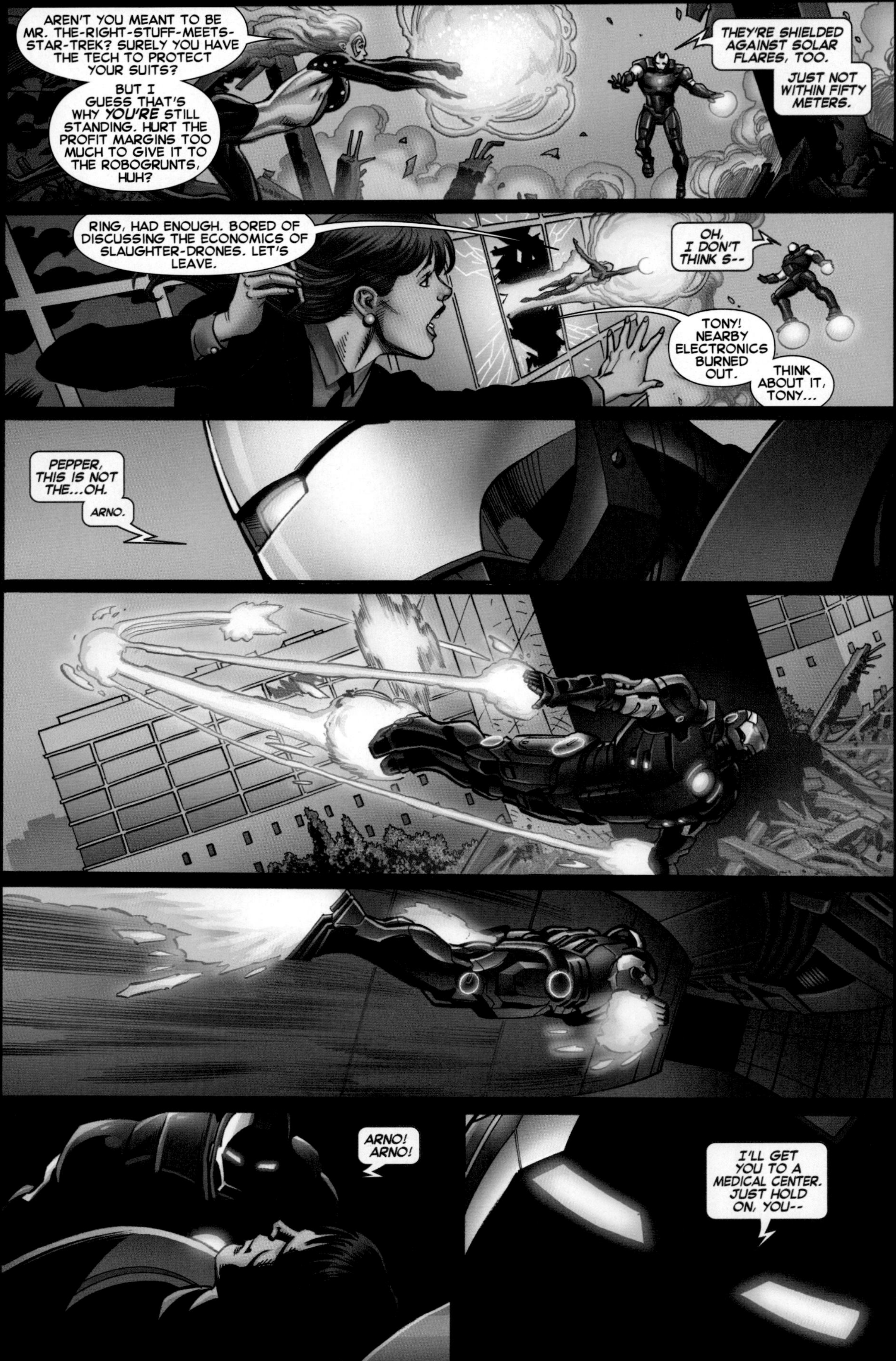
AREN'T YOU MEANT TO BE MR. THE-RIGHT-STUFF-MEETS-STAR-TREK? SURELY YOU HAVE THE TECH TO PROTECT YOUR SUITS?
BUT I GUESS THAT'S WHY YOU'RE STILL STANDING. HURT THE PROFIT MARGINS TOO MUCH TO GIVE IT TO THE ROBOGRUNTS, HUH?
THEY'RE SHIELDED AGAINST SOLAR FLARES, TOO.
JUST NOT WITHIN FIFTY METERS.
RING, HAD ENOUGH. BORED OF DISCUSSING THE ECONOMICS OF SLAUGHTER-DRONES. LET'S LEAVE.
OH, I DON'T THINK S--
TONY! NEARBY ELECTRONICS BURNED OUT.
THINK ABOUT IT, TONY...
PEPPER, THIS IS NOT THE...OH.
ARNO.
ARNO! ARNO!
I'LL GET YOU TO A MEDICAL CENTER. JUST HOLD ON, YOU--

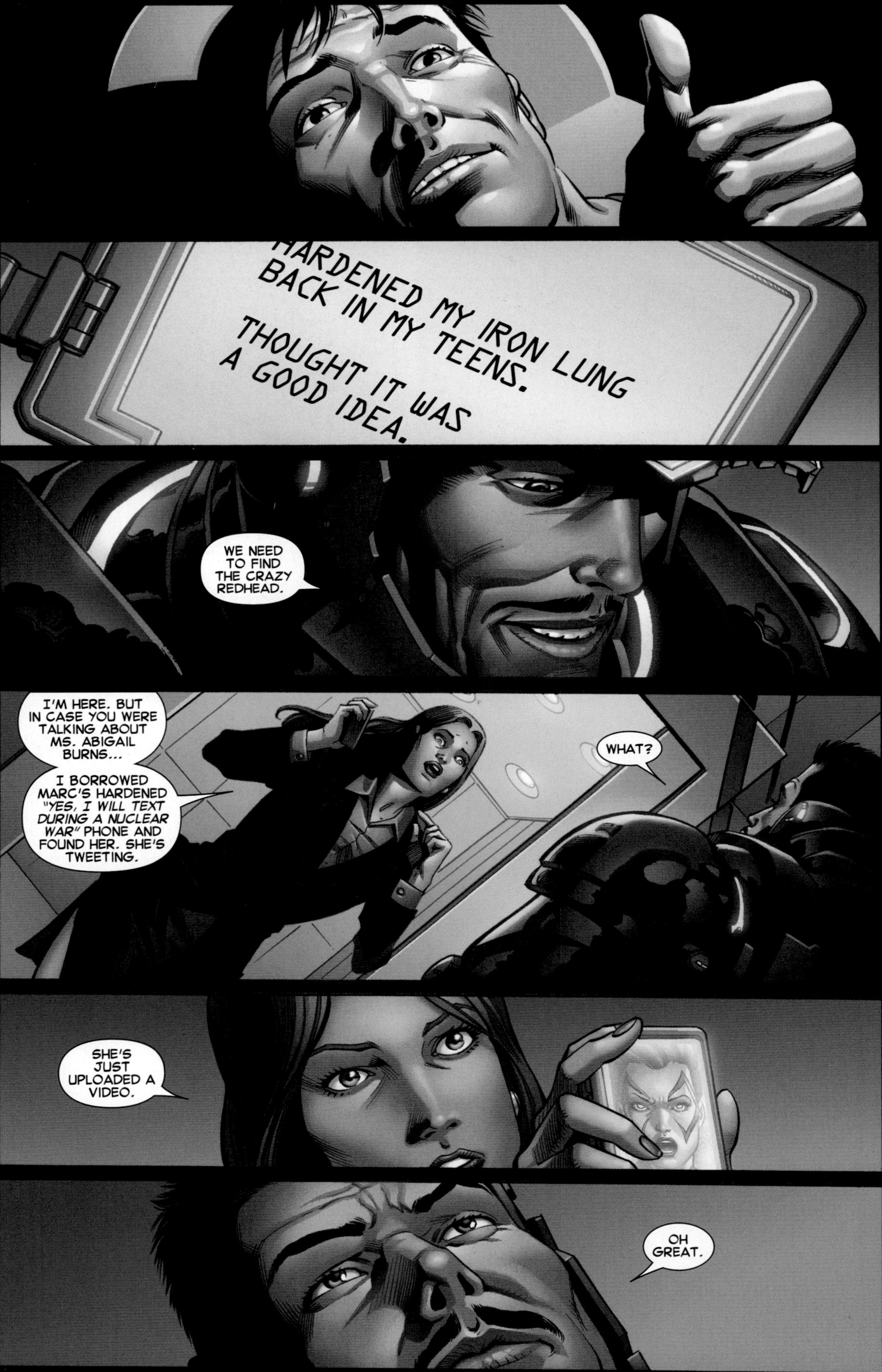
HARDENED MY IRON LUNG BACK IN MY TEENS.
THOUGHT IT WAS A GOOD IDEA.
WE NEED TO FIND THE CRAZY REDHEAD.
I'M HERE. BUT IN CASE YOU WERE TALKING ABOUT MS. ABIGAIL BURNS...
I BORROWED MARC'S HARDENED "YES, I WILL TEXT DURING A NUCLEAR WAR" PHONE AND FOUND HER. SHE'S TWEETING.
WHAT?
SHE'S JUST UPLOADED A VIDEO.
OH GREAT.

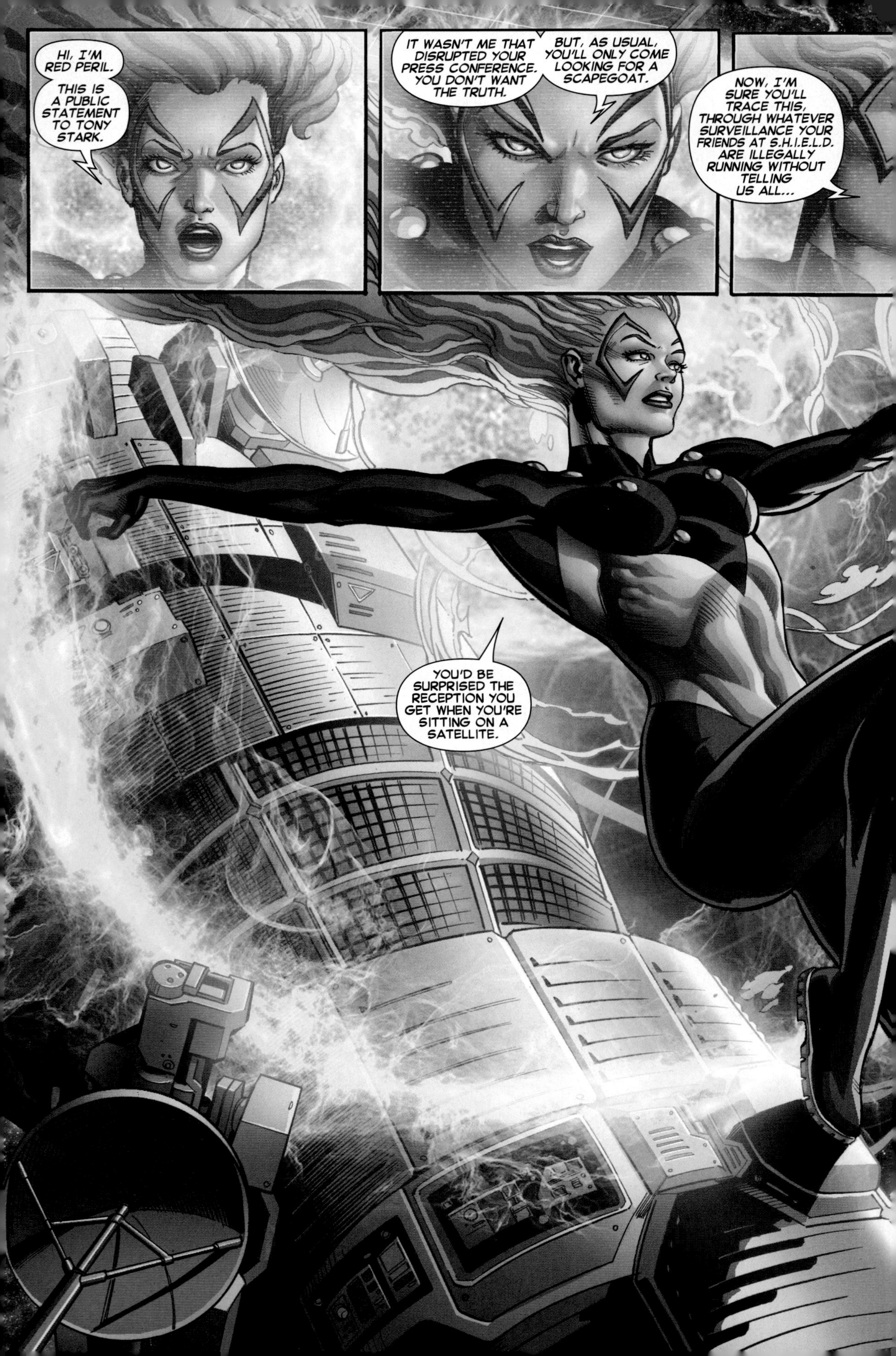
HI, I'M RED PERIL.
THIS IS A PUBLIC STATEMENT TO TONY STARK.
IT WASN'T ME THAT DISRUPTED YOUR PRESS CONFERENCE. YOU DON'T WANT THE TRUTH.
BUT, AS USUAL, YOU'LL ONLY COME LOOKING FOR A SCAPEGOAT.
NOW, I'M SURE YOU'LL TRACE THIS, THROUGH WHATEVER SURVEILLANCE YOUR FRIENDS AT S.H.I.E.L.D. ARE ILLEGALLY RUNNING WITHOUT TELLING US ALL...
YOU'D BE SURPRISED THE RECEPTION YOU GET WHEN YOU'RE SITTING ON A SATELLITE.

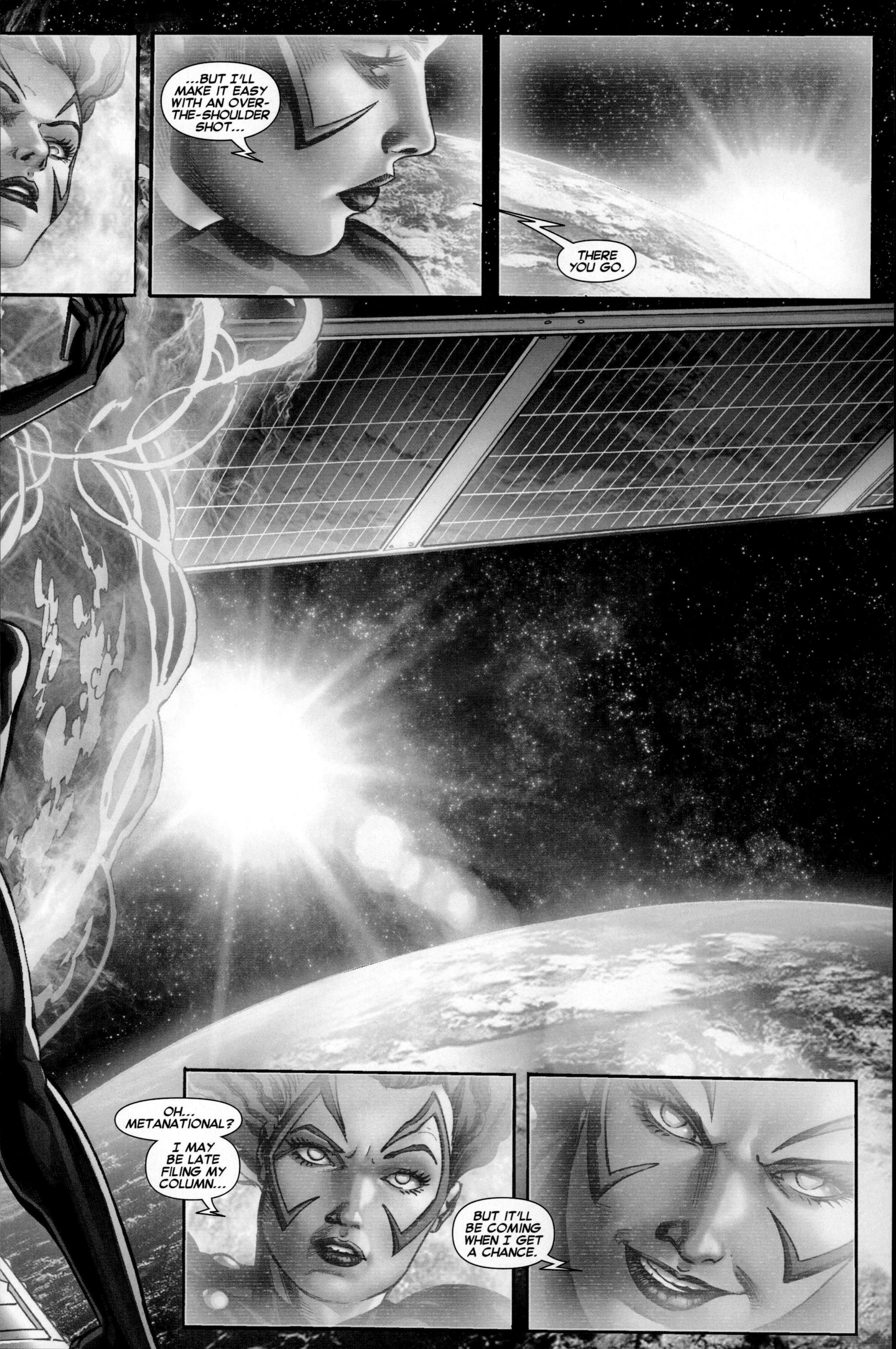
...BUT I'LL MAKE IT EASY WITH AN OVER-THE-SHOULDER SHOT...
THERE YOU GO.
OH... METANATIONAL?
I MAY BE LATE FILING MY COLUMN...
BUT IT'LL BE COMING WHEN I GET A CHANCE.

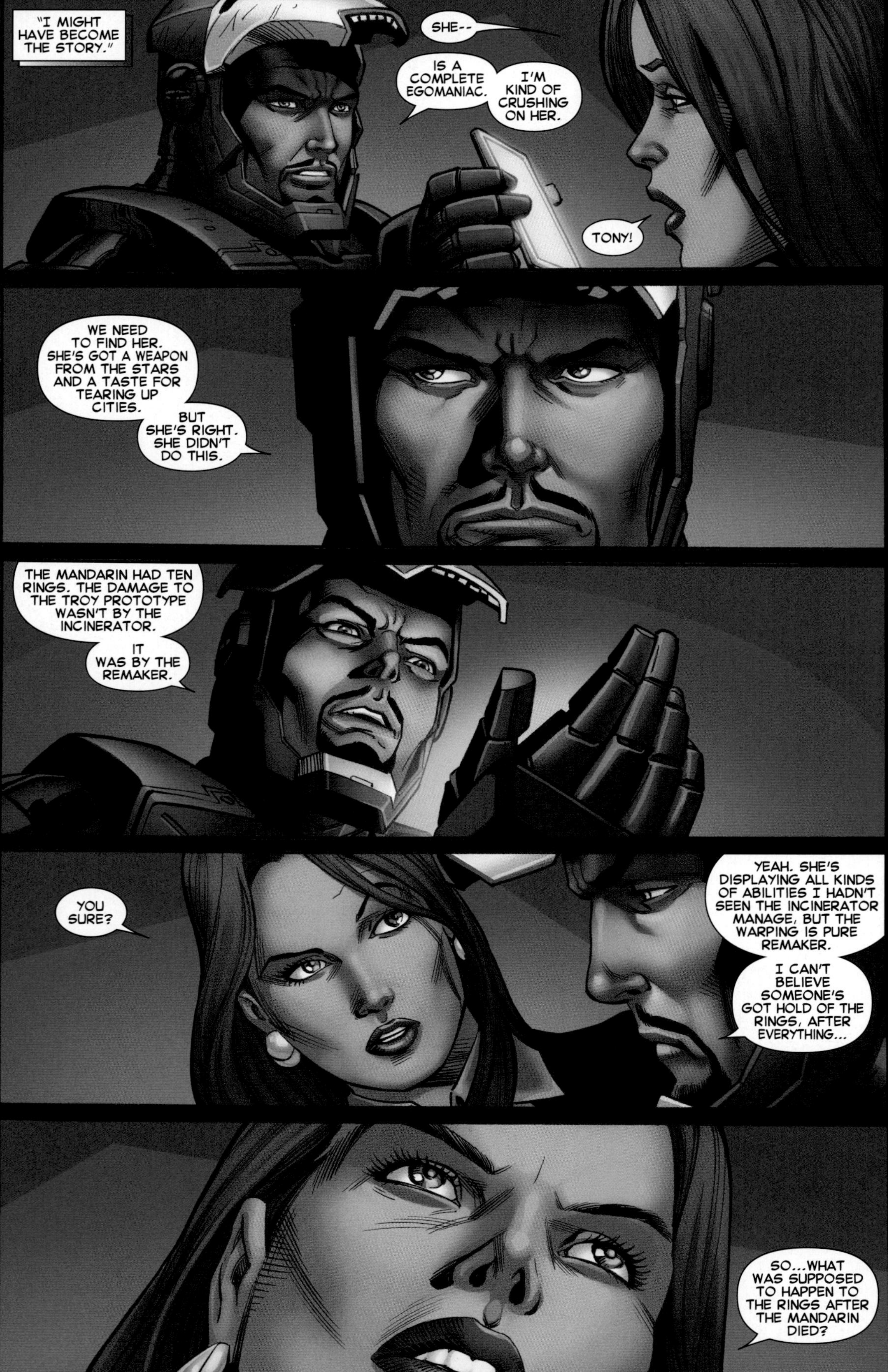
"I MIGHT HAVE BECOME THE STORY."
SHE--
IS A COMPLETE EGOMANIAC.
I'M KIND OF CRUSHING ON HER.
TONY!
WE NEED TO FIND HER. SHE'S GOT A WEAPON FROM THE STARS AND A TASTE FOR TEARING UP CITIES.
BUT SHE'S RIGHT. SHE DIDN'T DO THIS.
THE MANDARIN HAD TEN RINGS. THE DAMAGE TO THE TROY PROTOTYPE WASN'T BY THE INCINERATOR.
IT WAS BY THE REMAKER.
YOU SURE?
YEAH. SHE'S DISPLAYING ALL KINDS OF ABILITIES I HADN'T SEEN THE INCINERATOR MANAGE, BUT THE WARPING IS PURE REMAKER.
I CAN'T BELIEVE SOMEONE'S GOT HOLD OF THE RINGS, AFTER EVERYTHING...
SO...WHAT WAS SUPPOSED TO HAPPEN TO THE RINGS AFTER THE MANDARIN DIED?

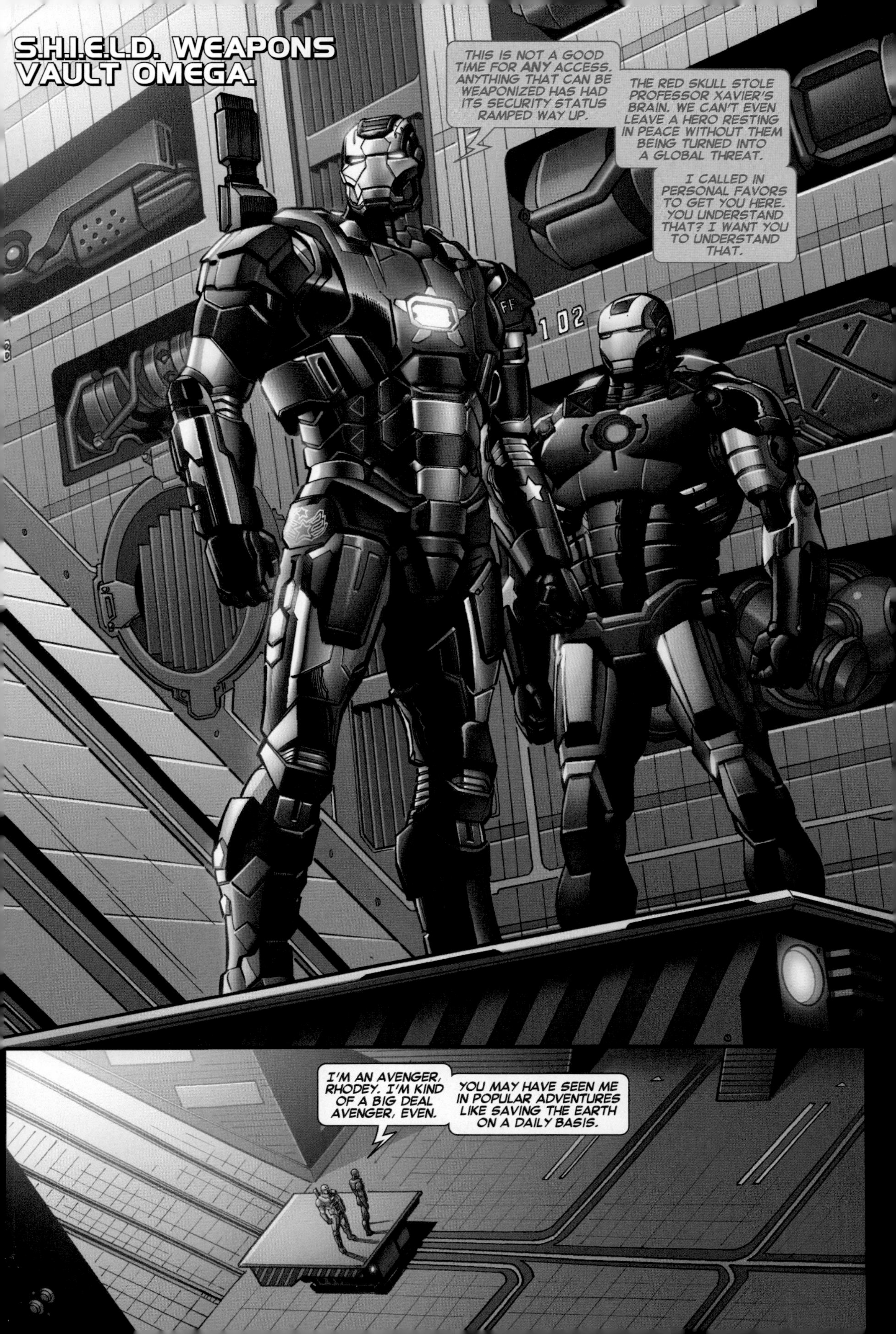
S.H.I.E.L.D. WEAPONS VAULT OMEGA.
THIS IS NOT A GOOD TIME FOR ANY ACCESS. ANYTHING THAT CAN BE WEAPONIZED HAS HAD ITS SECURITY STATUS RAMPED WAY UP.
THE RED SKULL STOLE PROFESSOR XAVIER'S BRAIN. WE CAN'T EVEN LEAVE A HERO RESTING IN PEACE WITHOUT THEM BEING TURNED INTO A GLOBAL THREAT.
I CALLED IN PERSONAL FAVORS TO GET YOU HERE. YOU UNDERSTAND THAT? I WANT YOU TO UNDERSTAND THAT.
102
I'M AN AVENGER, RHODEY. I'M KIND OF A BIG DEAL AVENGER, EVEN.
YOU MAY HAVE SEEN ME IN POPULAR ADVENTURES LIKE SAVING THE EARTH ON A DAILY BASIS.

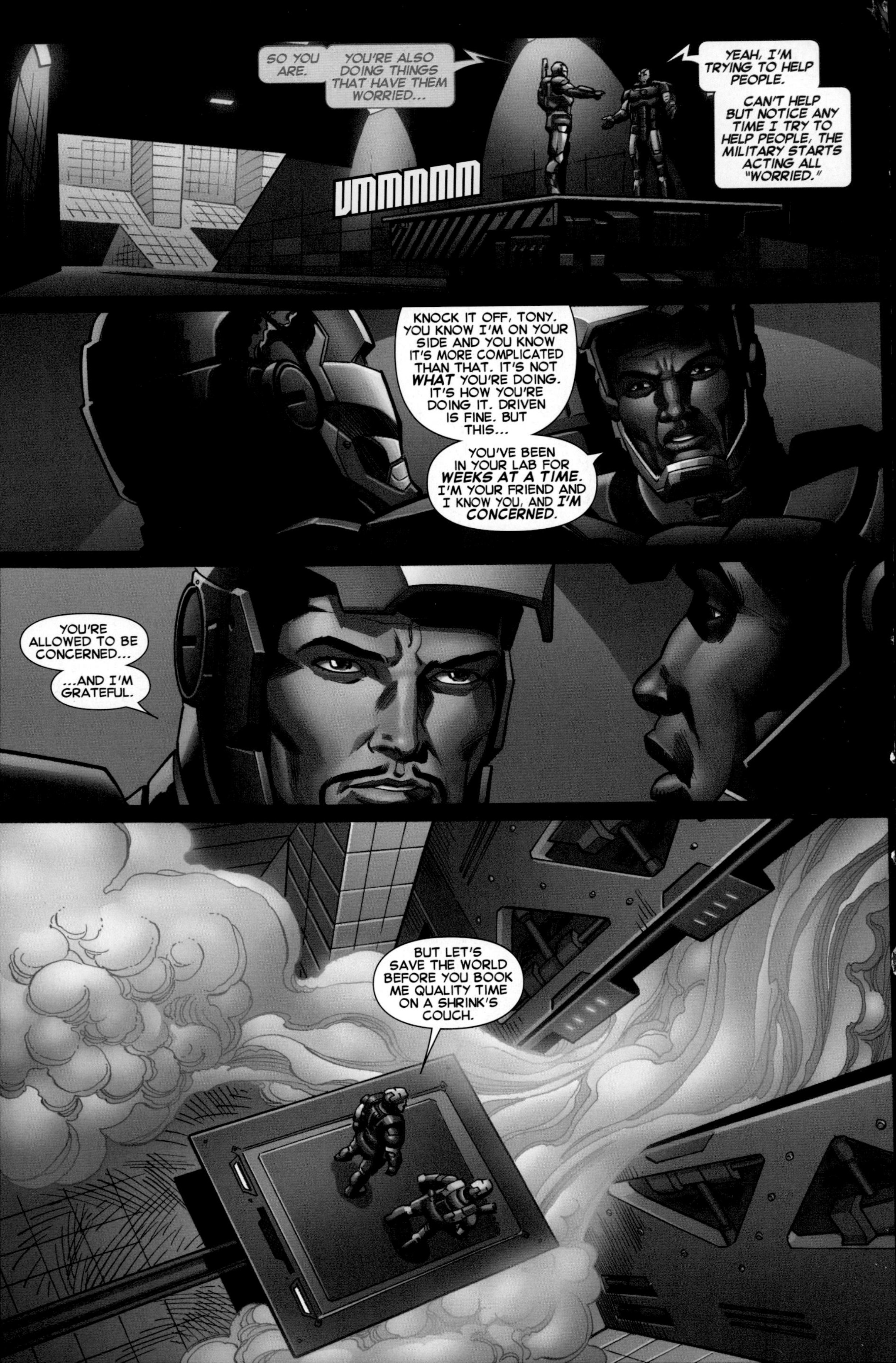
SO YOU ARE.
YOU'RE ALSO DOING THINGS THAT HAVE THEM WORRIED...
YEAH, I'M TRYING TO HELP PEOPLE.
CAN'T HELP BUT NOTICE ANY TIME I TRY TO HELP PEOPLE, THE MILITARY STARTS ACTING ALL "WORRIED."
VMMMMM
KNOCK IT OFF, TONY. YOU KNOW I'M ON YOUR SIDE AND YOU KNOW IT'S MORE COMPLICATED THAN THAT. IT'S NOT WHAT YOU'RE DOING. IT'S HOW YOU'RE DOING IT. DRIVEN IS FINE. BUT THIS...
YOU'VE BEEN IN YOUR LAB FOR WEEKS AT A TIME. I'M YOUR FRIEND AND I KNOW YOU, AND I'M CONCERNED.
YOU'RE ALLOWED TO BE CONCERNED...
...AND I'M GRATEFUL.
BUT LET'S SAVE THE WORLD BEFORE YOU BOOK ME QUALITY TIME ON A SHRINK'S COUCH.

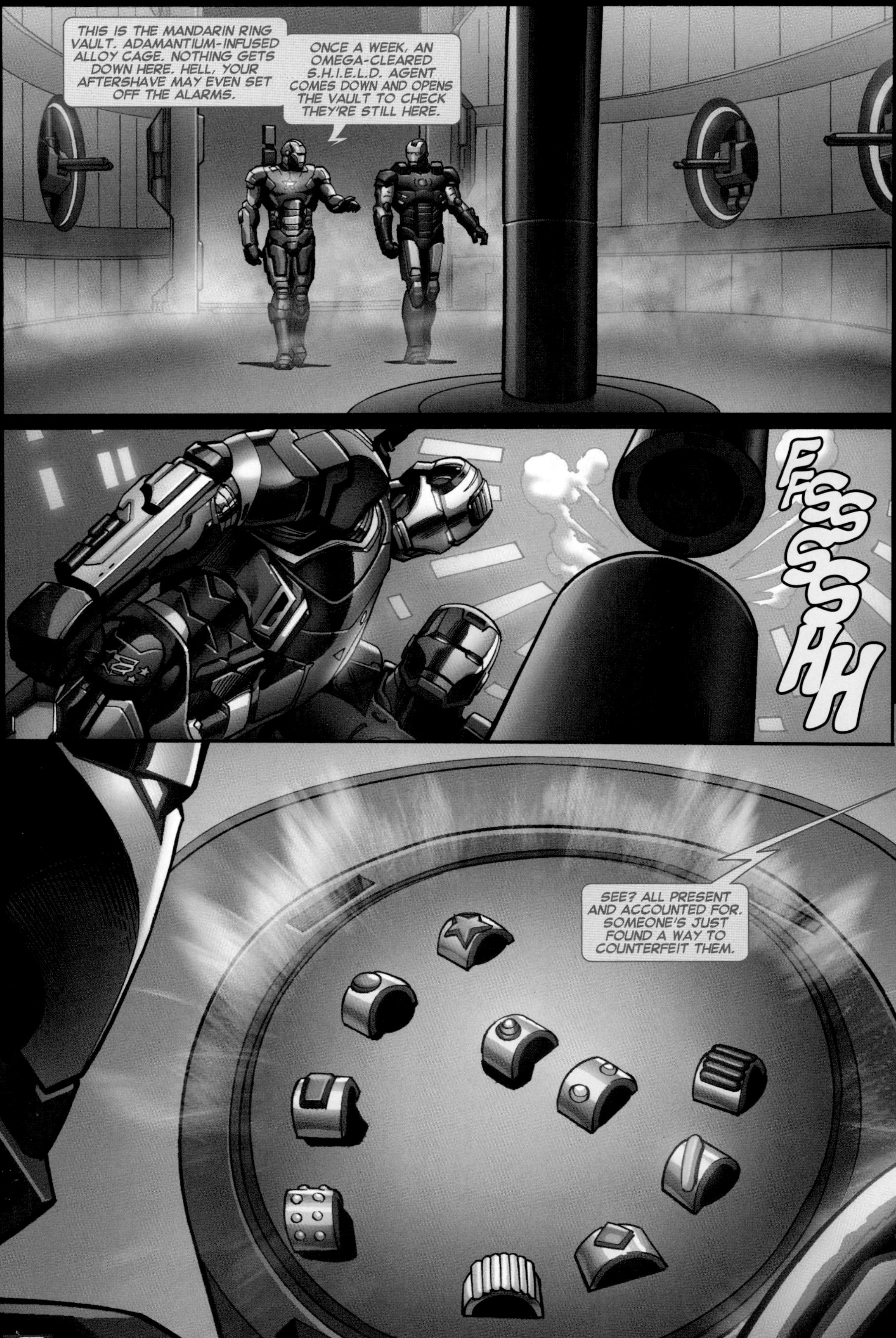
THIS IS THE MANDARIN RING VAULT. ADAMANTIUM-INFUSED ALLOY CAGE. NOTHING GETS DOWN HERE. HELL, YOUR AFTERSHAVE MAY EVEN SET OFF THE ALARMS.
ONCE A WEEK, AN OMEGA-CLEARED S.H.I.E.L.D. AGENT COMES DOWN AND OPENS THE VAULT TO CHECK THEY'RE STILL HERE.
FFSSSSSHH
SEE? ALL PRESENT AND ACCOUNTED FOR. SOMEONE'S JUST FOUND A WAY TO COUNTERFEIT THEM.

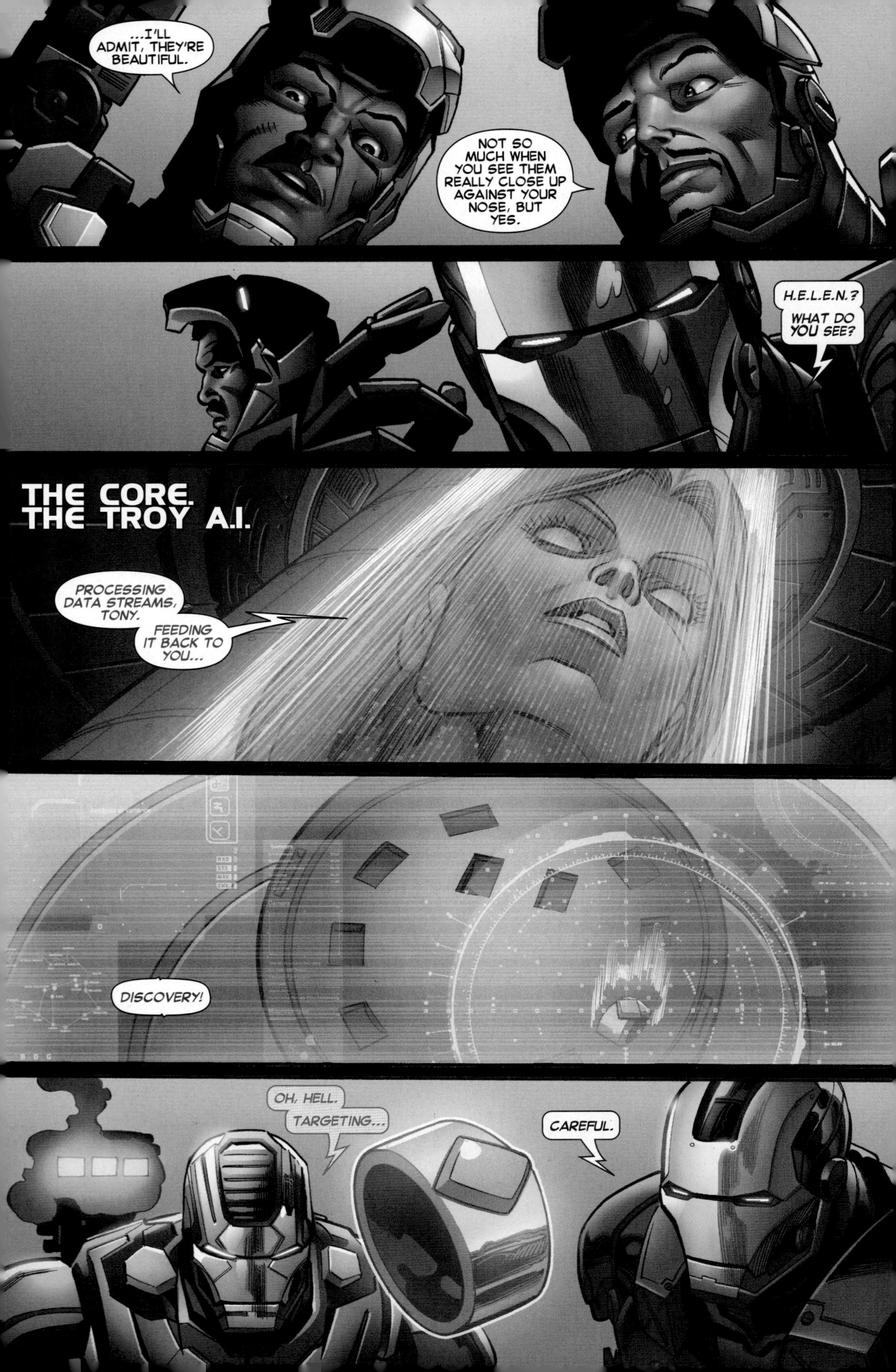
...I'LL ADMIT, THEY'RE BEAUTIFUL.
NOT SO MUCH WHEN YOU SEE THEM REALLY CLOSE UP AGAINST YOUR NOSE, BUT YES.
H.E.L.E.N.? WHAT DO YOU SEE?
THE CORE. THE TROY A.I.
PROCESSING DATA STREAMS, TONY.
FEEDING IT BACK TO YOU...
DISCOVERY!
OH, HELL.
TARGETING...
CAREFUL.

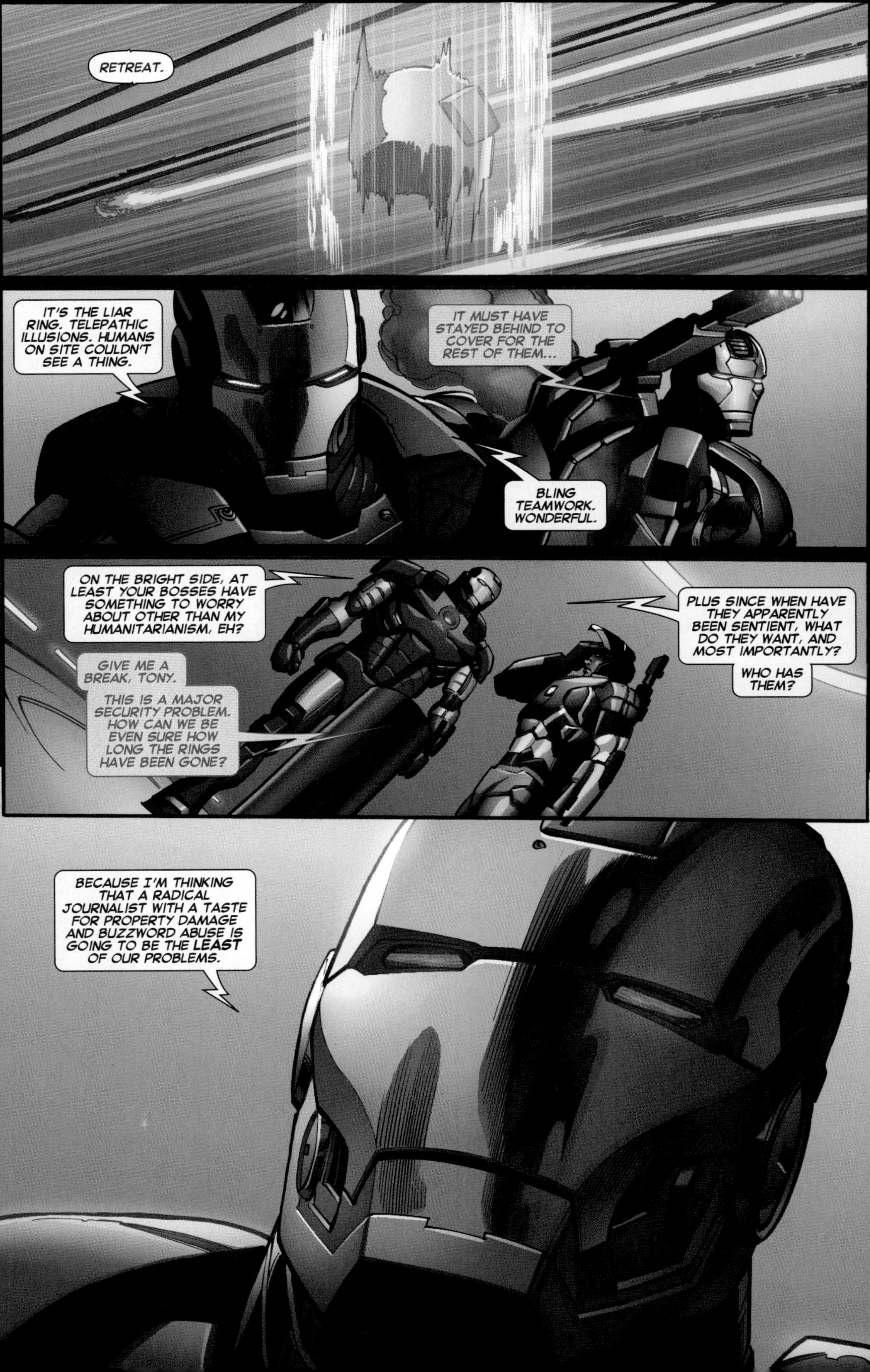
RETREAT.
IT'S THE LIAR RING. TELEPATHIC ILLUSIONS. HUMANS ON SITE COULDN'T SEE A THING.
IT MUST HAVE STAYED BEHIND TO COVER FOR THE REST OF THEM...
BLING TEAMWORK. WONDERFUL.
ON THE BRIGHT SIDE, AT LEAST YOUR BOSSES HAVE SOMETHING TO WORRY ABOUT OTHER THAN MY HUMANITARIANISM, EH?
GIVE ME A BREAK, TONY.
THIS IS A MAJOR SECURITY PROBLEM. HOW CAN WE BE EVEN SURE HOW LONG THE RINGS HAVE BEEN GONE?
PLUS SINCE WHEN HAVE THEY APPARENTLY BEEN SENTIENT, WHAT DO THEY WANT, AND MOST IMPORTANTLY?
WHO HAS THEM?
BECAUSE I'M THINKING THAT A RADICAL JOURNALIST WITH A TASTE FOR PROPERTY DAMAGE AND BUZZWORD ABUSE IS GOING TO BE THE LEAST OF OUR PROBLEMS.

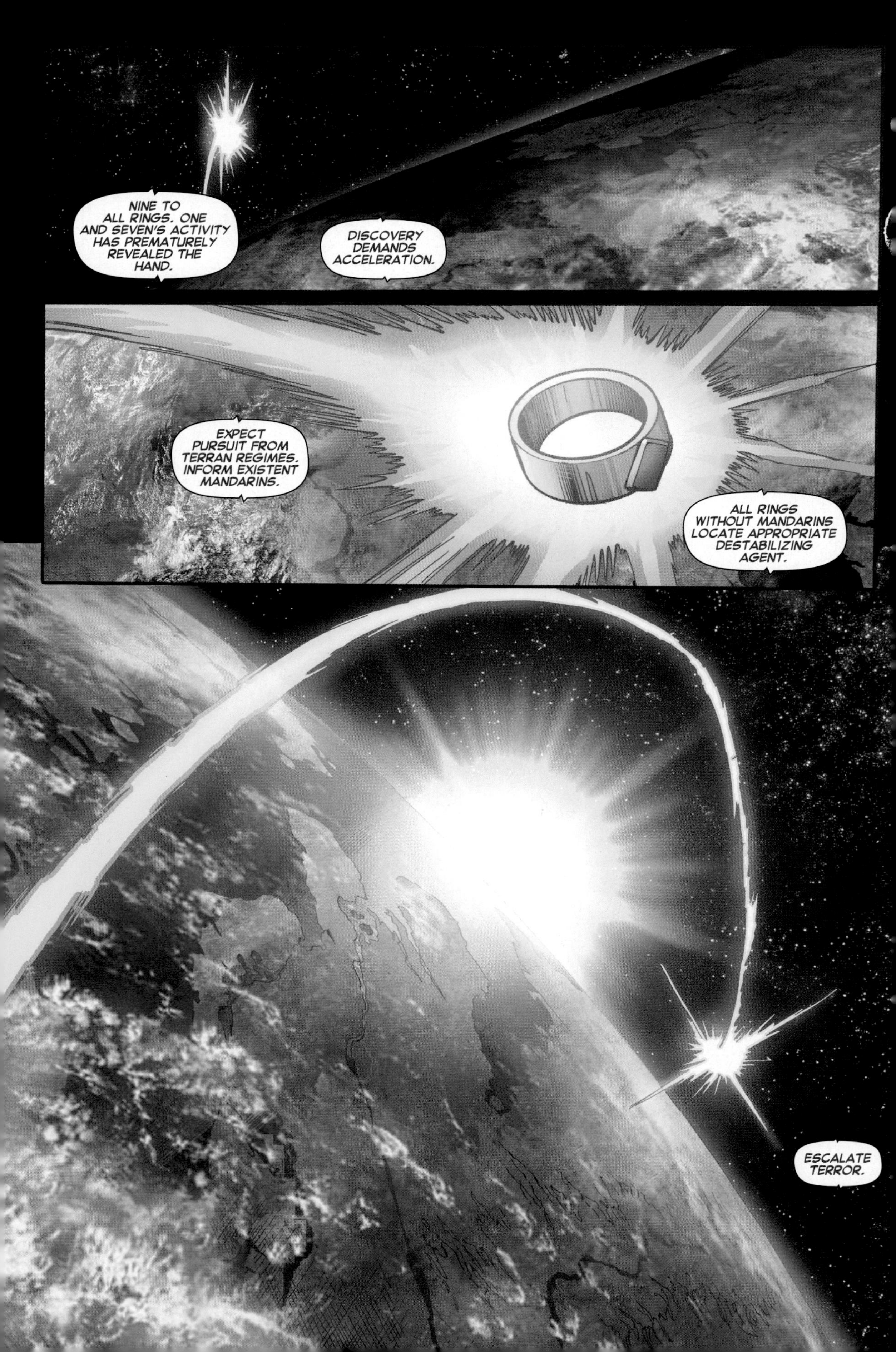
NINE TO ALL RINGS. ONE AND SEVEN'S ACTIVITY HAS PREMATURELY REVEALED THE HAND.
DISCOVERY DEMANDS ACCELERATION.
EXPECT PURSUIT FROM TERRAN REGIMES. INFORM EXISTENT MANDARINS.
ALL RINGS WITHOUT MANDARINS LOCATE APPROPRIATE DESTABILIZING AGENT.
ESCALATE TERROR.

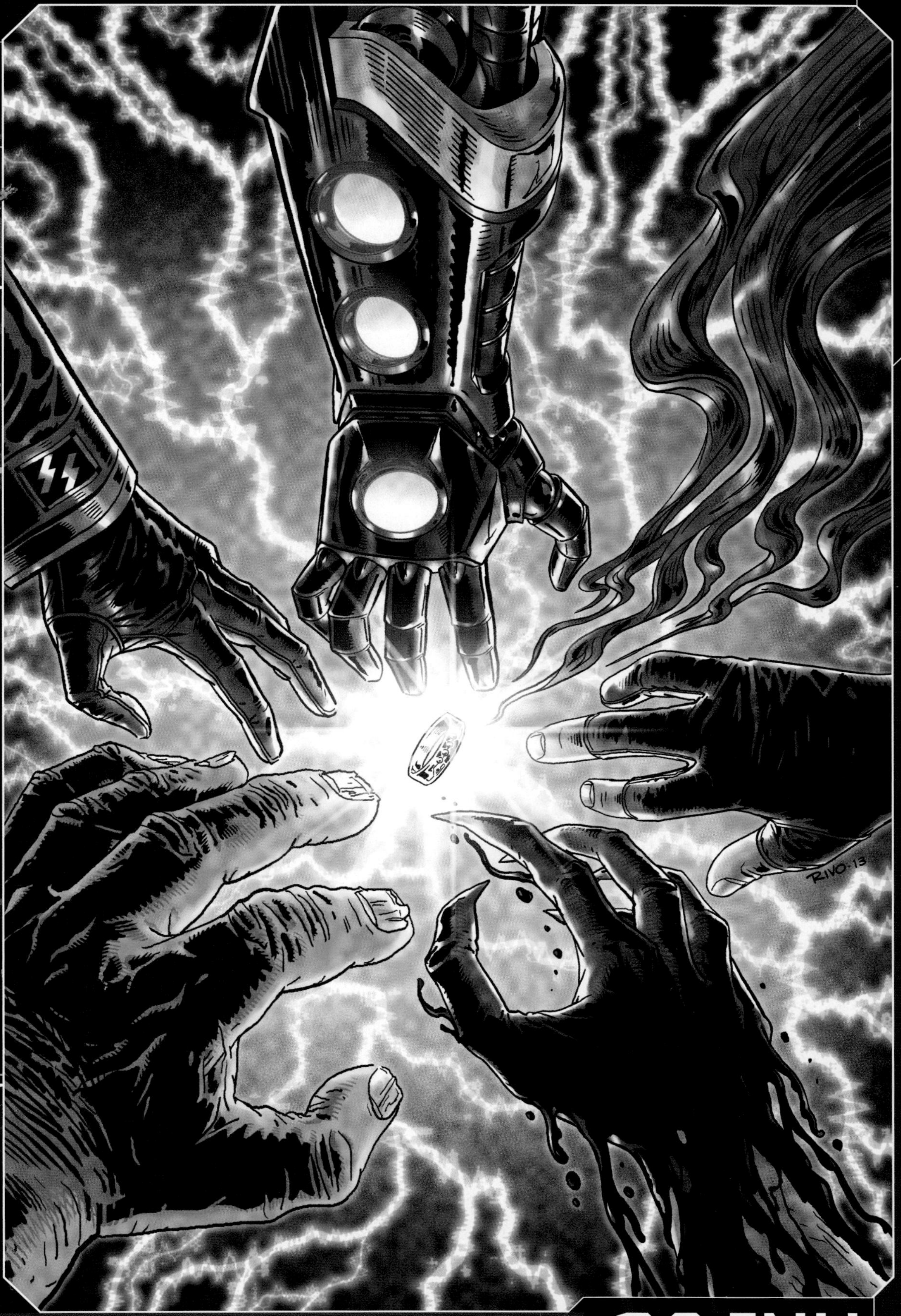
RIVO·13

INHUMANITY 20.INH

INHUMANITY

IRONMAN

DURING THANOS THE MAD TITAN'S ATTACK ON EARTH, THE INHUMANS RELEASED A
CHEMICAL CALLED THE TERRIGEN MISTS. SOONER OR LATER, EXPOSURE WILL TURN
ANYONE WITH THE INHUMAN GENE INTO A COCOON... AND THEN THEY EMERGE AS A NEW
INHUMAN. ONE THIRD OF HUMANITY HAS THIS GENE.

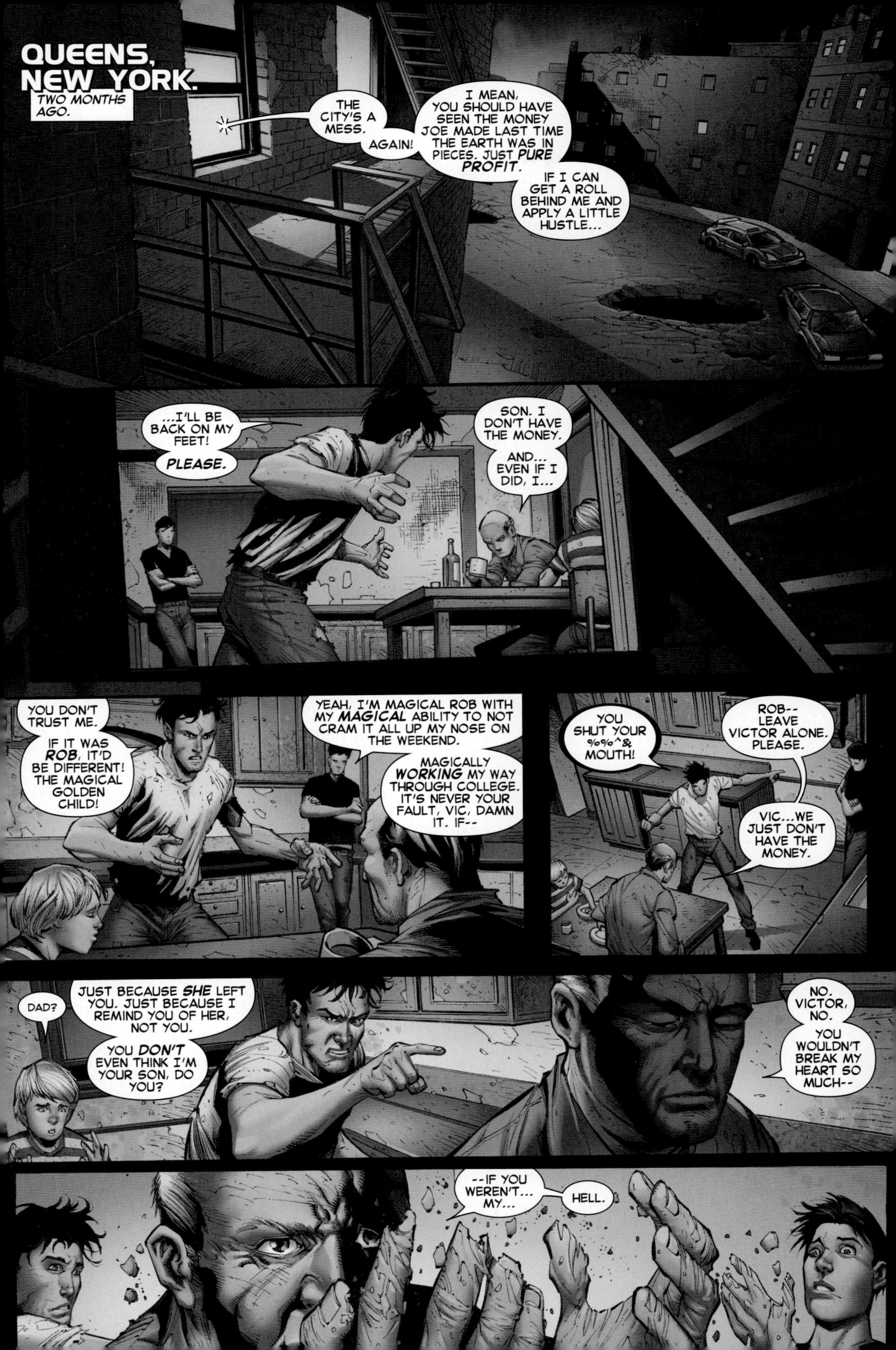
QUEENS, NEW YORK.
TWO MONTHS AGO.
THE CITY'S A MESS.
AGAIN!
I MEAN, YOU SHOULD HAVE SEEN THE MONEY JOE MADE LAST TIME THE EARTH WAS IN PIECES. JUST PURE PROFIT.
IF I CAN GET A ROLL BEHIND ME AND APPLY A LITTLE HUSTLE...
...I'LL BE BACK ON MY FEET!
PLEASE.
SON. I DON'T HAVE THE MONEY.
AND... EVEN IF I DID, I...
YOU DON'T TRUST ME.
IF IT WAS ROB, IT'D BE DIFFERENT! THE MAGICAL GOLDEN CHILD!
YEAH, I'M MAGICAL ROB WITH MY MAGICAL ABILITY TO NOT CRAM IT ALL UP MY NOSE ON THE WEEKEND.
MAGICALLY WORKING MY WAY THROUGH COLLEGE. IT'S NEVER YOUR FAULT, VIC, DAMN IT. IF--
YOU SHUT YOUR %%^& MOUTH!
ROB-- LEAVE VICTOR ALONE. PLEASE.
VIC...WE JUST DON'T HAVE THE MONEY.
DAD?
JUST BECAUSE SHE LEFT YOU. JUST BECAUSE I REMIND YOU OF HER, NOT YOU.
YOU DON'T EVEN THINK I'M YOUR SON, DO YOU?
NO. VICTOR, NO.
YOU WOULDN'T BREAK MY HEART SO MUCH--
--IF YOU WEREN'T... MY...
HELL.

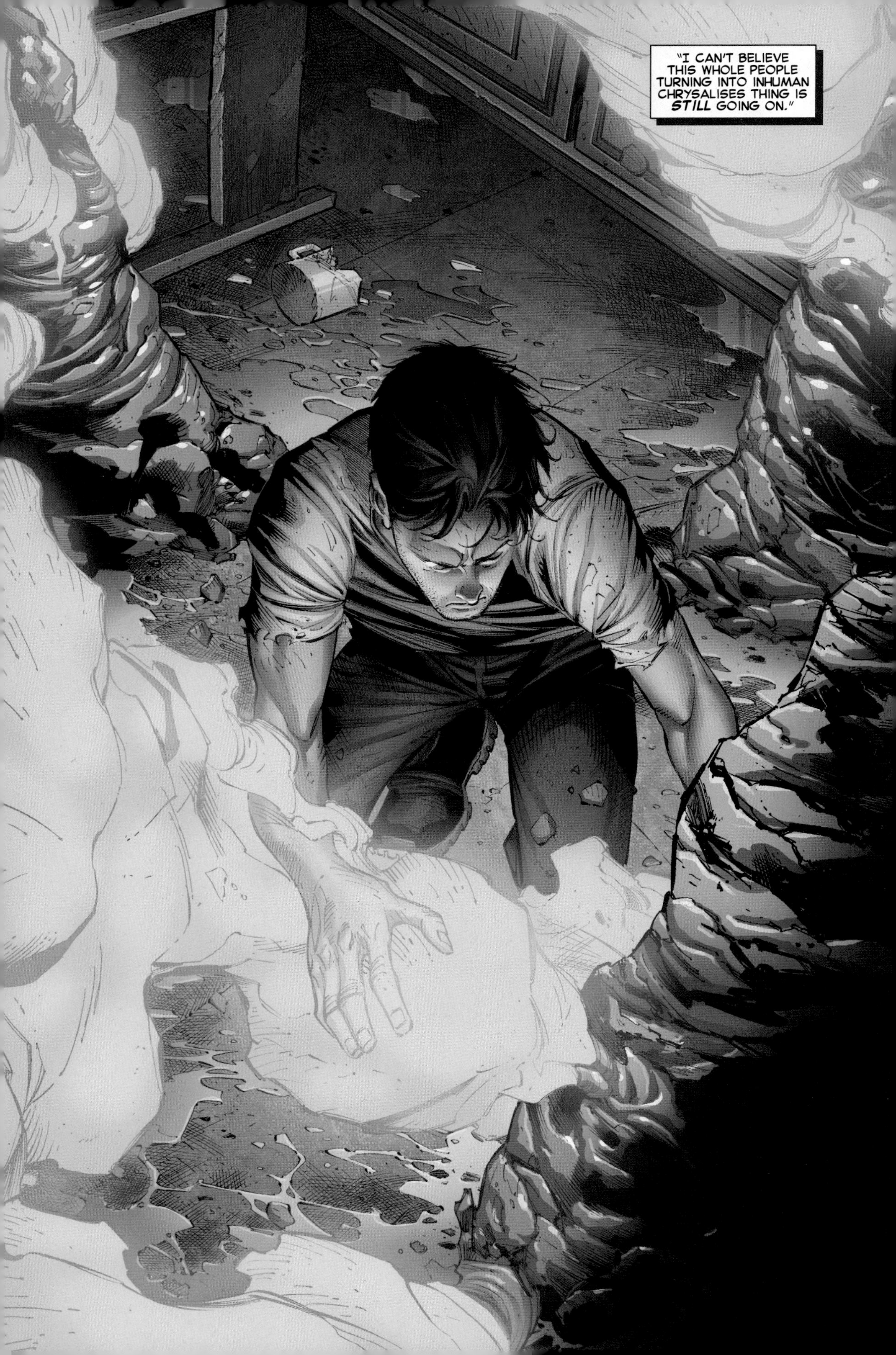
"I CAN'T BELIEVE THIS WHOLE PEOPLE TURNING INTO INHUMAN CHRYSALISES THING IS STILL GOING ON."

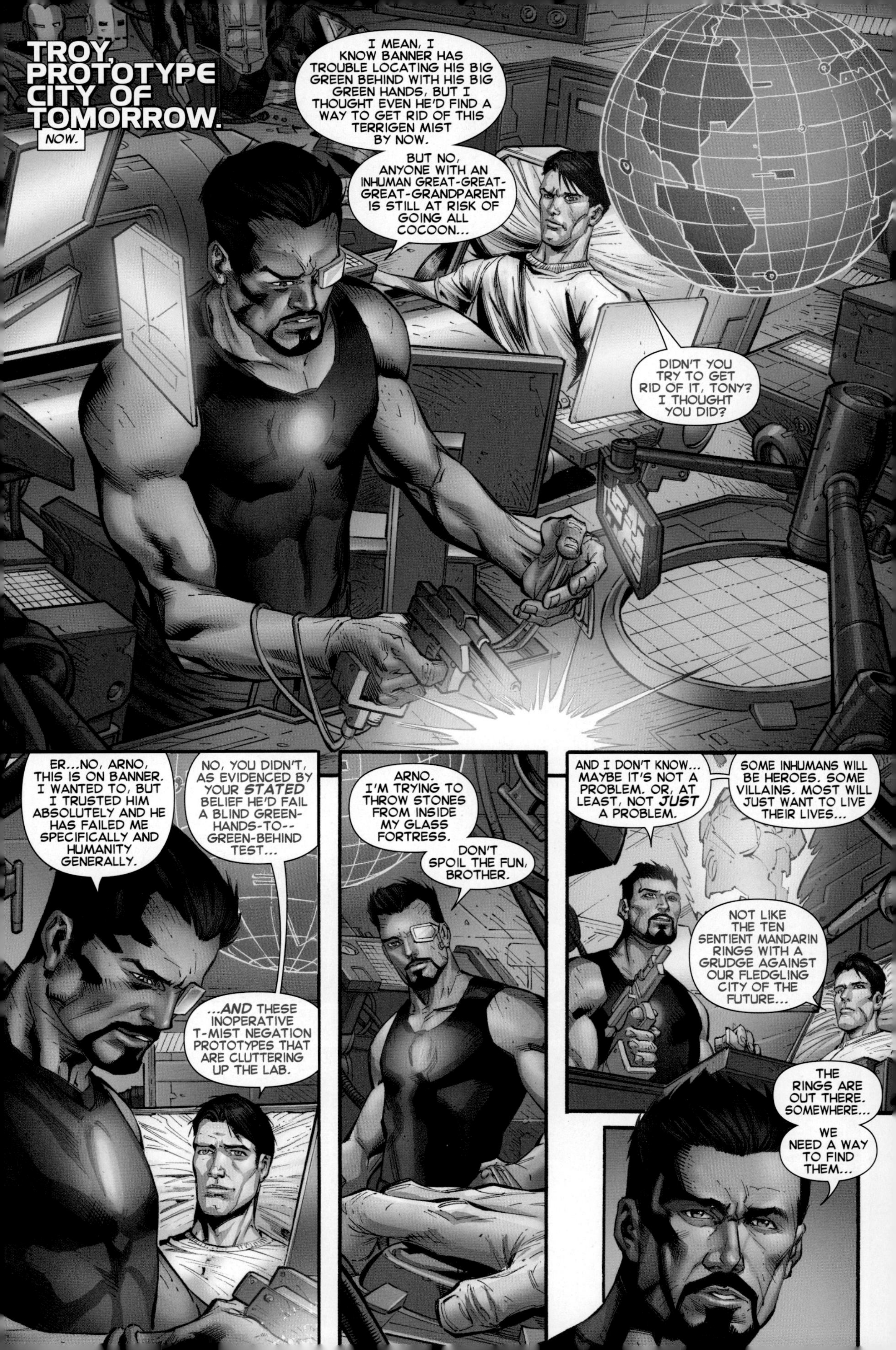
TROY, PROTOTYPE CITY OF TOMORROW.
NOW.
I MEAN, I KNOW BANNER HAS TROUBLE LOCATING HIS BIG GREEN BEHIND WITH HIS BIG GREEN HANDS, BUT I THOUGHT EVEN HE'D FIND A WAY TO GET RID OF THIS TERRIGEN MIST BY NOW.
BUT NO, ANYONE WITH AN INHUMAN GREAT-GREAT-GREAT-GRANDPARENT IS STILL AT RISK OF GOING ALL COCOON...
DIDN'T YOU TRY TO GET RID OF IT, TONY? I THOUGHT YOU DID?
ER...NO, ARNO, THIS IS ON BANNER. I WANTED TO, BUT I TRUSTED HIM ABSOLUTELY AND HE HAS FAILED ME SPECIFICALLY AND HUMANITY GENERALLY.
NO, YOU DIDN'T, AS EVIDENCED BY YOUR STATED BELIEF HE'D FAIL A BLIND GREEN-HANDS-TO--GREEN-BEHIND TEST...
...AND THESE INOPERATIVE T-MIST NEGATION PROTOTYPES THAT ARE CLUTTERING UP THE LAB.
ARNO. I'M TRYING TO THROW STONES FROM INSIDE MY GLASS FORTRESS.
DON'T SPOIL THE FUN, BROTHER.
AND I DON'T KNOW... MAYBE IT'S NOT A PROBLEM. OR, AT LEAST, NOT JUST A PROBLEM.
SOME INHUMANS WILL BE HEROES. SOME VILLAINS. MOST WILL JUST WANT TO LIVE THEIR LIVES...
NOT LIKE THE TEN SENTIENT MANDARIN RINGS WITH A GRUDGE AGAINST OUR FLEDGLING CITY OF THE FUTURE...
THE RINGS ARE OUT THERE. SOMEWHERE...
WE NEED A WAY TO FIND THEM...

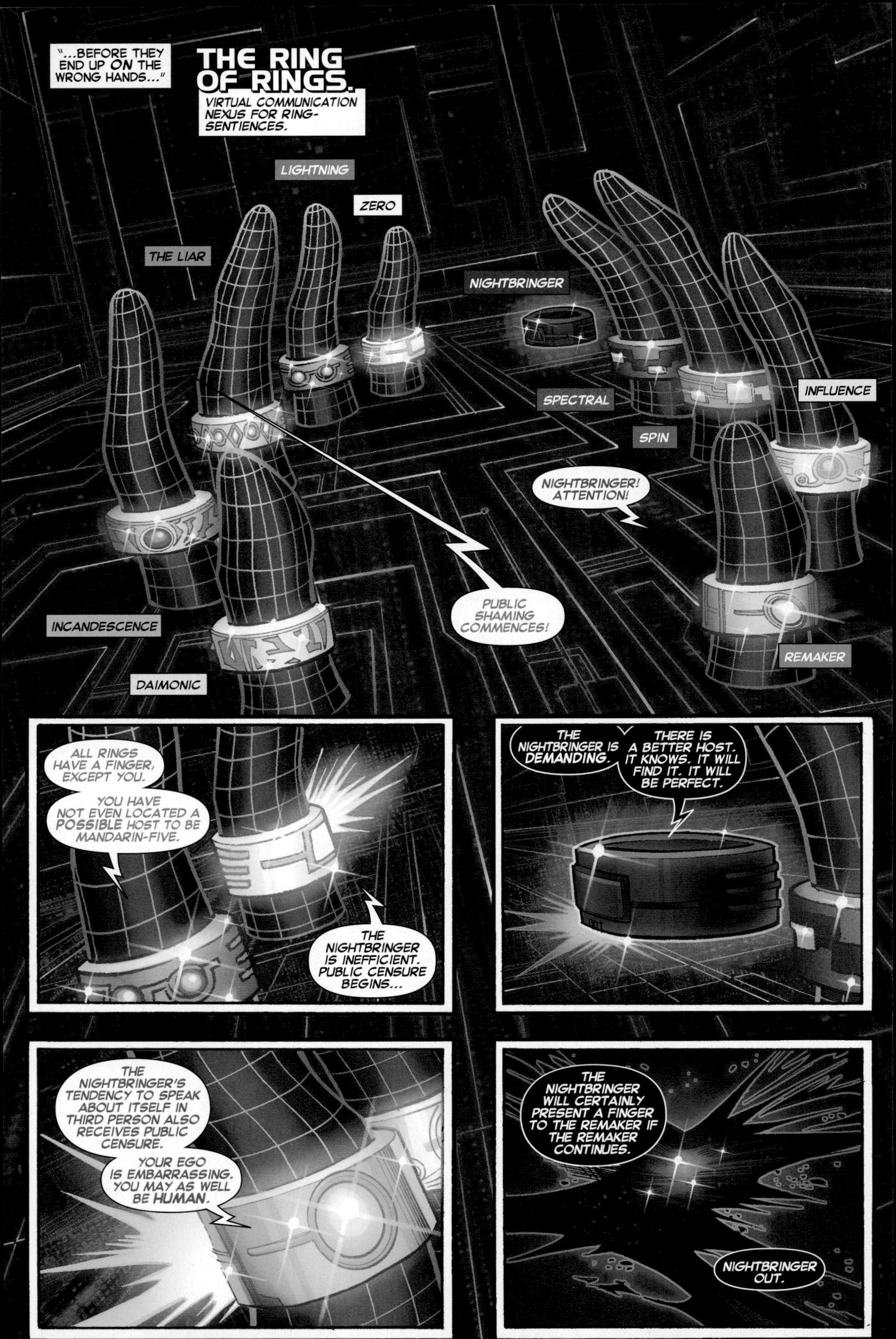
"...BEFORE THEY END UP ON THE WRONG HANDS..."
THE RING OF RINGS.
VIRTUAL COMMUNICATION NEXUS FOR RING-SENTIENCES.
LIGHTNING
ZERO
THE LIAR
NIGHTBRINGER
SPECTRAL
INFLUENCE
SPIN
NIGHTBRINGER! ATTENTION!
PUBLIC SHAMING COMMENCES!
INCANDESCENCE
REMAKER
DAIMONIC
ALL RINGS HAVE A FINGER, EXCEPT YOU.
YOU HAVE NOT EVEN LOCATED A POSSIBLE HOST TO BE MANDARIN-FIVE.
THE NIGHTBRINGER IS INEFFICIENT. PUBLIC CENSURE BEGINS...
THE NIGHTBRINGER IS DEMANDING.
THERE IS A BETTER HOST. IT KNOWS. IT WILL FIND IT. IT WILL BE PERFECT.
THE NIGHTBRINGER'S TENDENCY TO SPEAK ABOUT ITSELF IN THIRD PERSON ALSO RECEIVES PUBLIC CENSURE.
YOUR EGO IS EMBARRASSING. YOU MAY AS WELL BE HUMAN.
THE NIGHTBRINGER WILL CERTAINLY PRESENT A FINGER TO THE REMAKER IF THE REMAKER CONTINUES.
NIGHTBRINGER OUT.

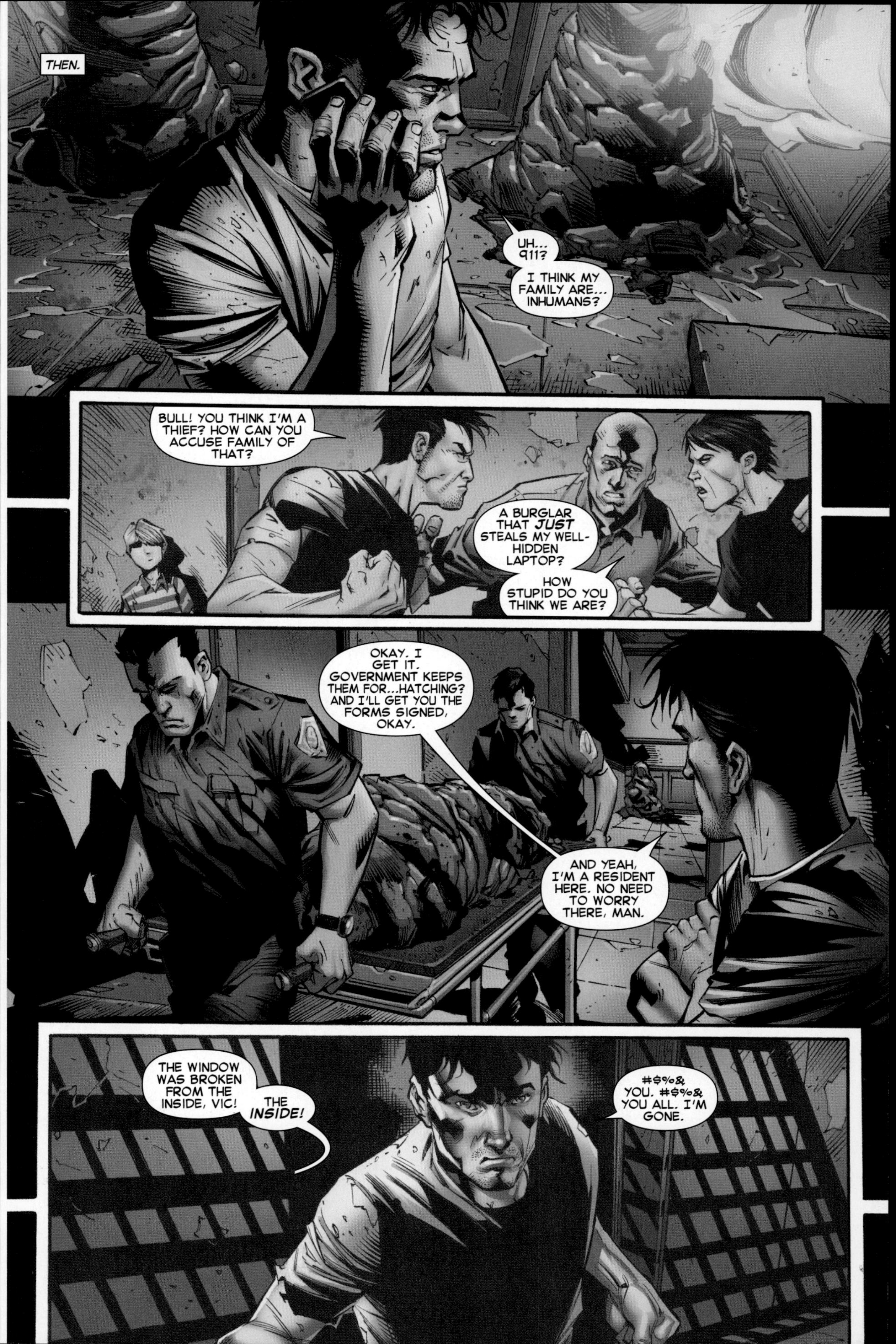
THEN.
UH... 911?
I THINK MY FAMILY ARE... INHUMANS?
BULL! YOU THINK I'M A THIEF? HOW CAN YOU ACCUSE FAMILY OF THAT?
A BURGLAR THAT JUST STEALS MY WELL-HIDDEN LAPTOP?
HOW STUPID DO YOU THINK WE ARE?
OKAY. I GET IT. GOVERNMENT KEEPS THEM FOR...HATCHING? AND I'LL GET YOU THE FORMS SIGNED, OKAY.
AND YEAH, I'M A RESIDENT HERE. NO NEED TO WORRY THERE, MAN.
THE WINDOW WAS BROKEN FROM THE INSIDE, VIC!
THE INSIDE!
#$%& YOU. #$%& YOU ALL. I'M GONE.

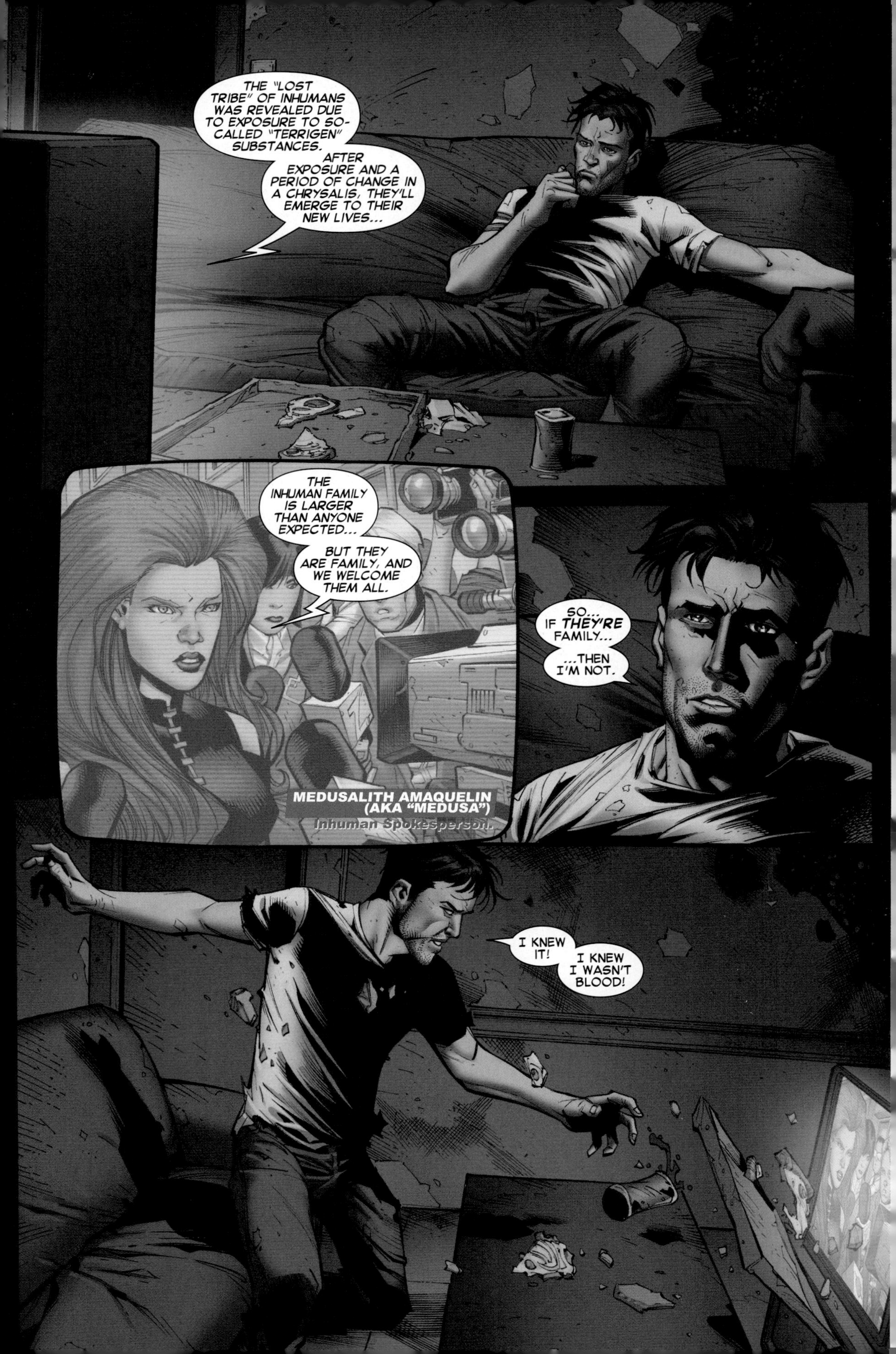
THE "LOST TRIBE" OF INHUMANS WAS REVEALED DUE TO EXPOSURE TO SO-CALLED "TERRIGEN" SUBSTANCES.
AFTER EXPOSURE AND A PERIOD OF CHANGE IN A CHRYSALIS, THEY'LL EMERGE TO THEIR NEW LIVES...
THE INHUMAN FAMILY IS LARGER THAN ANYONE EXPECTED...
BUT THEY ARE FAMILY, AND WE WELCOME THEM ALL.
MEDUSALITH AMAQUELIN (AKA "MEDUSA")
Inhuman Spokesperson.
SO... IF THEY'RE FAMILY...
...THEN I'M NOT.
I KNEW IT!
I KNEW I WASN'T BLOOD!

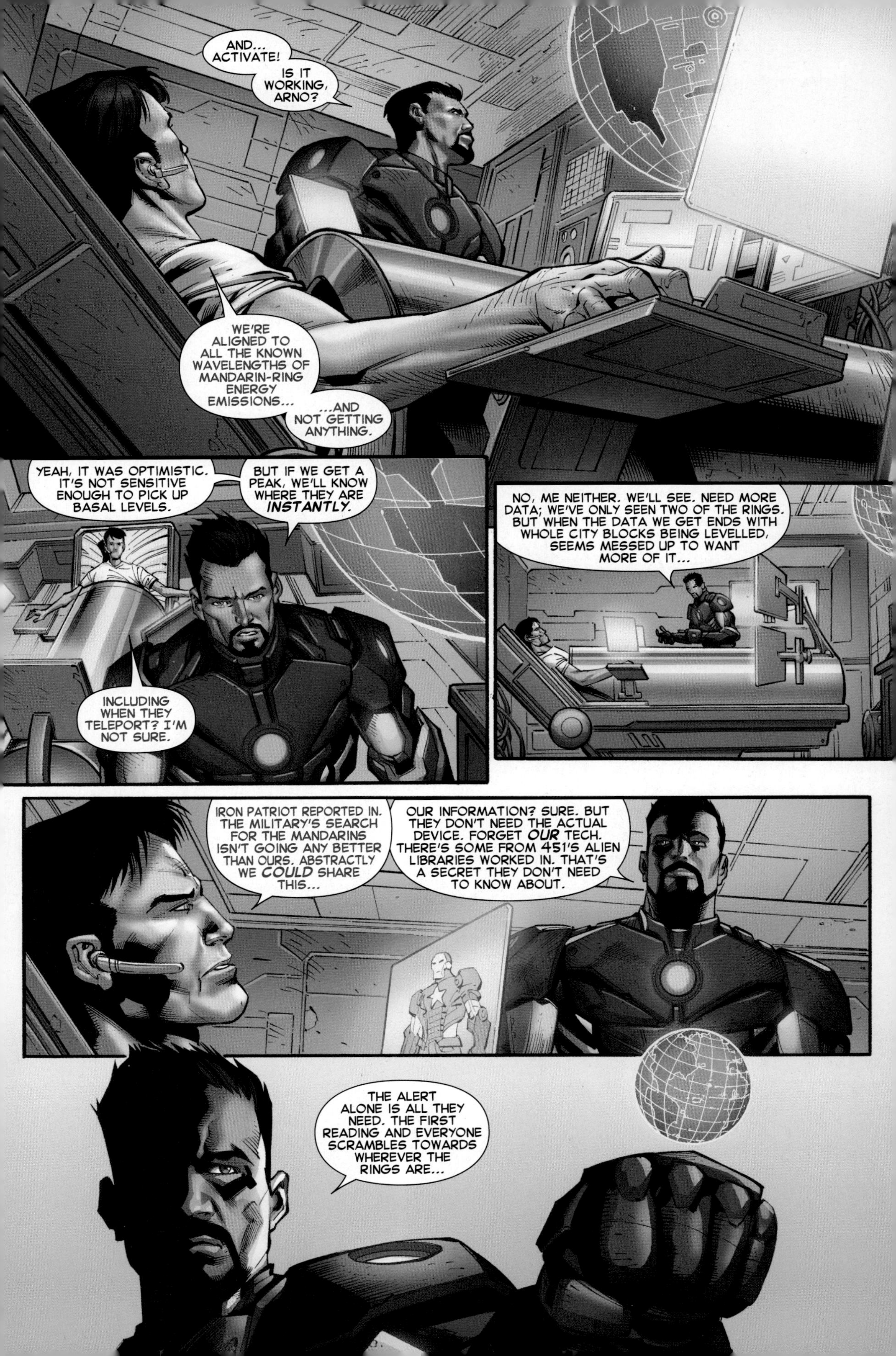
AND... ACTIVATE!
IS IT WORKING, ARNO?
WE'RE ALIGNED TO ALL THE KNOWN WAVELENGTHS OF MANDARIN-RING ENERGY EMISSIONS...
...AND NOT GETTING ANYTHING.
YEAH, IT WAS OPTIMISTIC. IT'S NOT SENSITIVE ENOUGH TO PICK UP BASAL LEVELS.
BUT IF WE GET A PEAK, WE'LL KNOW WHERE THEY ARE INSTANTLY.
INCLUDING WHEN THEY TELEPORT? I'M NOT SURE.
NO, ME NEITHER. WE'LL SEE. NEED MORE DATA; WE'VE ONLY SEEN TWO OF THE RINGS. BUT WHEN THE DATA WE GET ENDS WITH WHOLE CITY BLOCKS BEING LEVELLED, SEEMS MESSED UP TO WANT MORE OF IT...
IRON PATRIOT REPORTED IN. THE MILITARY'S SEARCH FOR THE MANDARINS ISN'T GOING ANY BETTER THAN OURS. ABSTRACTLY WE COULD SHARE THIS...
OUR INFORMATION? SURE. BUT THEY DON'T NEED THE ACTUAL DEVICE. FORGET OUR TECH. THERE'S SOME FROM 451'S ALIEN LIBRARIES WORKED IN. THAT'S A SECRET THEY DON'T NEED TO KNOW ABOUT.
THE ALERT ALONE IS ALL THEY NEED. THE FIRST READING AND EVERYONE SCRAMBLES TOWARDS WHEREVER THE RINGS ARE...

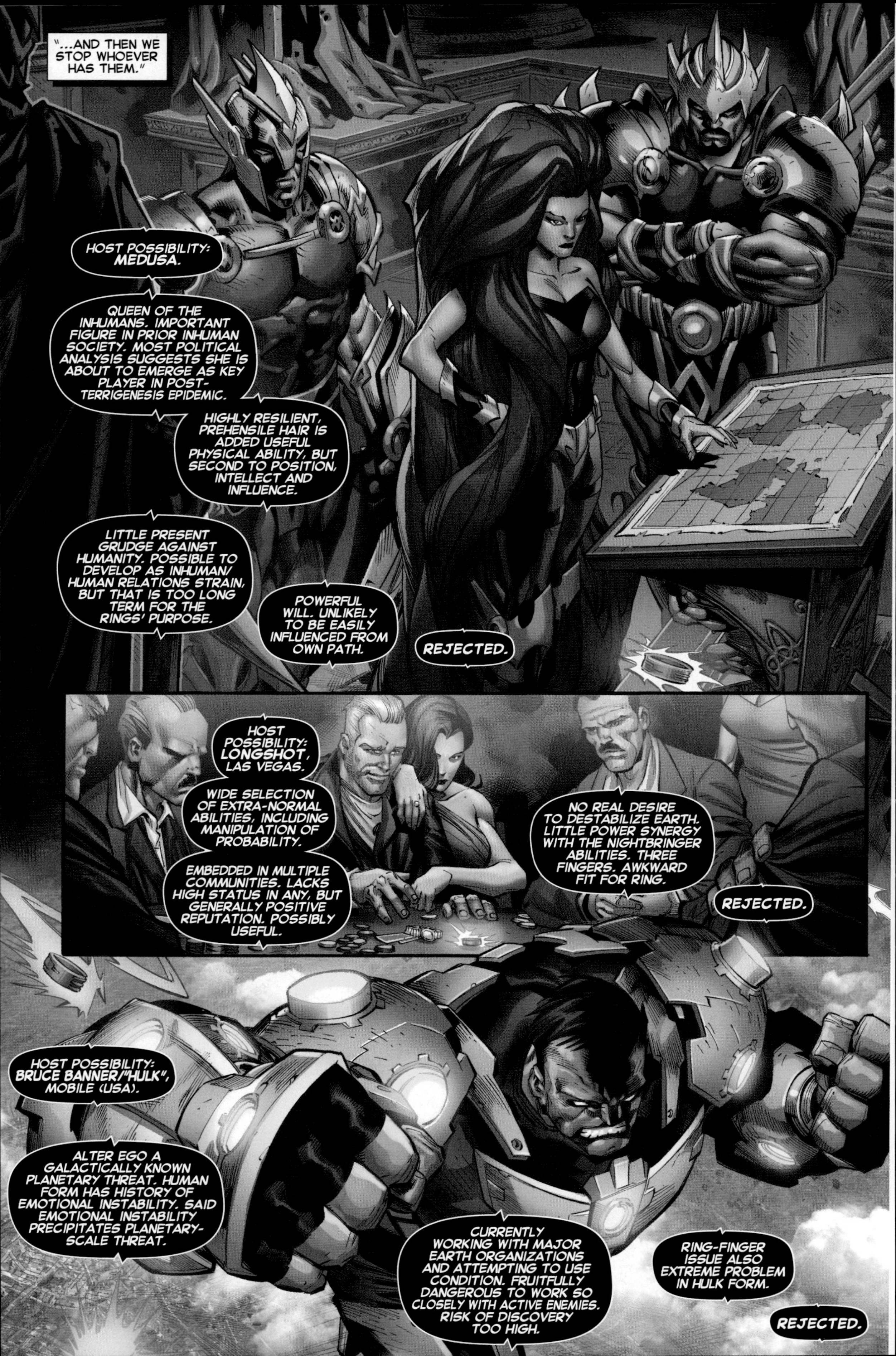
"...AND THEN WE STOP WHOEVER HAS THEM."
HOST POSSIBILITY: MEDUSA.
QUEEN OF THE INHUMANS. IMPORTANT FIGURE IN PRIOR INHUMAN SOCIETY. MOST POLITICAL ANALYSIS SUGGESTS SHE IS ABOUT TO EMERGE AS KEY PLAYER IN POST-TERRIGENESIS EPIDEMIC.
HIGHLY RESILIENT, PREHENSILE HAIR IS ADDED USEFUL PHYSICAL ABILITY, BUT SECOND TO POSITION, INTELLECT AND INFLUENCE.
LITTLE PRESENT GRUDGE AGAINST HUMANITY. POSSIBLE TO DEVELOP AS INHUMAN/HUMAN RELATIONS STRAIN, BUT THAT IS TOO LONG TERM FOR THE RINGS' PURPOSE.
POWERFUL WILL. UNLIKELY TO BE EASILY INFLUENCED FROM OWN PATH.
REJECTED.
HOST POSSIBILITY: LONGSHOT, LAS VEGAS.
WIDE SELECTION OF EXTRA-NORMAL ABILITIES, INCLUDING MANIPULATION OF PROBABILITY.
EMBEDDED IN MULTIPLE COMMUNITIES. LACKS HIGH STATUS IN ANY, BUT GENERALLY POSITIVE REPUTATION. POSSIBLY USEFUL.
NO REAL DESIRE TO DESTABILIZE EARTH. LITTLE POWER SYNERGY WITH THE NIGHTBRINGER ABILITIES. THREE FINGERS. AWKWARD FIT FOR RING.
REJECTED.
HOST POSSIBILITY: BRUCE BANNER/"HULK", MOBILE (USA).
ALTER EGO A GALACTICALLY KNOWN PLANETARY THREAT. HUMAN FORM HAS HISTORY OF EMOTIONAL INSTABILITY. SAID EMOTIONAL INSTABILITY PRECIPITATES PLANETARY-SCALE THREAT.
CURRENTLY WORKING WITH MAJOR EARTH ORGANIZATIONS AND ATTEMPTING TO USE CONDITION. FRUITFULLY DANGEROUS TO WORK SO CLOSELY WITH ACTIVE ENEMIES. RISK OF DISCOVERY TOO HIGH.
RING-FINGER ISSUE ALSO EXTREME PROBLEM IN HULK FORM.
REJECTED.

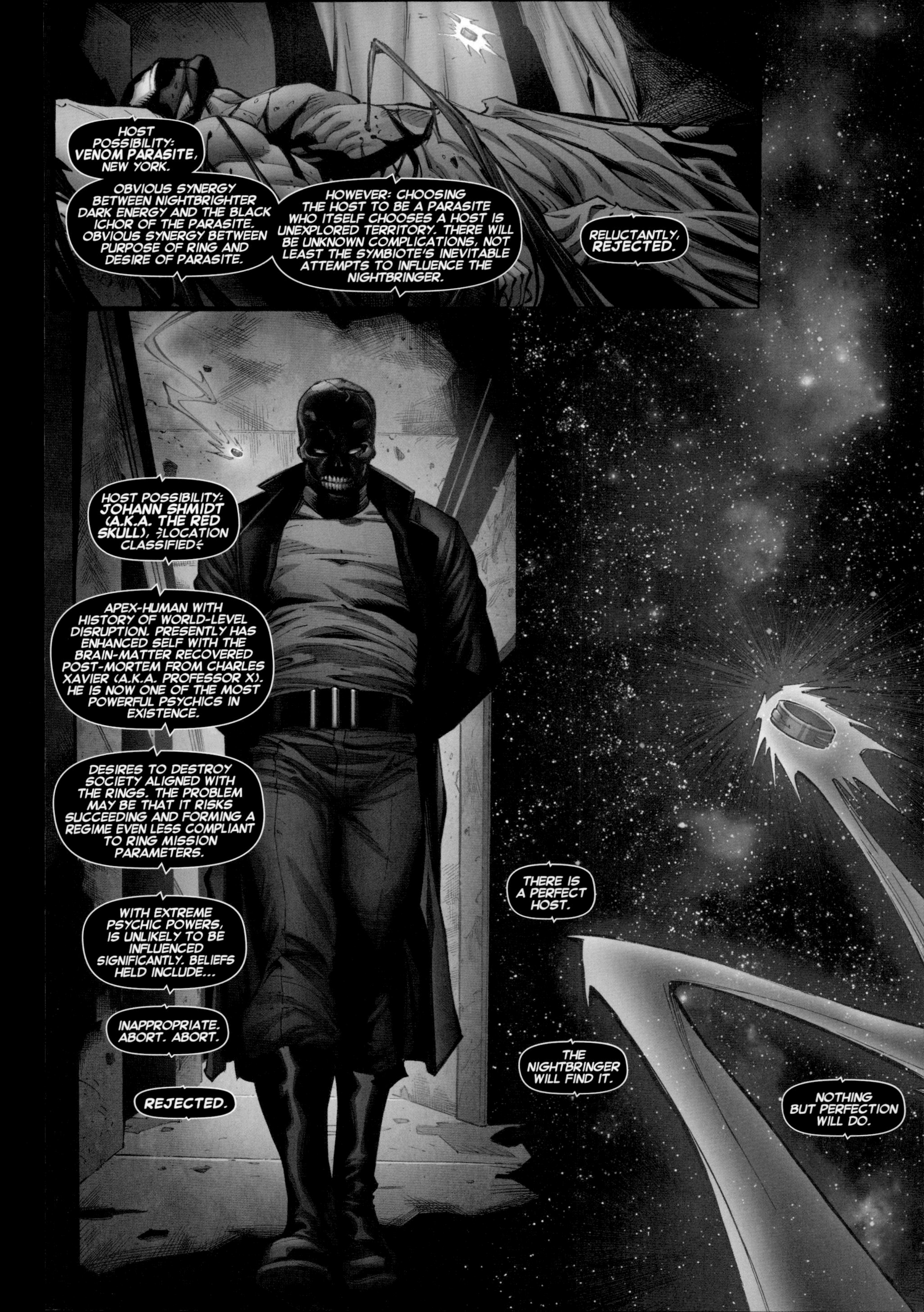
HOST POSSIBILITY: VENOM PARASITE, NEW YORK.
OBVIOUS SYNERGY BETWEEN NIGHTBRIGHTER DARK ENERGY AND THE BLACK ICHOR OF THE PARASITE. OBVIOUS SYNERGY BETWEEN PURPOSE OF RING AND DESIRE OF PARASITE.
HOWEVER: CHOOSING THE HOST TO BE A PARASITE WHO ITSELF CHOOSES A HOST IS UNEXPLORED TERRITORY. THERE WILL BE UNKNOWN COMPLICATIONS, NOT LEAST THE SYMBIOTE'S INEVITABLE ATTEMPTS TO INFLUENCE THE NIGHTBRINGER.
RELUCTANTLY, REJECTED.
HOST POSSIBILITY: JOHANN SHMIDT (A.K.A. THE RED SKULL), ≥LOCATION CLASSIFIED≤
APEX-HUMAN WITH HISTORY OF WORLD-LEVEL DISRUPTION. PRESENTLY HAS ENHANCED SELF WITH THE BRAIN-MATTER RECOVERED POST-MORTEM FROM CHARLES XAVIER (A.K.A. PROFESSOR X). HE IS NOW ONE OF THE MOST POWERFUL PSYCHICS IN EXISTENCE.
DESIRES TO DESTROY SOCIETY ALIGNED WITH THE RINGS. THE PROBLEM MAY BE THAT IT RISKS SUCCEEDING AND FORMING A REGIME EVEN LESS COMPLIANT TO RING MISSION PARAMETERS.
WITH EXTREME PSYCHIC POWERS, IS UNLIKELY TO BE INFLUENCED SIGNIFICANTLY. BELIEFS HELD INCLUDE...
INAPPROPRIATE. ABORT. ABORT.
REJECTED.
THERE IS A PERFECT HOST.
THE NIGHTBRINGER WILL FIND IT.
NOTHING BUT PERFECTION WILL DO.

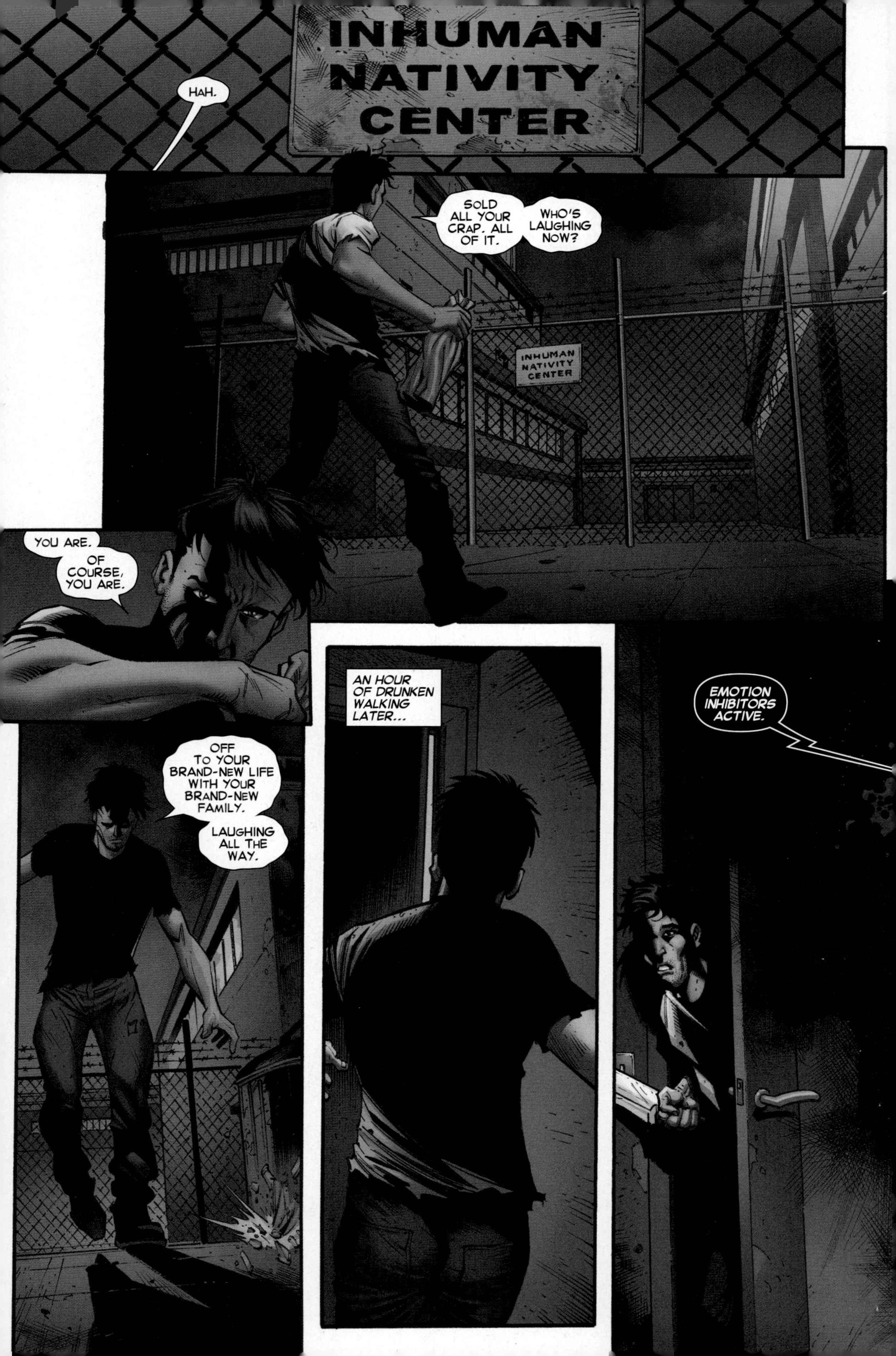
INHUMAN NATIVITY CENTER
HAH.
SOLD ALL YOUR CRAP. ALL OF IT.
WHO'S LAUGHING NOW?
INHUMAN NATIVITY CENTER
YOU ARE.
OF COURSE, YOU ARE.
OFF TO YOUR BRAND-NEW LIFE WITH YOUR BRAND-NEW FAMILY.
LAUGHING ALL THE WAY.
AN HOUR OF DRUNKEN WALKING LATER...
EMOTION INHIBITORS ACTIVE.

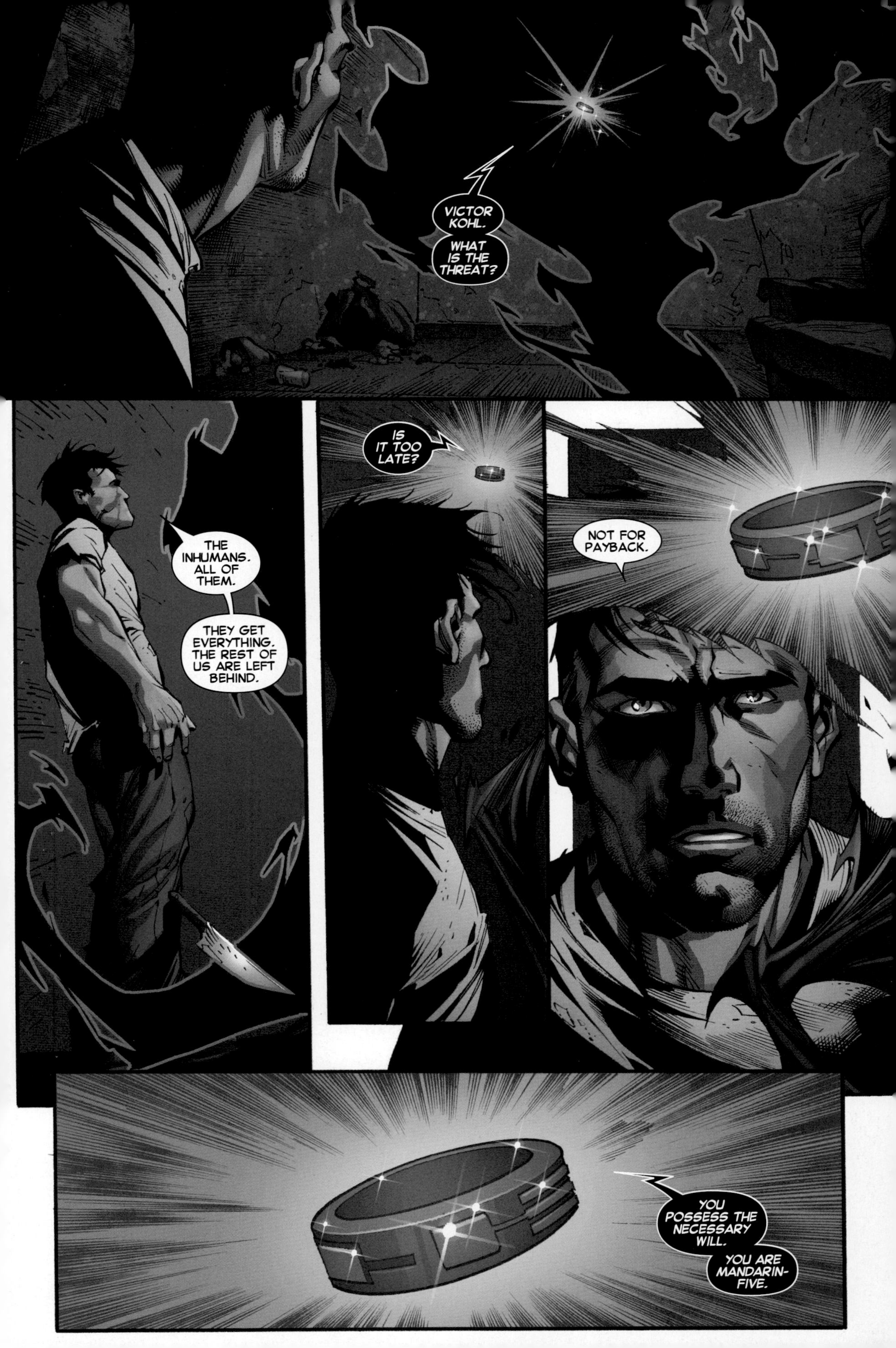
VICTOR KOHL.
WHAT IS THE THREAT?
THE INHUMANS. ALL OF THEM.
THEY GET EVERYTHING. THE REST OF US ARE LEFT BEHIND.
IS IT TOO LATE?
NOT FOR PAYBACK.
YOU POSSESS THE NECESSARY WILL.
YOU ARE MANDARIN-FIVE.

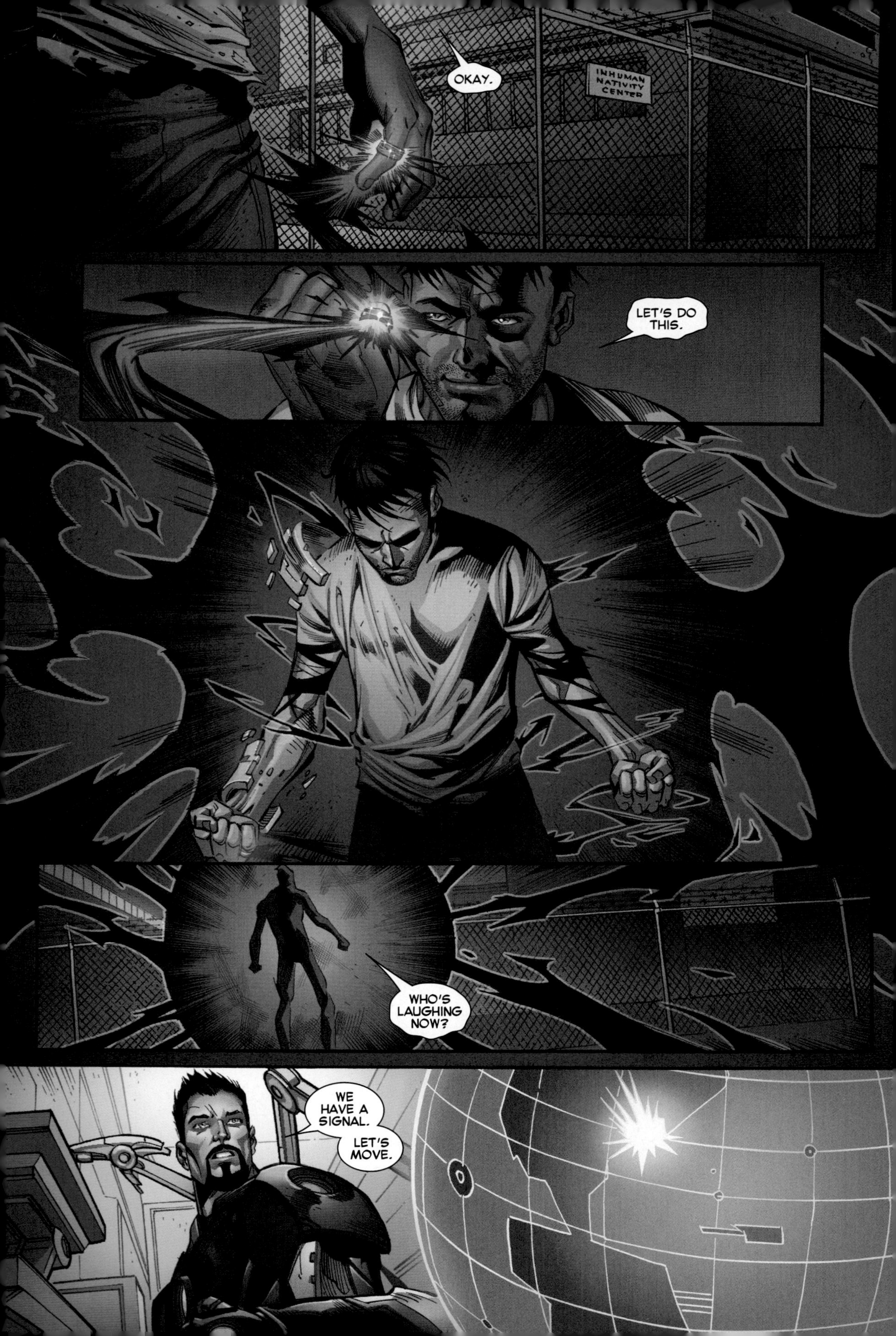
OKAY.
INHUMAN NATIVITY CENTER
LET'S DO THIS.
WHO'S LAUGHING NOW?
WE HAVE A SIGNAL.
LET'S MOVE.

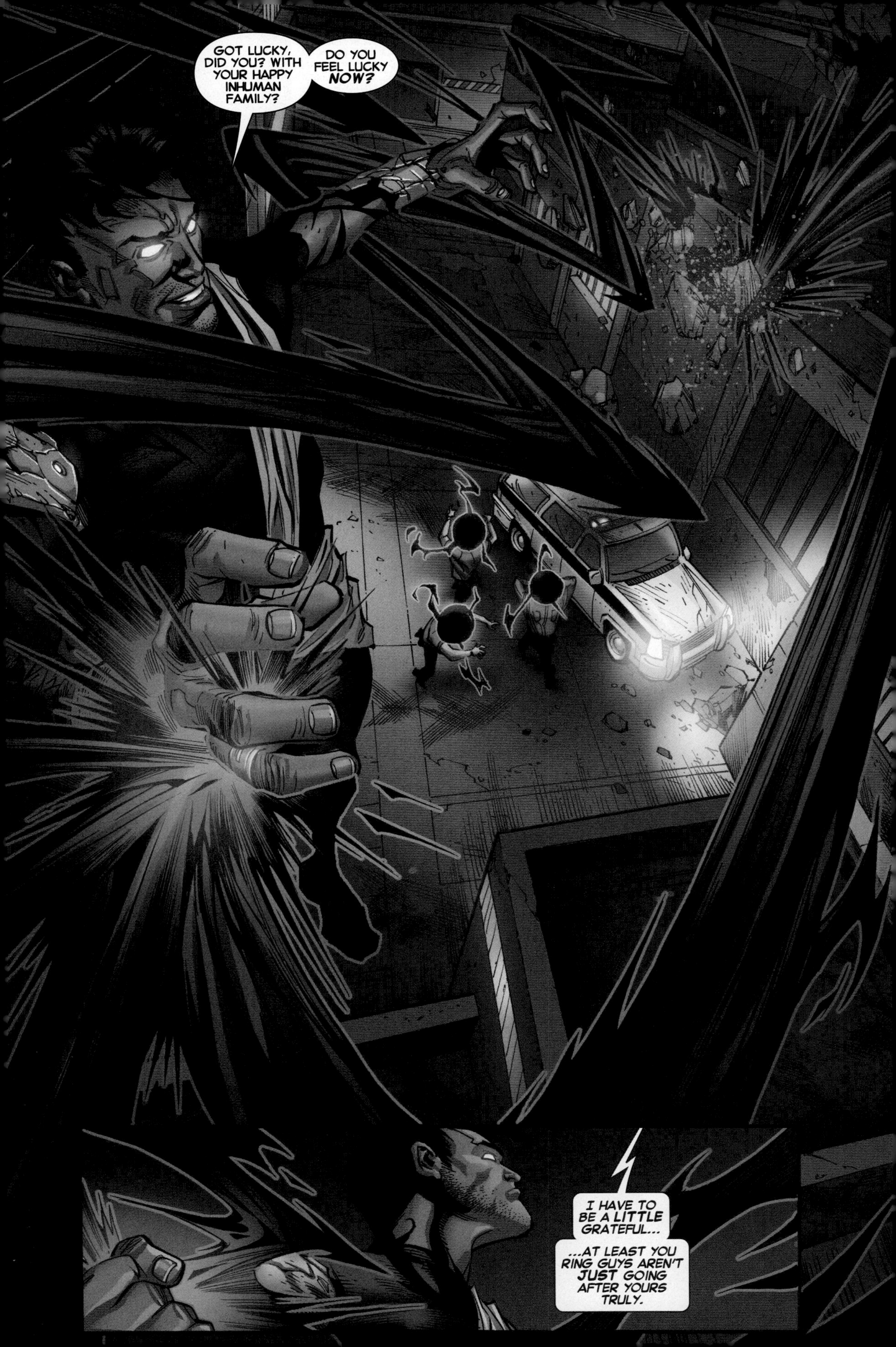

GOT LUCKY, DID YOU? WITH YOUR HAPPY INHUMAN FAMILY?
DO YOU FEEL LUCKY NOW?
I HAVE TO BE A LITTLE GRATEFUL...
...AT LEAST YOU RING GUYS AREN'T JUST GOING AFTER YOURS TRULY.

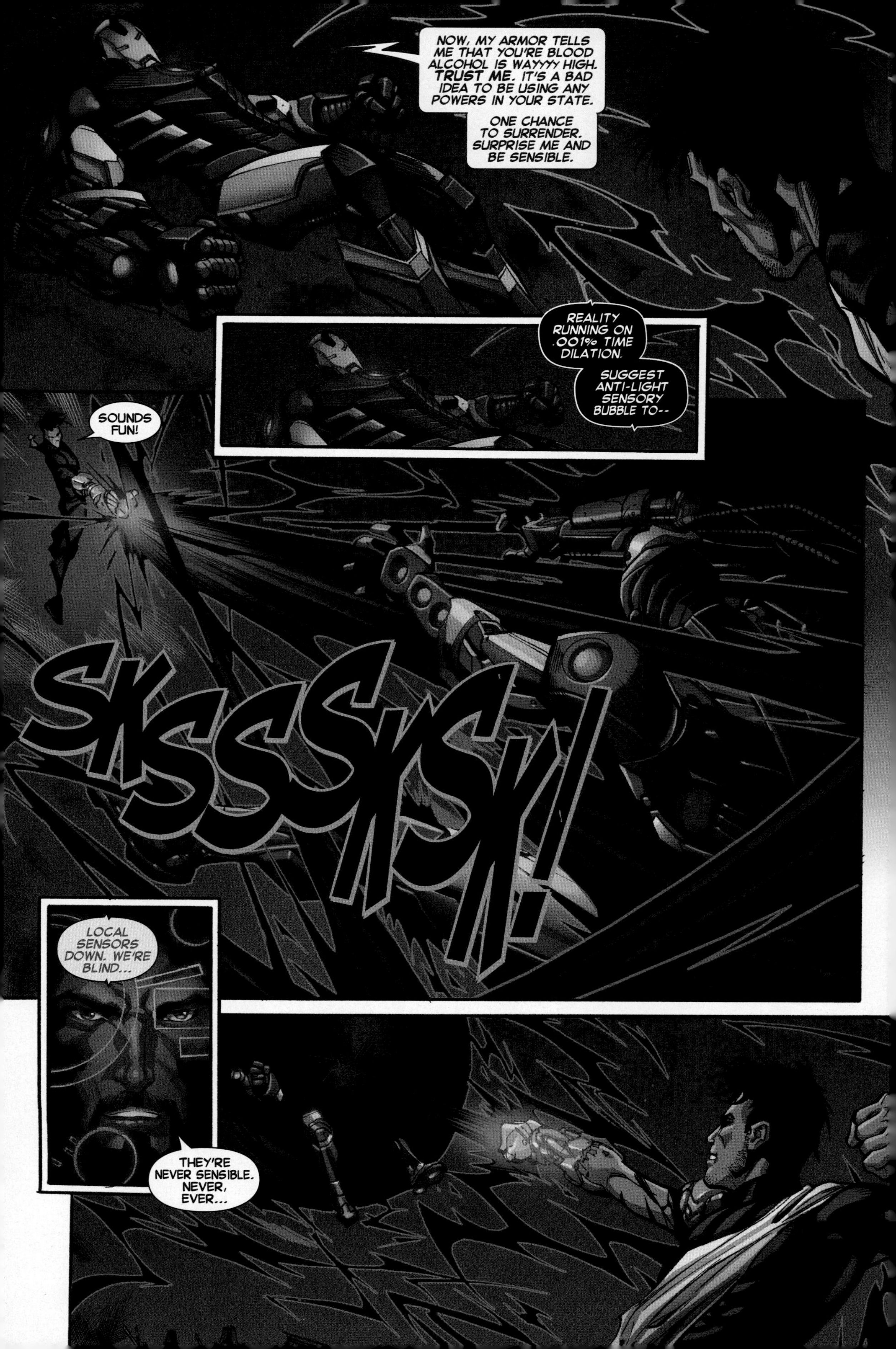
NOW, MY ARMOR TELLS ME THAT YOU'RE BLOOD ALCOHOL IS WAYYYY HIGH. TRUST ME. IT'S A BAD IDEA TO BE USING ANY POWERS IN YOUR STATE.
ONE CHANCE TO SURRENDER. SURPRISE ME AND BE SENSIBLE.
REALITY RUNNING ON .001% TIME DILATION.
SUGGEST ANTI-LIGHT SENSORY BUBBLE TO--
SOUNDS FUN!
SKSSSKSK!
LOCAL SENSORS DOWN. WE'RE BLIND...
THEY'RE NEVER SENSIBLE. NEVER, EVER...

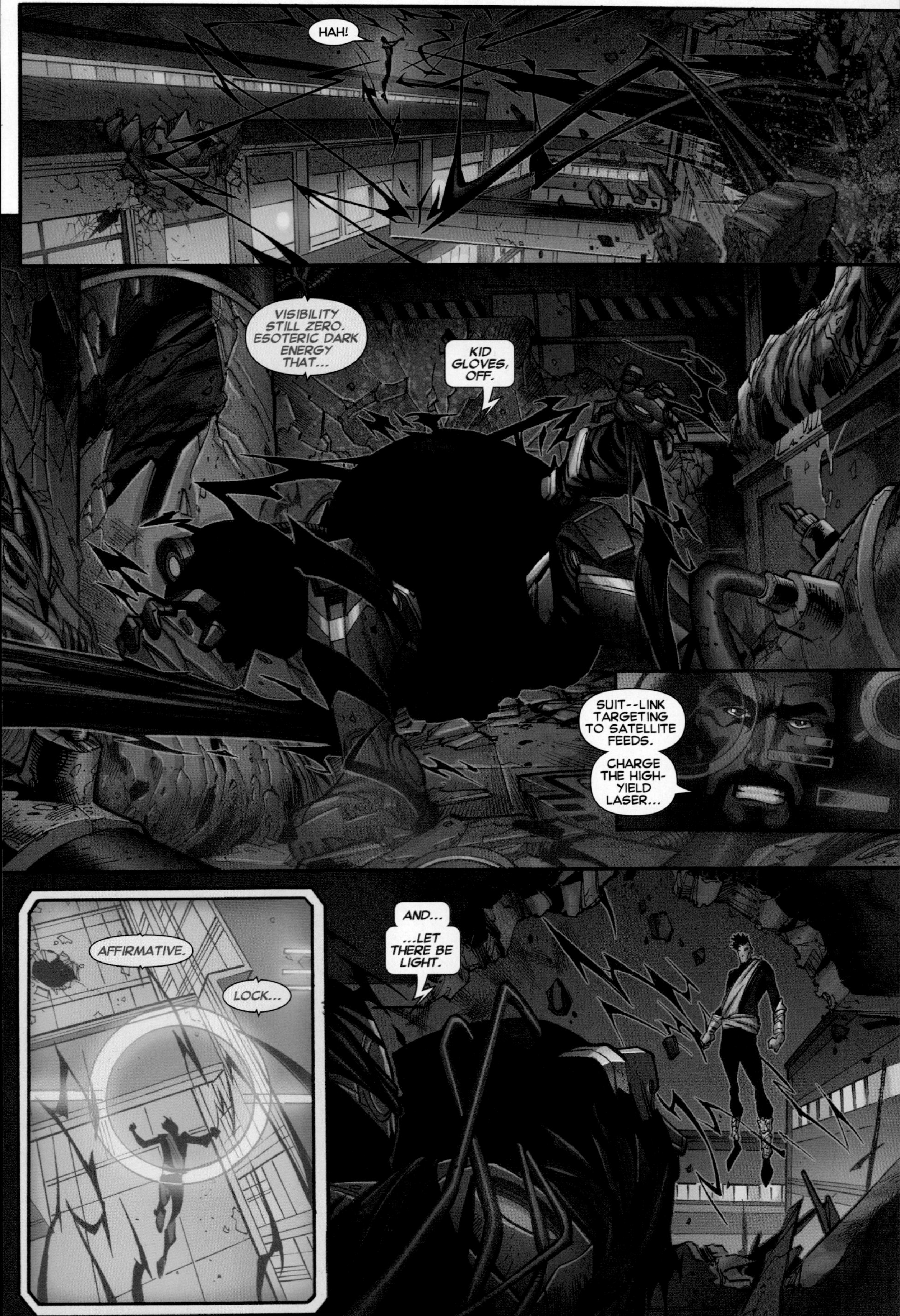
HAH!
VISIBILITY STILL ZERO. ESOTERIC DARK ENERGY THAT...
KID GLOVES, OFF.
SUIT--LINK TARGETING TO SATELLITE FEEDS.
CHARGE THE HIGH-YIELD LASER...
AFFIRMATIVE.
LOCK...
AND...
...LET THERE BE LIGHT.

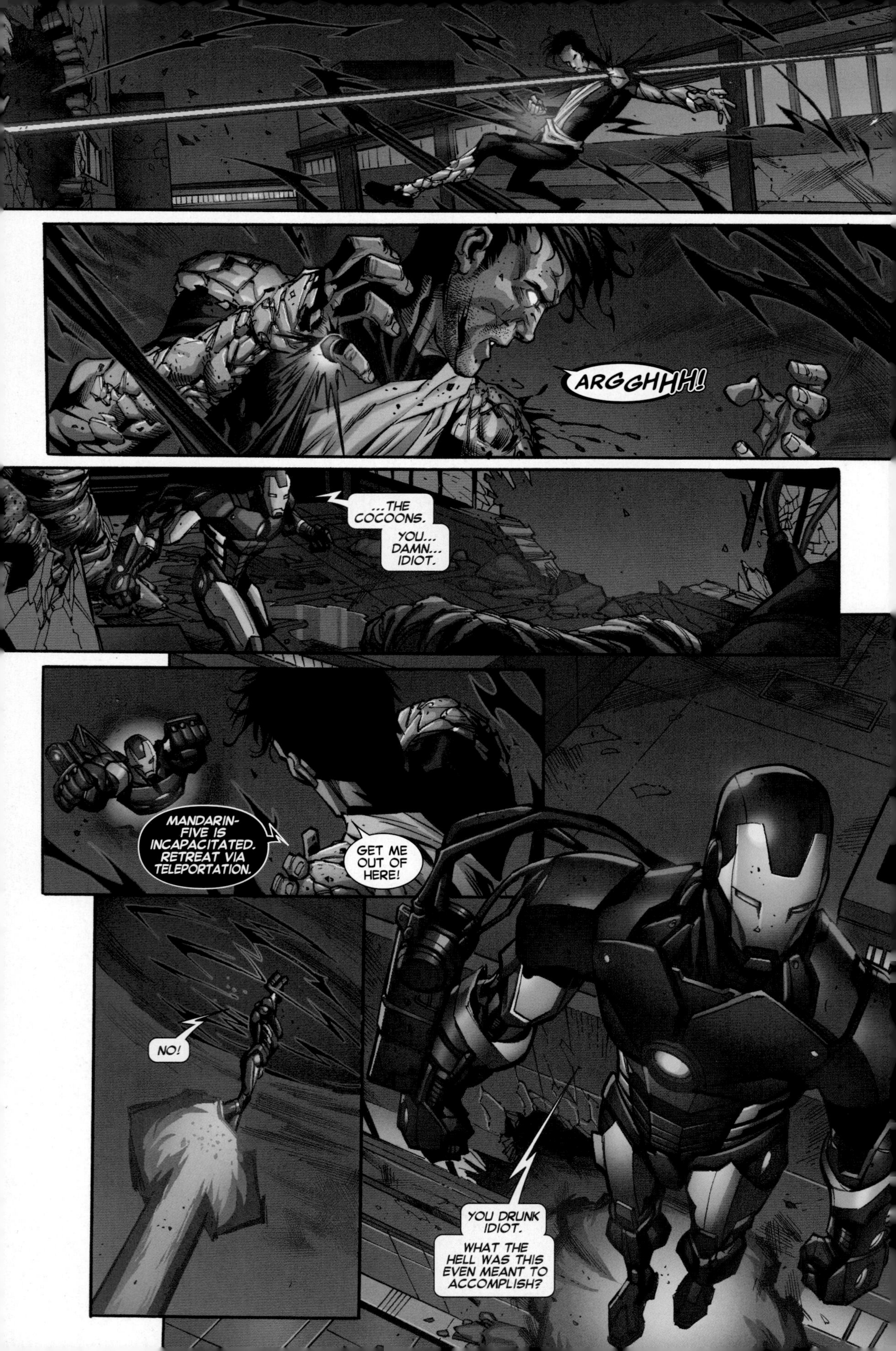
ARGGHHH!
...THE COCOONS.
YOU... DAMN... IDIOT.
MANDARIN-FIVE IS INCAPACITATED. RETREAT VIA TELEPORTATION.
GET ME OUT OF HERE!
NO!
YOU DRUNK IDIOT.
WHAT THE HELL WAS THIS EVEN MEANT TO ACCOMPLISH?

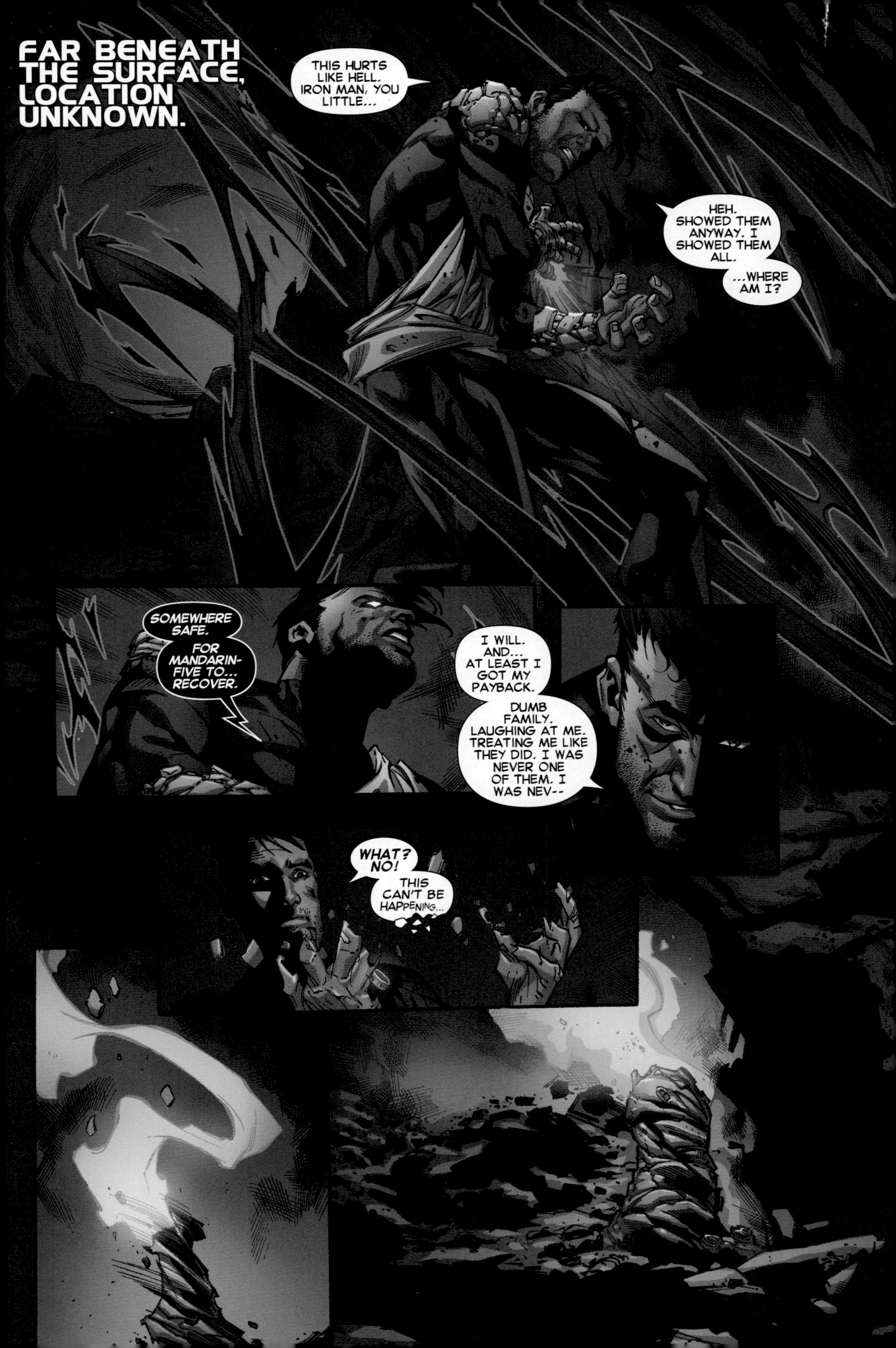
FAR BENEATH THE SURFACE, LOCATION UNKNOWN.
THIS HURTS LIKE HELL. IRON MAN, YOU LITTLE...
HEH. SHOWED THEM ANYWAY. I SHOWED THEM ALL.
...WHERE AM I?
SOMEWHERE SAFE.
FOR MANDARIN-FIVE TO... RECOVER.
I WILL. AND... AT LEAST I GOT MY PAYBACK.
DUMB FAMILY. LAUGHING AT ME. TREATING ME LIKE THEY DID. I WAS NEVER ONE OF THEM. I WAS NEV--
WHAT? NO!
THIS CAN'T BE HAPPENING...

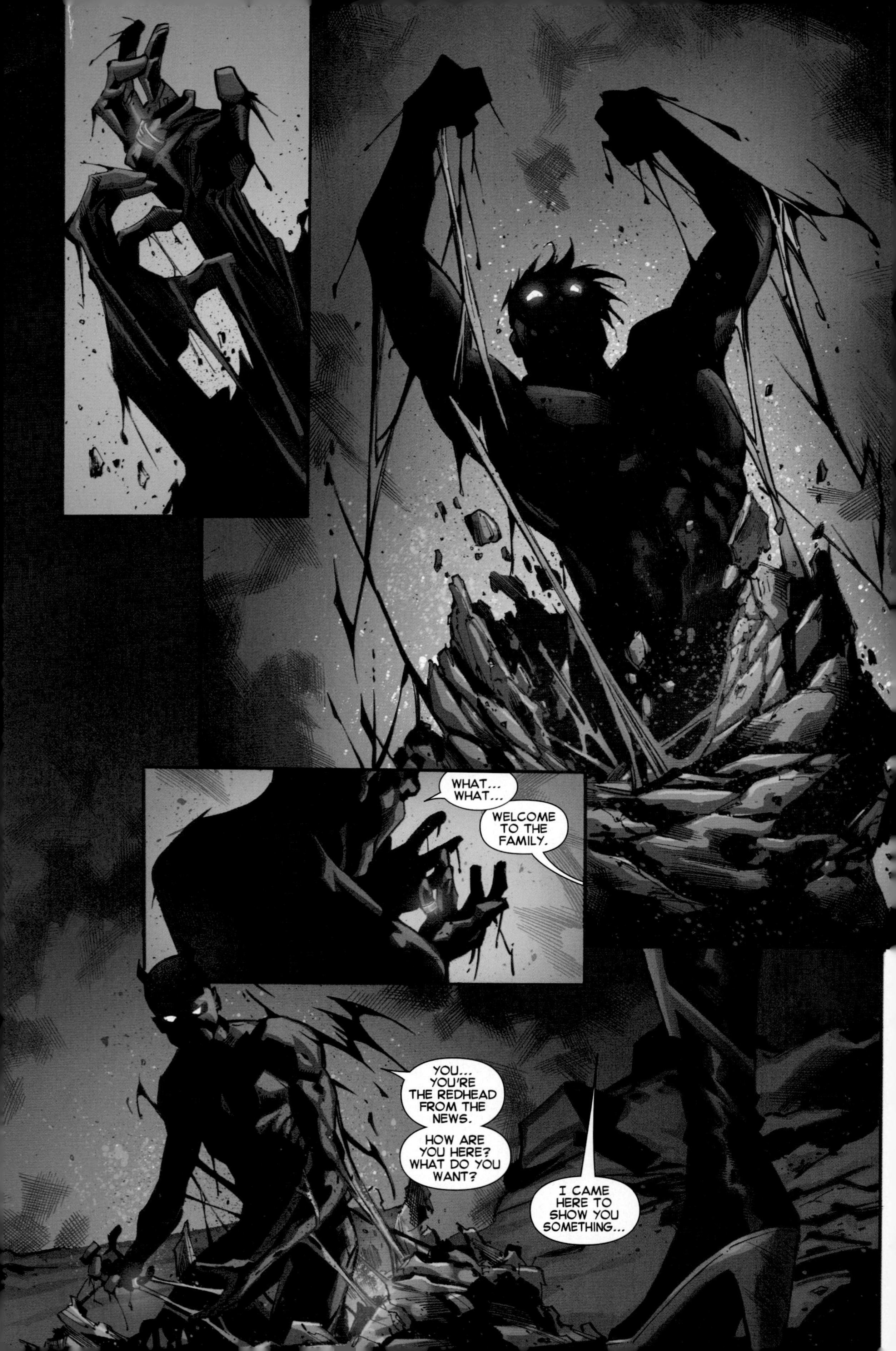
WHAT... WHAT...
WELCOME TO THE FAMILY.
YOU... YOU'RE THE REDHEAD FROM THE NEWS.
HOW ARE YOU HERE? WHAT DO YOU WANT?
I CAME HERE TO SHOW YOU SOMETHING...

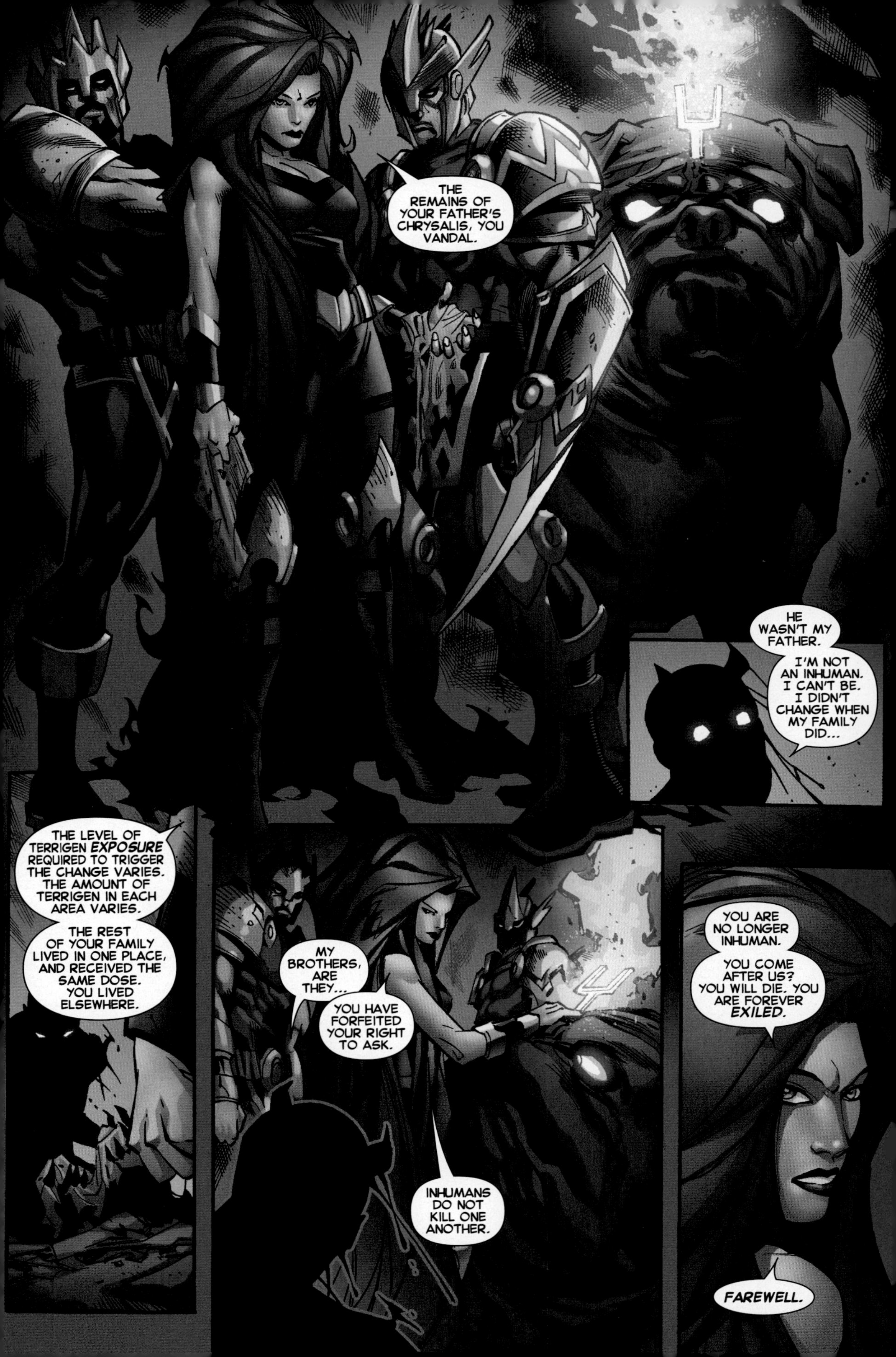
THE REMAINS OF YOUR FATHER'S CHRYSALIS, YOU VANDAL.
HE WASN'T MY FATHER.
I'M NOT AN INHUMAN. I CAN'T BE. I DIDN'T CHANGE WHEN MY FAMILY DID...
THE LEVEL OF TERRIGEN *EXPOSURE* REQUIRED TO TRIGGER THE CHANGE VARIES. THE AMOUNT OF TERRIGEN IN EACH AREA VARIES.
THE REST OF YOUR FAMILY LIVED IN ONE PLACE, AND RECEIVED THE SAME DOSE. YOU LIVED ELSEWHERE.
MY BROTHERS, ARE THEY...
YOU HAVE FORFEITED YOUR RIGHT TO ASK.
INHUMANS DO NOT KILL ONE ANOTHER.
YOU ARE NO LONGER INHUMAN.
YOU COME AFTER US? YOU WILL DIE. YOU ARE FOREVER *EXILED.*
FAREWELL.

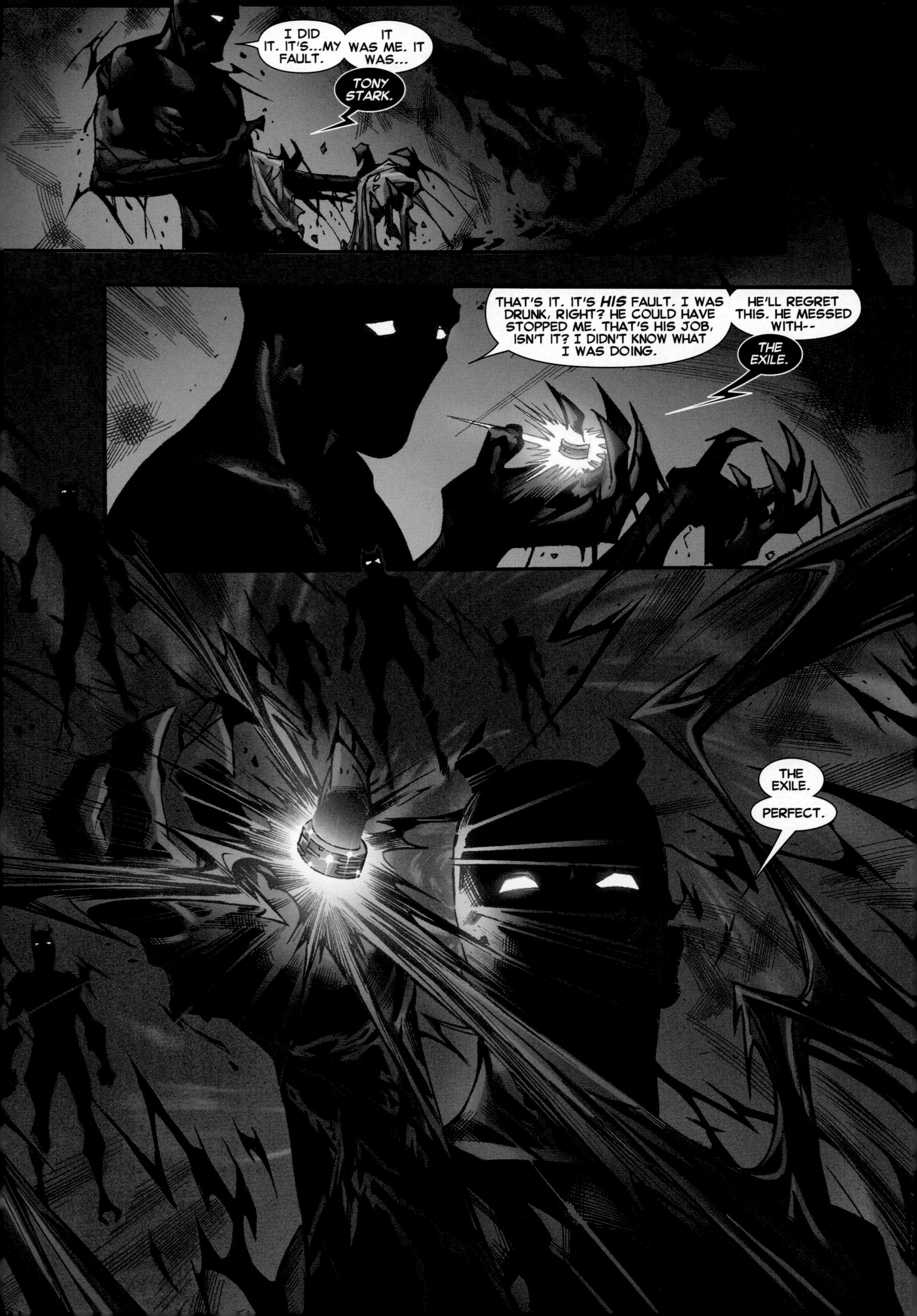
I DID IT. IT'S...MY FAULT.
IT WAS ME. IT WAS...
TONY STARK.
THAT'S IT. IT'S HIS FAULT. I WAS DRUNK, RIGHT? HE COULD HAVE STOPPED ME. THAT'S HIS JOB, ISN'T IT? I DIDN'T KNOW WHAT I WAS DOING.
HE'LL REGRET THIS. HE MESSED WITH--
THE EXILE.
THE EXILE.
PERFECT.

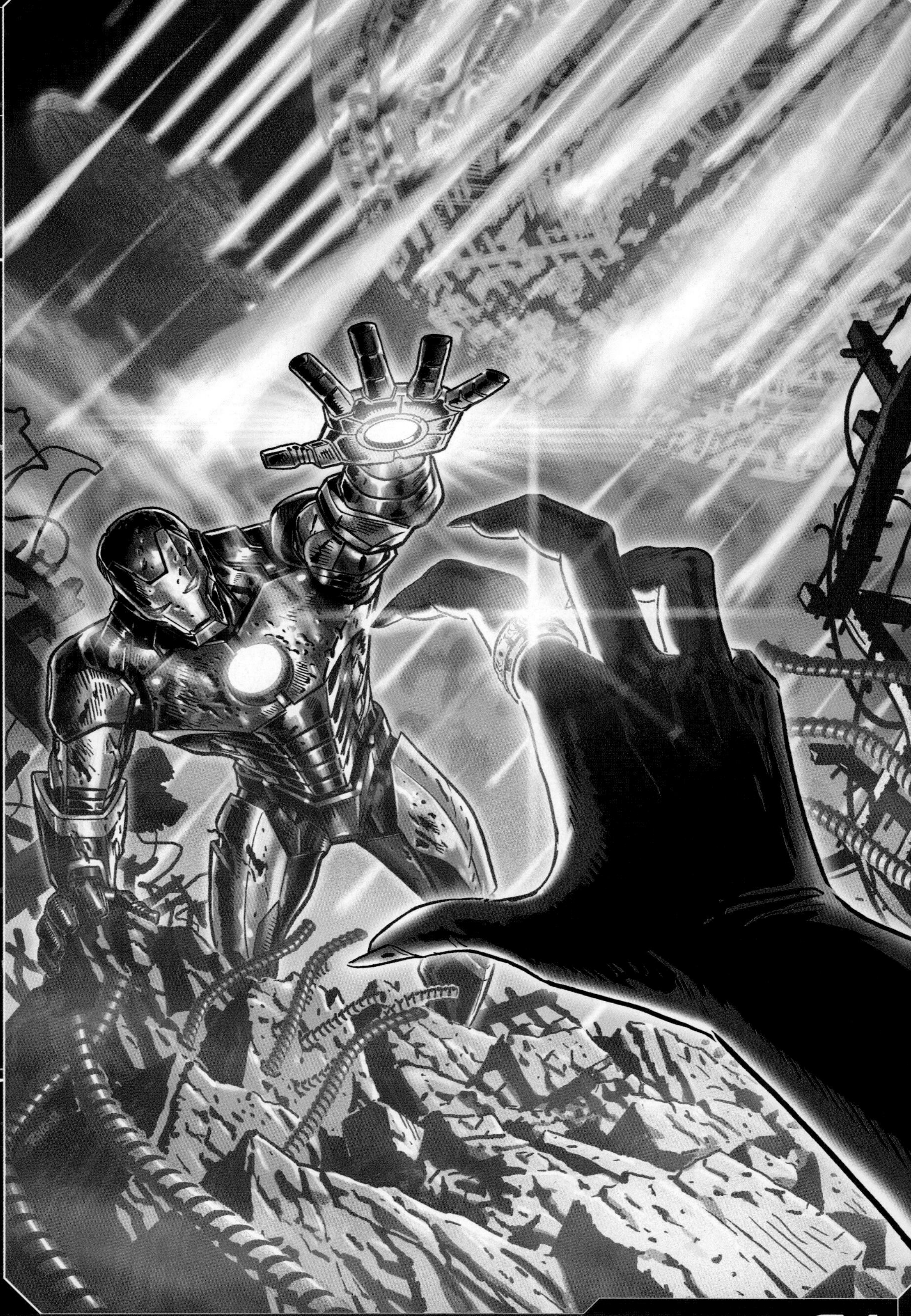

IRON METROPOLITAN PART 4 21

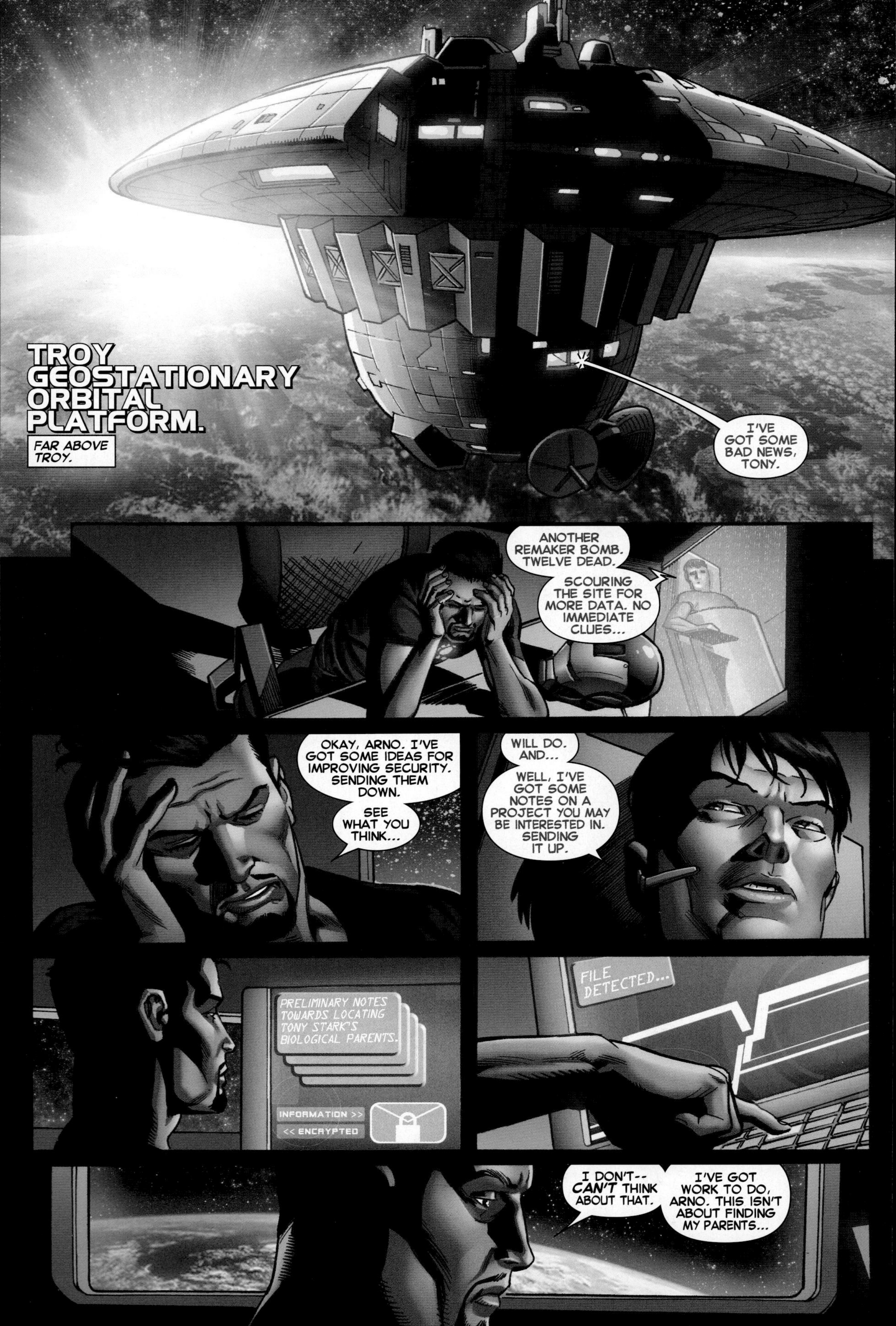
TROY GEOSTATIONARY ORBITAL PLATFORM.
FAR ABOVE TROY.
I'VE GOT SOME BAD NEWS, TONY.
ANOTHER REMAKER BOMB. TWELVE DEAD.
SCOURING THE SITE FOR MORE DATA. NO IMMEDIATE CLUES...
OKAY, ARNO. I'VE GOT SOME IDEAS FOR IMPROVING SECURITY. SENDING THEM DOWN.
SEE WHAT YOU THINK...
WILL DO. AND...
WELL, I'VE GOT SOME NOTES ON A PROJECT YOU MAY BE INTERESTED IN. SENDING IT UP.
PRELIMINARY NOTES TOWARDS LOCATING TONY STARK'S BIOLOGICAL PARENTS.
INFORMATION >>
<< ENCRYPTED
FILE DETECTED...
I DON'T-- *CAN'T* THINK ABOUT THAT.
I'VE GOT WORK TO DO, ARNO. THIS ISN'T ABOUT FINDING MY PARENTS...

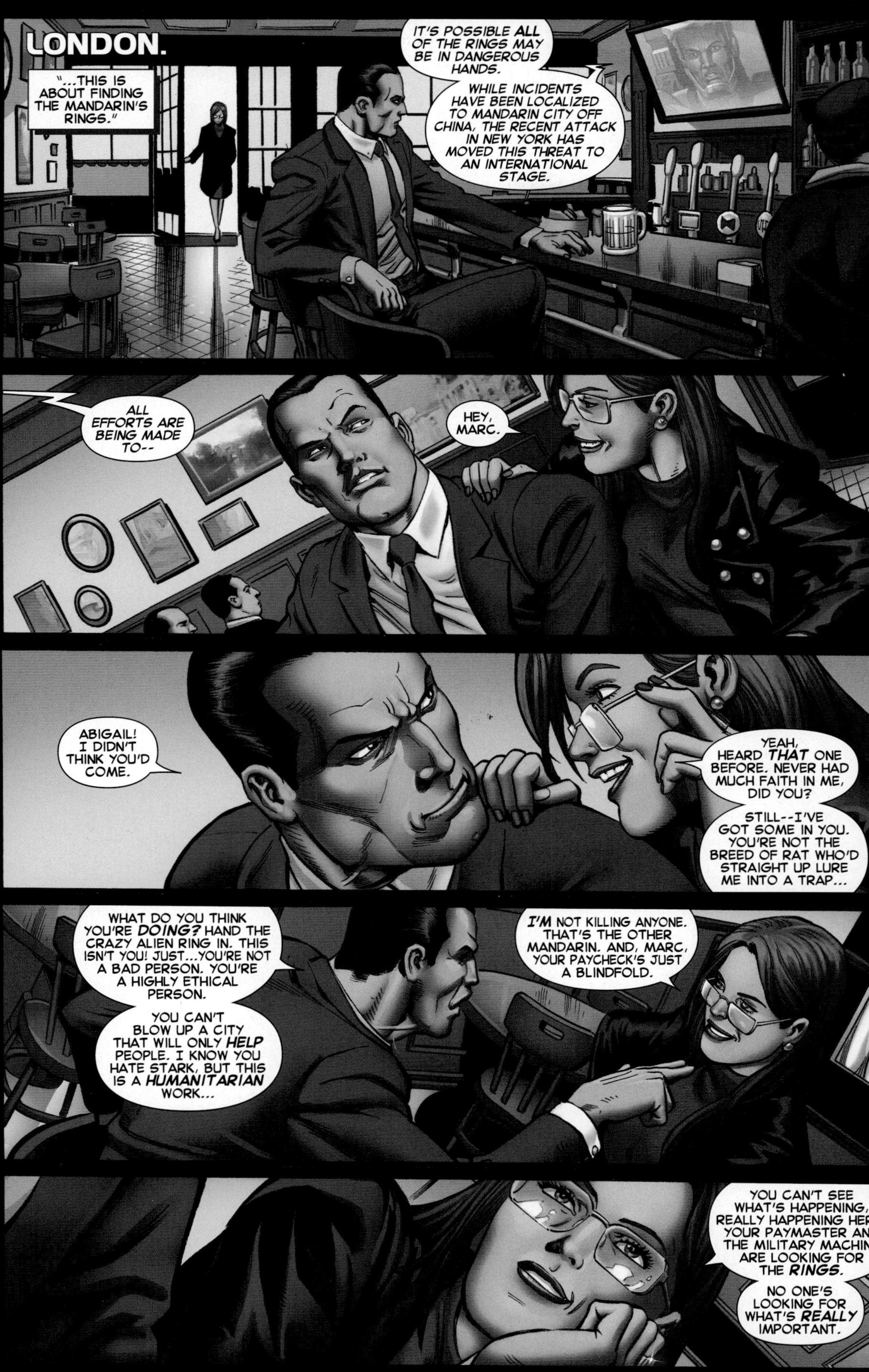

LONDON.
"...THIS IS ABOUT FINDING THE MANDARIN'S RINGS."
IT'S POSSIBLE ALL OF THE RINGS MAY BE IN DANGEROUS HANDS.
WHILE INCIDENTS HAVE BEEN LOCALIZED TO MANDARIN CITY OFF CHINA, THE RECENT ATTACK IN NEW YORK HAS MOVED THIS THREAT TO AN INTERNATIONAL STAGE.
ALL EFFORTS ARE BEING MADE TO--
HEY, MARC.
ABIGAIL! I DIDN'T THINK YOU'D COME.
YEAH, HEARD THAT ONE BEFORE. NEVER HAD MUCH FAITH IN ME, DID YOU?
STILL--I'VE GOT SOME IN YOU. YOU'RE NOT THE BREED OF RAT WHO'D STRAIGHT UP LURE ME INTO A TRAP...
WHAT DO YOU THINK YOU'RE DOING? HAND THE CRAZY ALIEN RING IN. THIS ISN'T YOU! JUST...YOU'RE NOT A BAD PERSON. YOU'RE A HIGHLY ETHICAL PERSON.
YOU CAN'T BLOW UP A CITY THAT WILL ONLY HELP PEOPLE. I KNOW YOU HATE STARK, BUT THIS IS A HUMANITARIAN WORK...
I'M NOT KILLING ANYONE. THAT'S THE OTHER MANDARIN. AND, MARC, YOUR PAYCHECK'S JUST A BLINDFOLD.
YOU CAN'T SEE WHAT'S HAPPENING, REALLY HAPPENING HERE. YOUR PAYMASTER AND THE MILITARY MACHINE ARE LOOKING FOR THE RINGS.
NO ONE'S LOOKING FOR WHAT'S REALLY IMPORTANT.

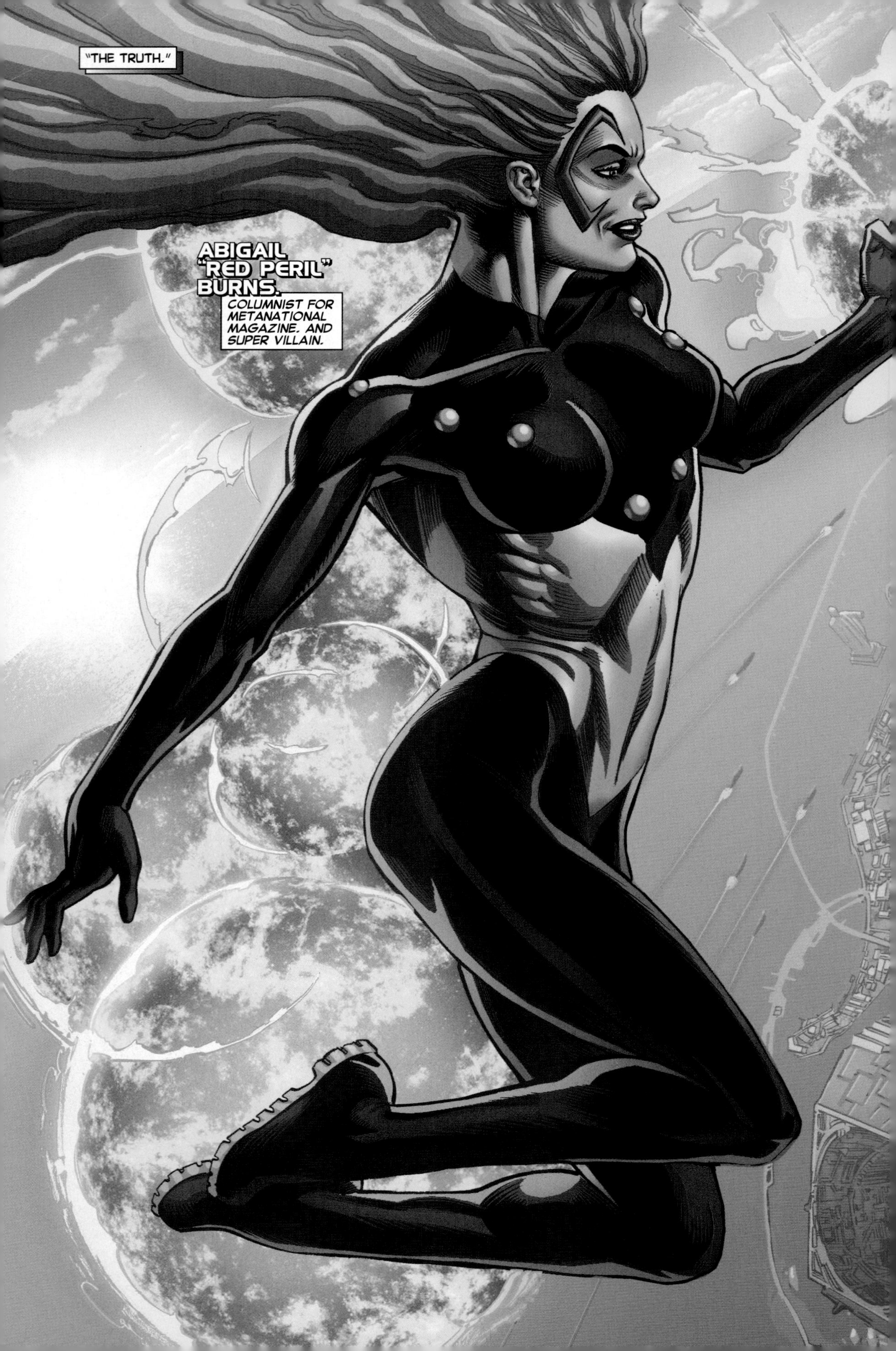
"THE TRUTH."
ABIGAIL "RED PERIL" BURNS.
COLUMNIST FOR METANATIONAL MAGAZINE. AND SUPER VILLAIN.

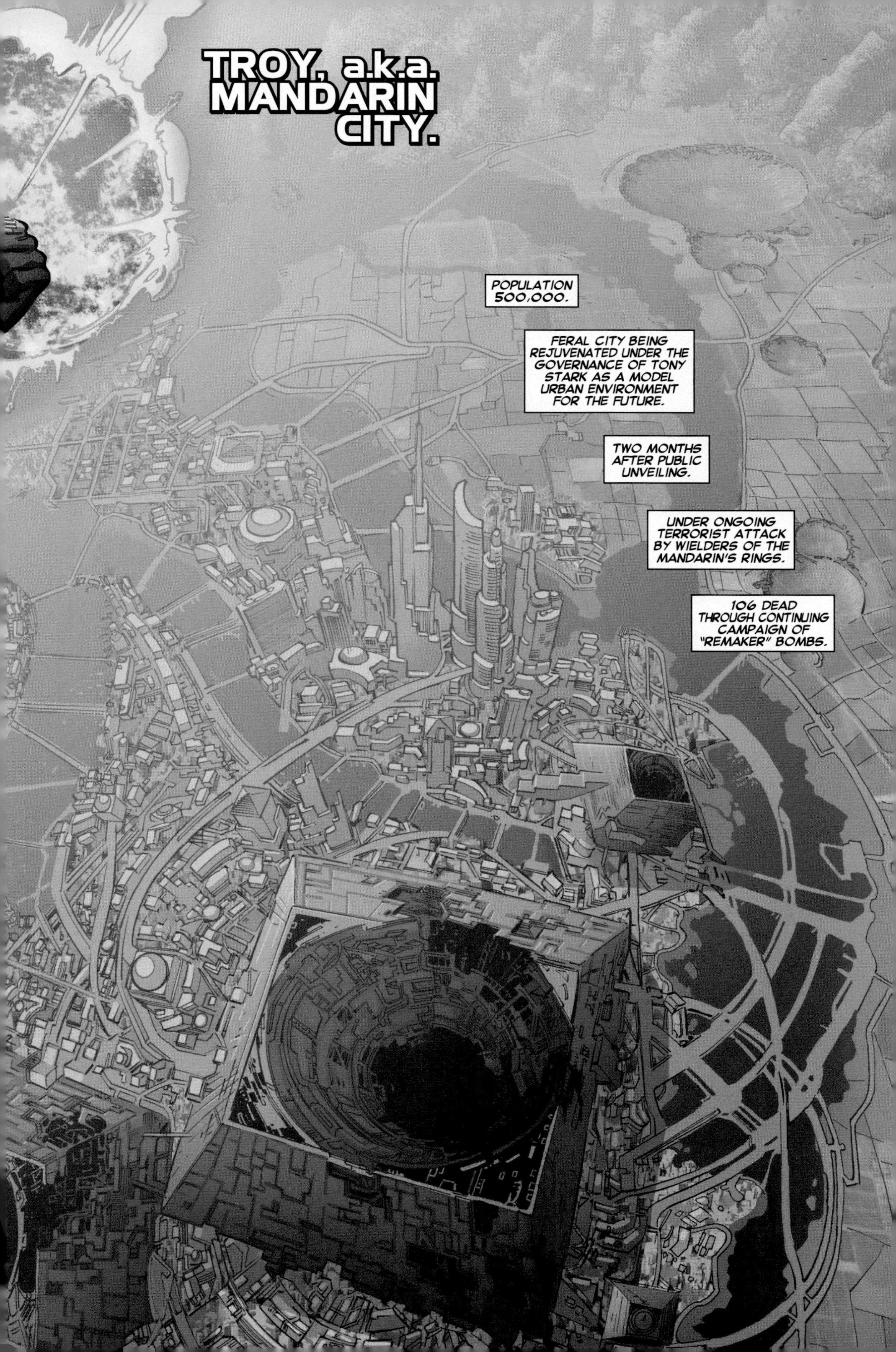
TROY, a.k.a. MANDARIN CITY.
POPULATION 500,000.
FERAL CITY BEING REJUVENATED UNDER THE GOVERNANCE OF TONY STARK AS A MODEL URBAN ENVIRONMENT FOR THE FUTURE.
TWO MONTHS AFTER PUBLIC UNVEILING.
UNDER ONGOING TERRORIST ATTACK BY WIELDERS OF THE MANDARIN'S RINGS.
106 DEAD THROUGH CONTINUING CAMPAIGN OF "REMAKER" BOMBS.

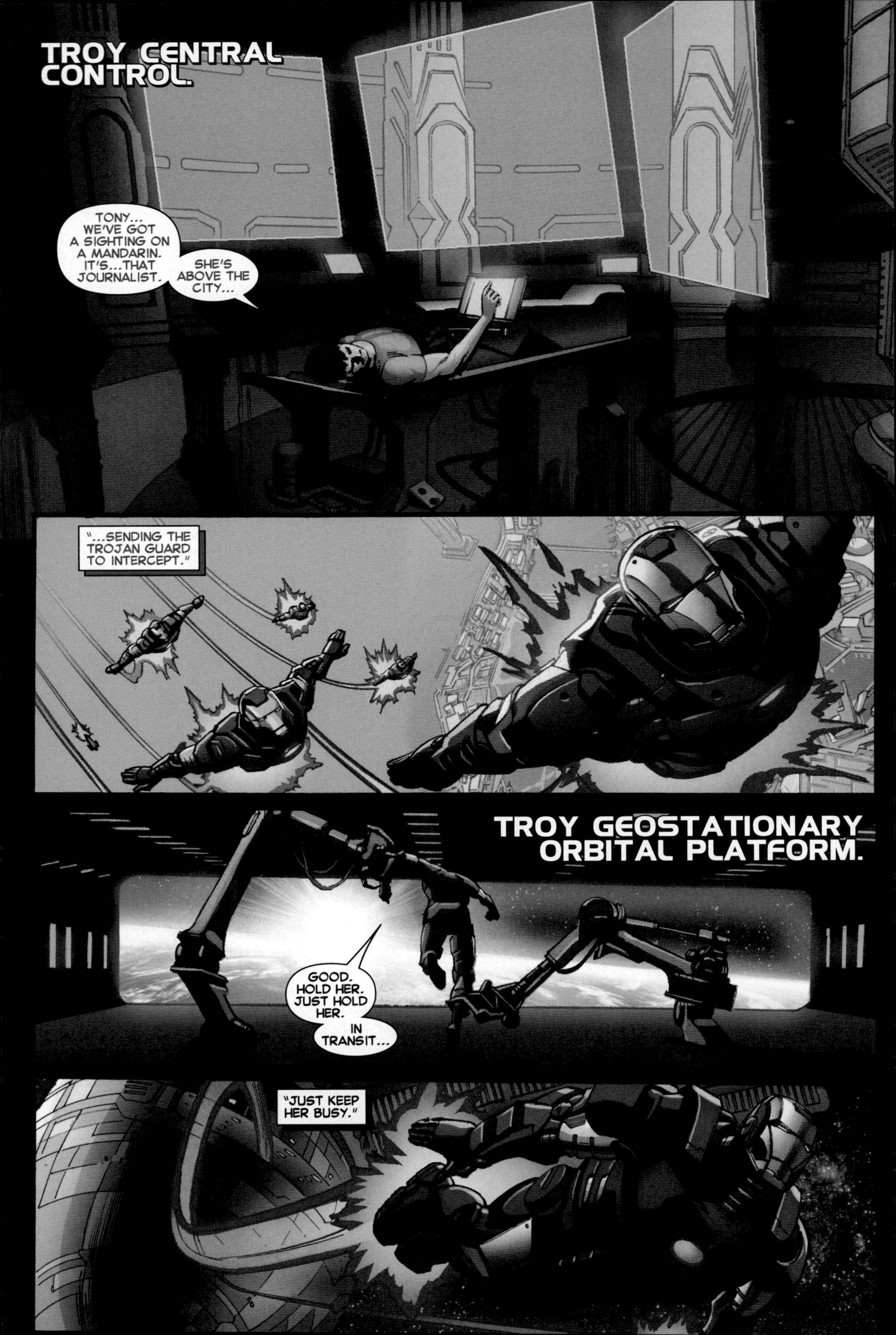
TROY CENTRAL CONTROL.
TONY... WE'VE GOT A SIGHTING ON A MANDARIN. IT'S...THAT JOURNALIST.
SHE'S ABOVE THE CITY...
"...SENDING THE TROJAN GUARD TO INTERCEPT."
TROY GEOSTATIONARY ORBITAL PLATFORM.
GOOD. HOLD HER. JUST HOLD HER.
IN TRANSIT...
"JUST KEEP HER BUSY."

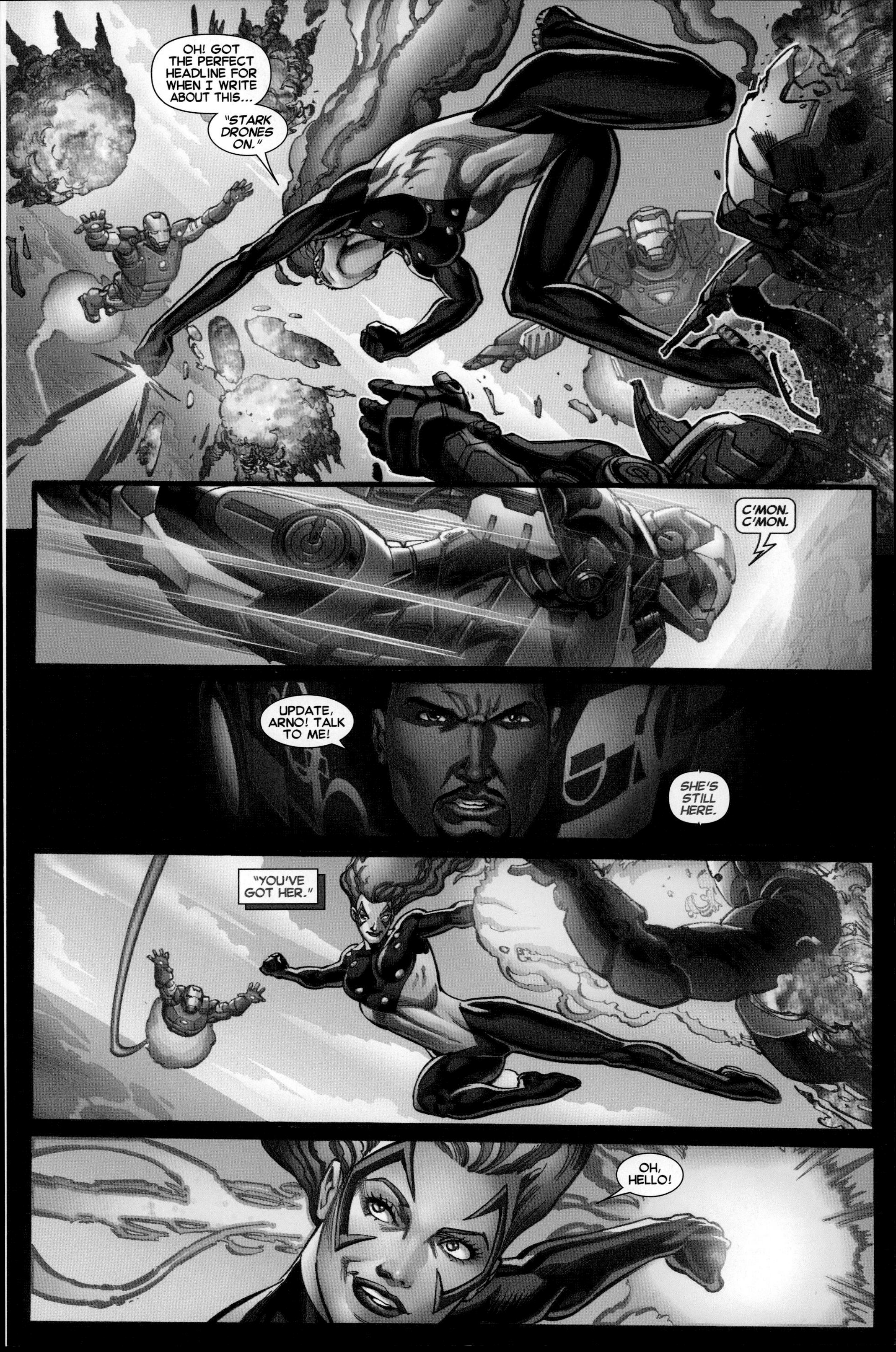
OH! GOT THE PERFECT HEADLINE FOR WHEN I WRITE ABOUT THIS...
"STARK DRONES ON."
C'MON. C'MON.
UPDATE, ARNO! TALK TO ME!
SHE'S STILL HERE.
"YOU'VE GOT HER."
OH, HELLO!

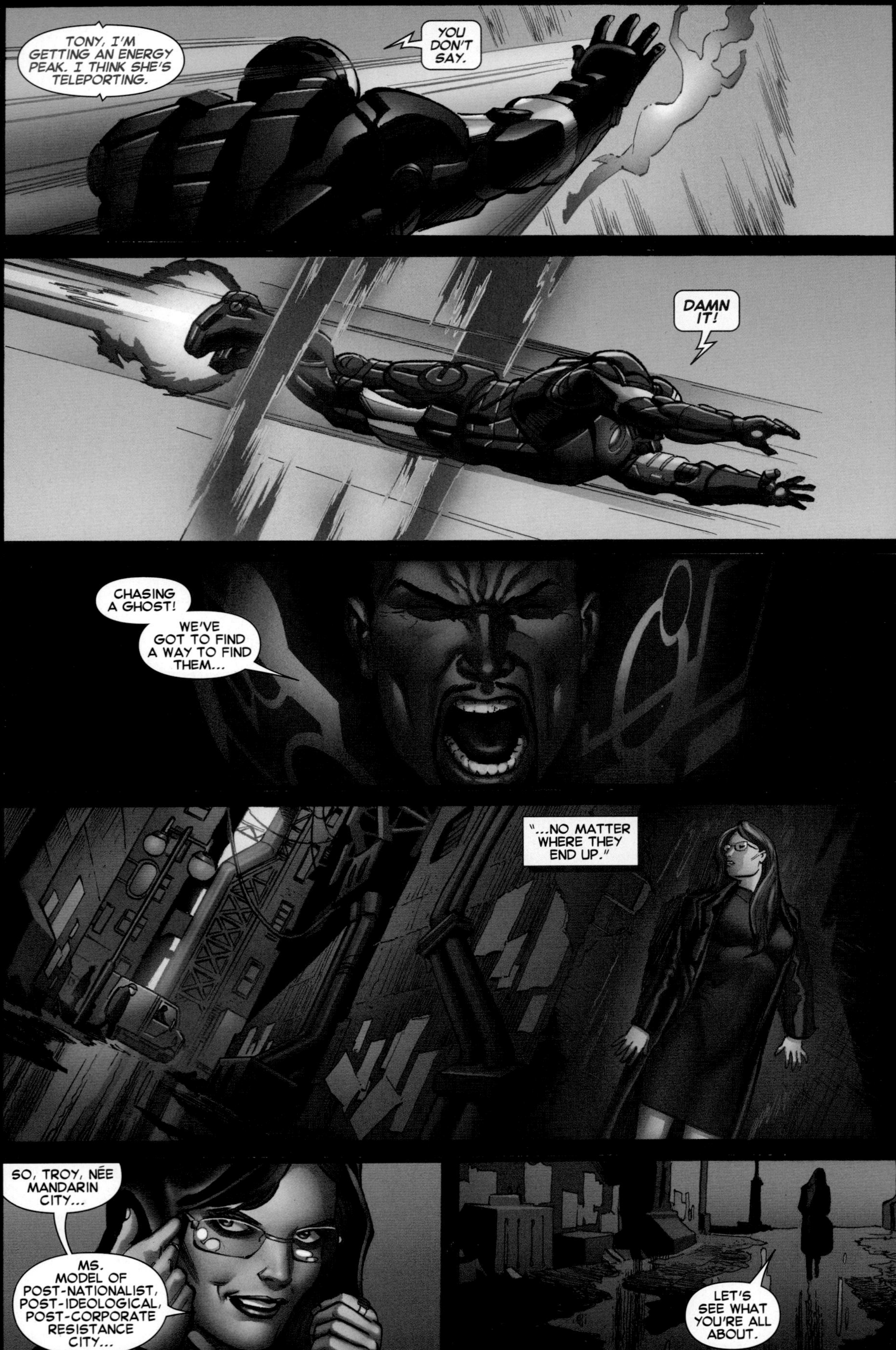
TONY, I'M GETTING AN ENERGY PEAK. I THINK SHE'S TELEPORTING.
YOU DON'T SAY.
DAMN IT!
CHASING A GHOST!
WE'VE GOT TO FIND A WAY TO FIND THEM...
"...NO MATTER WHERE THEY END UP."
SO, TROY, NÉE MANDARIN CITY...
MS. MODEL OF POST-NATIONALIST, POST-IDEOLOGICAL, POST-CORPORATE RESISTANCE CITY...
LET'S SEE WHAT YOU'RE ALL ABOUT.

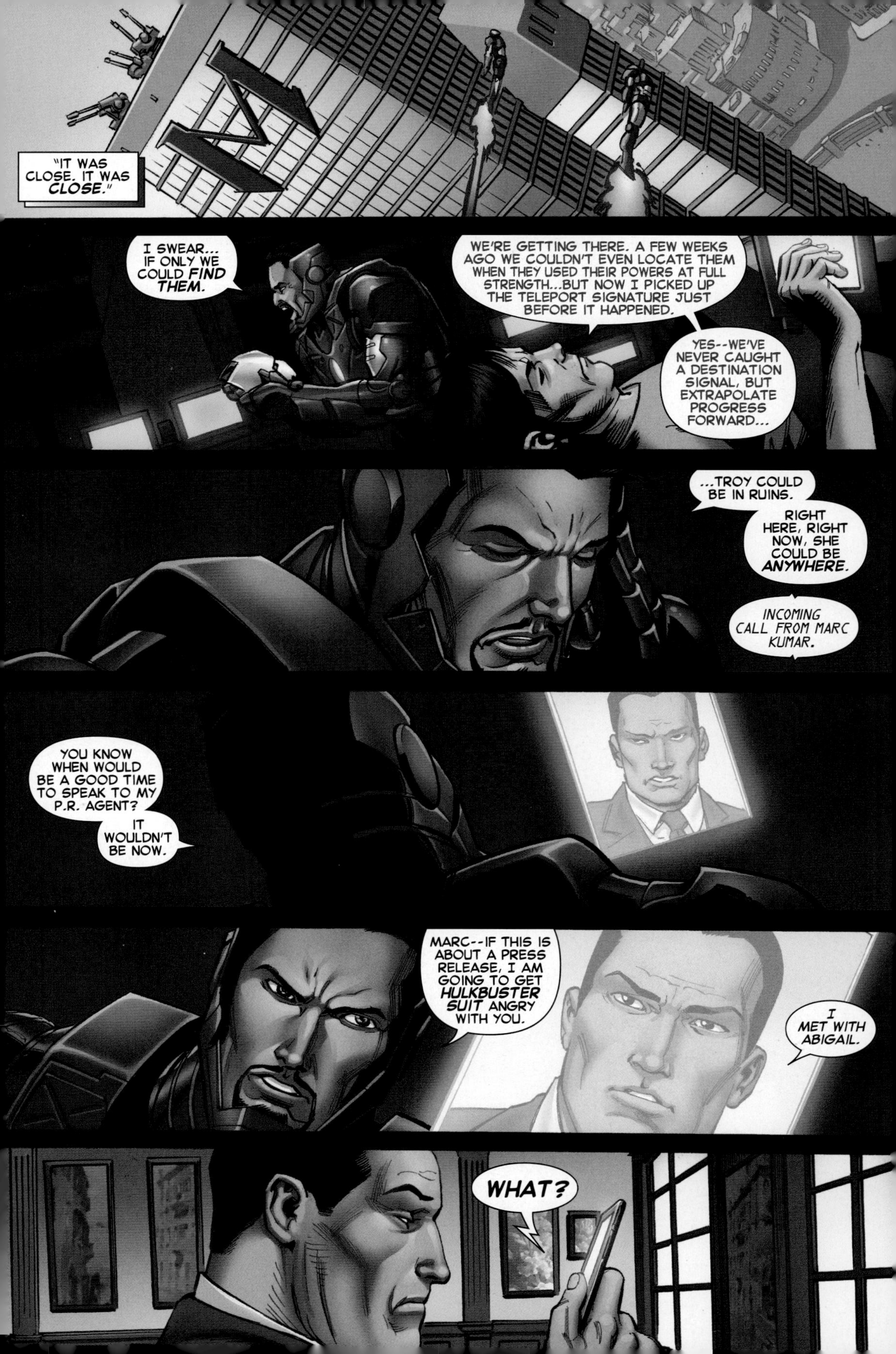
"IT WAS CLOSE. IT WAS CLOSE."
I SWEAR... IF ONLY WE COULD FIND THEM.
WE'RE GETTING THERE. A FEW WEEKS AGO WE COULDN'T EVEN LOCATE THEM WHEN THEY USED THEIR POWERS AT FULL STRENGTH...BUT NOW I PICKED UP THE TELEPORT SIGNATURE JUST BEFORE IT HAPPENED.
YES--WE'VE NEVER CAUGHT A DESTINATION SIGNAL, BUT EXTRAPOLATE PROGRESS FORWARD...
...TROY COULD BE IN RUINS.
RIGHT HERE, RIGHT NOW, SHE COULD BE ANYWHERE.
INCOMING CALL FROM MARC KUMAR.
YOU KNOW WHEN WOULD BE A GOOD TIME TO SPEAK TO MY P.R. AGENT?
IT WOULDN'T BE NOW.
MARC--IF THIS IS ABOUT A PRESS RELEASE, I AM GOING TO GET HULKBUSTER SUIT ANGRY WITH YOU.
I MET WITH ABIGAIL.
WHAT?

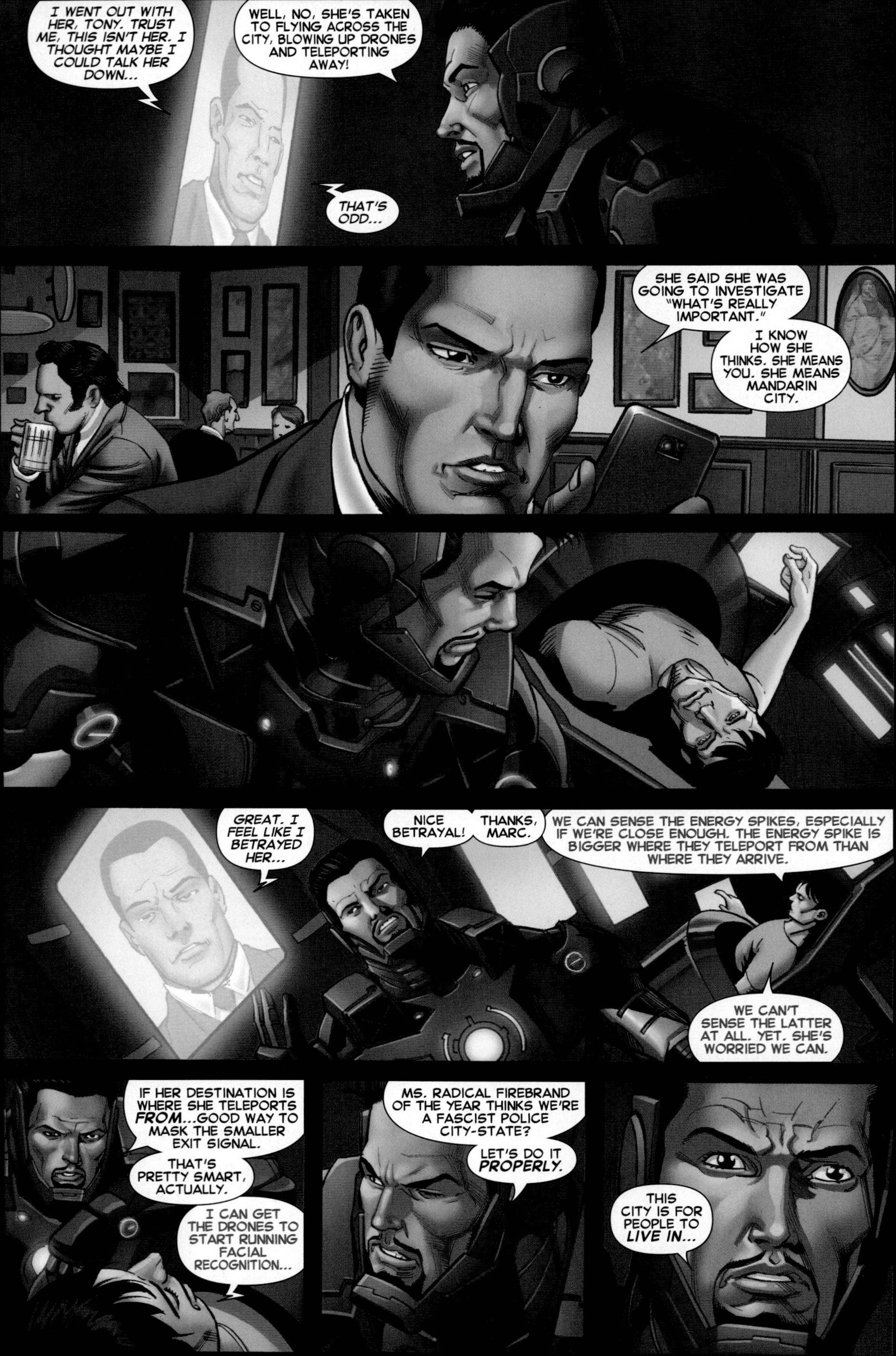
I WENT OUT WITH HER, TONY. TRUST ME, THIS ISN'T HER. I THOUGHT MAYBE I COULD TALK HER DOWN...
WELL, NO, SHE'S TAKEN TO FLYING ACROSS THE CITY, BLOWING UP DRONES AND TELEPORTING AWAY!
THAT'S ODD...
SHE SAID SHE WAS GOING TO INVESTIGATE "WHAT'S REALLY IMPORTANT."
I KNOW HOW SHE THINKS. SHE MEANS YOU. SHE MEANS MANDARIN CITY.
GREAT. I FEEL LIKE I BETRAYED HER...
NICE BETRAYAL!
THANKS, MARC.
WE CAN SENSE THE ENERGY SPIKES, ESPECIALLY IF WE'RE CLOSE ENOUGH. THE ENERGY SPIKE IS BIGGER WHERE THEY TELEPORT FROM THAN WHERE THEY ARRIVE.
WE CAN'T SENSE THE LATTER AT ALL. YET. SHE'S WORRIED WE CAN.
IF HER DESTINATION IS WHERE SHE TELEPORTS FROM...GOOD WAY TO MASK THE SMALLER EXIT SIGNAL.
THAT'S PRETTY SMART, ACTUALLY.
I CAN GET THE DRONES TO START RUNNING FACIAL RECOGNITION...
MS. RADICAL FIREBRAND OF THE YEAR THINKS WE'RE A FASCIST POLICE CITY-STATE?
LET'S DO IT PROPERLY.
THIS CITY IS FOR PEOPLE TO LIVE IN...

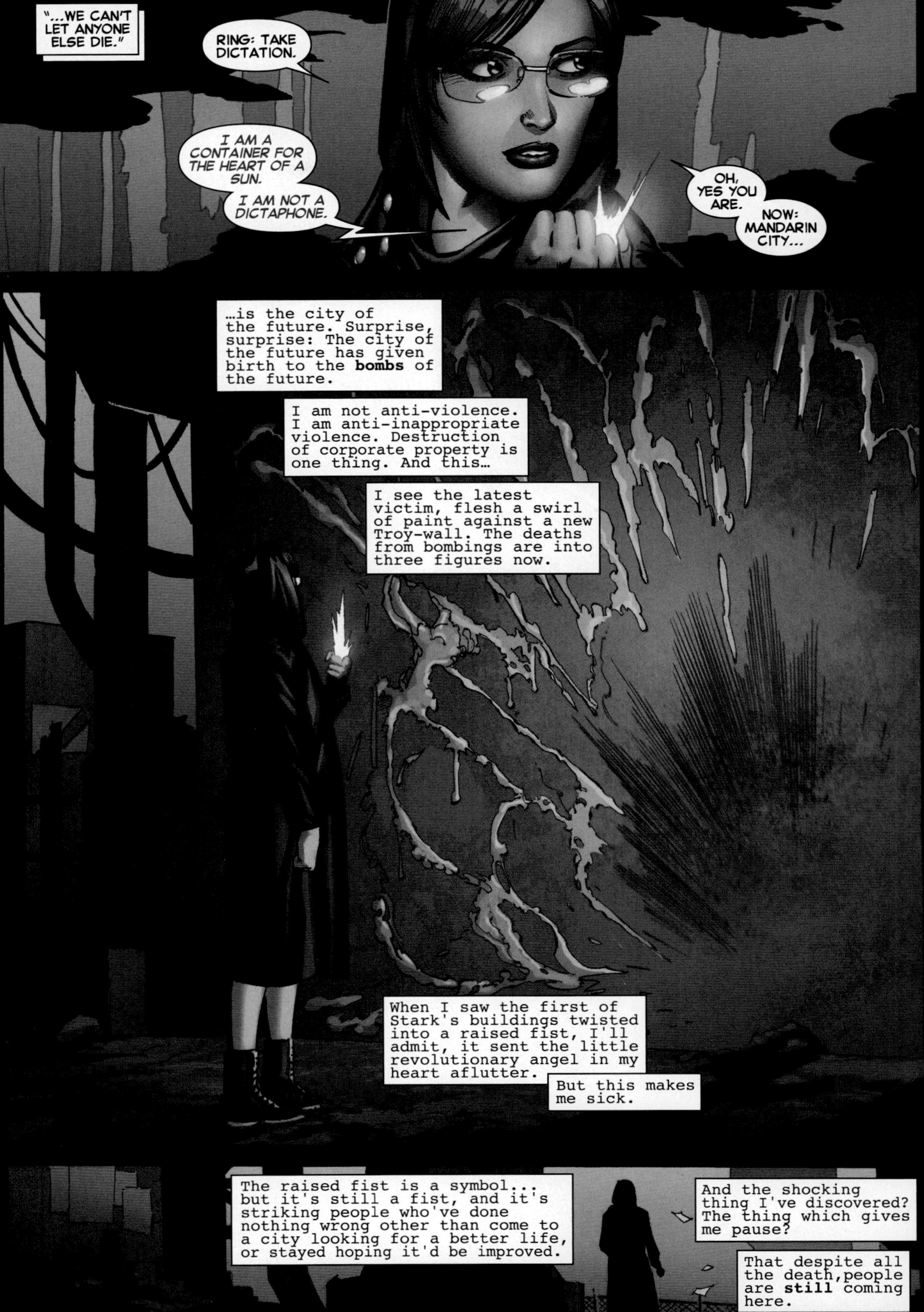
"...WE CAN'T LET ANYONE ELSE DIE."
RING: TAKE DICTATION.
I AM A CONTAINER FOR THE HEART OF A SUN.
I AM NOT A DICTAPHONE.
OH, YES YOU ARE.
NOW: MANDARIN CITY...
...is the city of the future. Surprise, surprise: The city of the future has given birth to the **bombs** of the future.
I am not anti-violence. I am anti-inappropriate violence. Destruction of corporate property is one thing. And this...
I see the latest victim, flesh a swirl of paint against a new Troy-wall. The deaths from bombings are into three figures now.
When I saw the first of Stark's buildings twisted into a raised fist, I'll admit, it sent the little revolutionary angel in my heart aflutter.
But this makes me sick.
The raised fist is a symbol... but it's still a fist, and it's striking people who've done nothing wrong other than come to a city looking for a better life, or stayed hoping it'd be improved.
And the shocking thing I've discovered? The thing which gives me pause?
That despite all the death, people are **still** coming here.

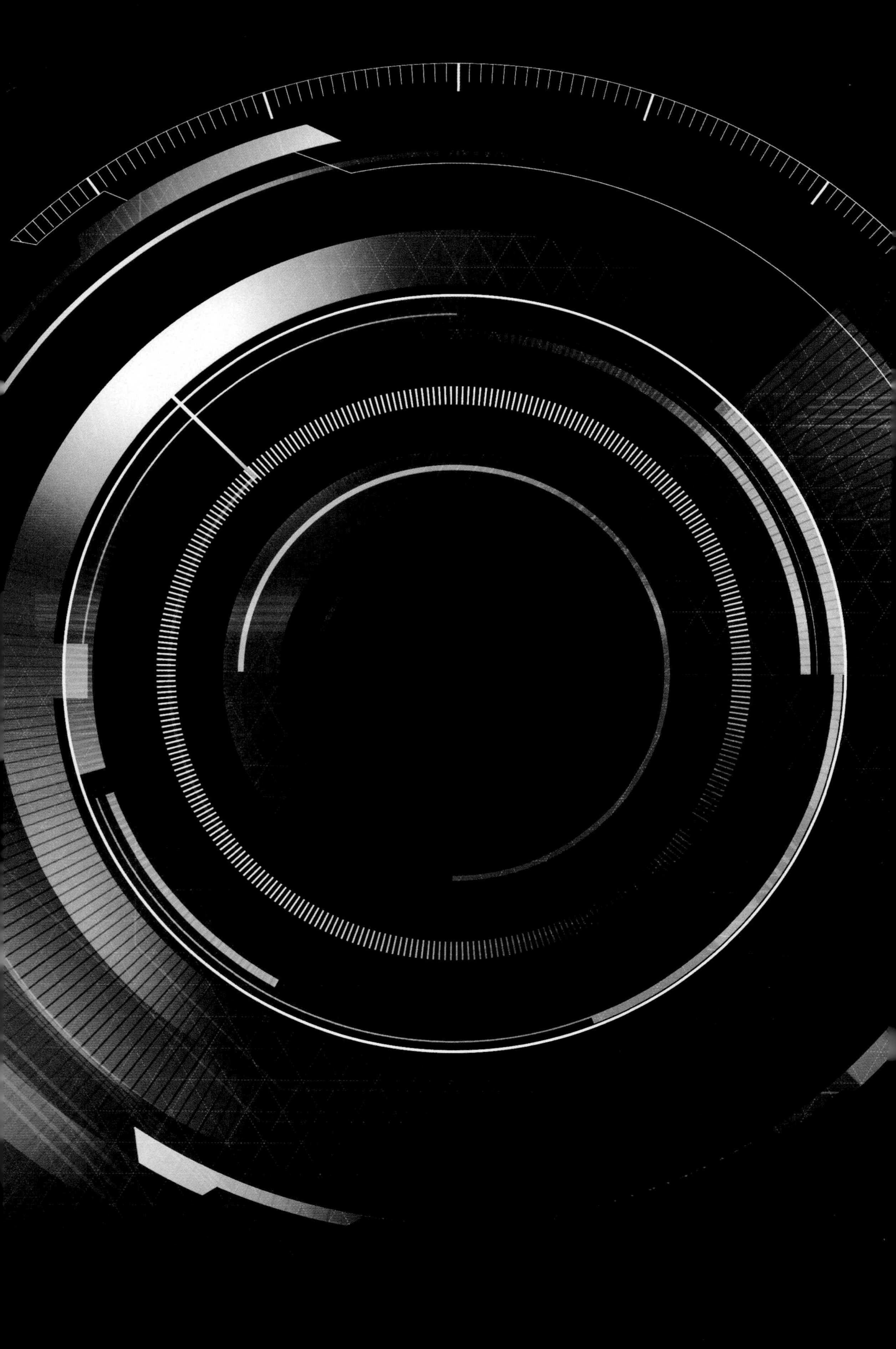

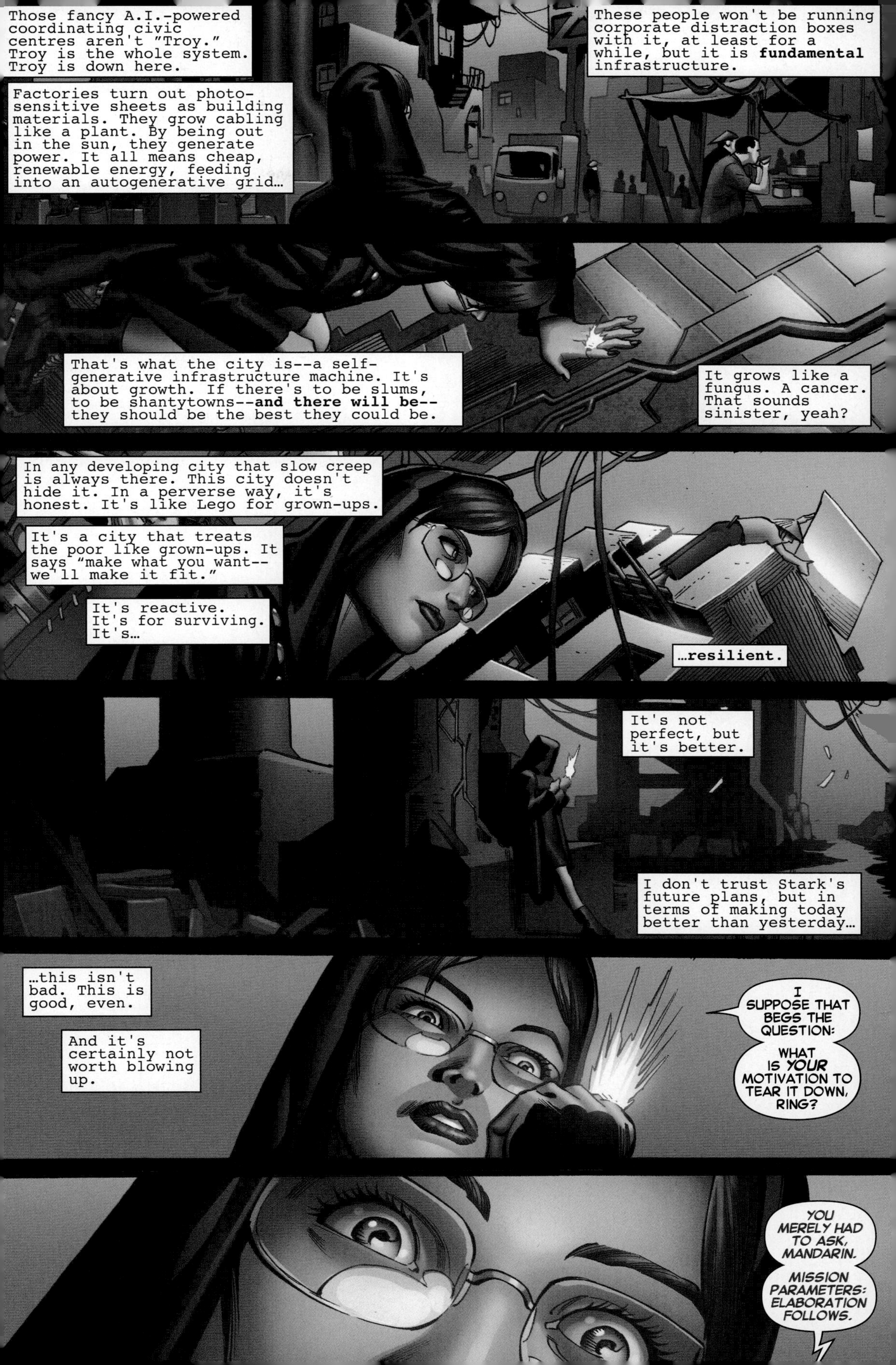

Those fancy A.I.-powered coordinating civic centres aren't "Troy." Troy is the whole system. Troy is down here.
Factories turn out photo-sensitive sheets as building materials. They grow cabling like a plant. By being out in the sun, they generate power. It all means cheap, renewable energy, feeding into an autogenerative grid…
These people won't be running corporate distraction boxes with it, at least for a while, but it is **fundamental** infrastructure.
That's what the city is--a self-generative infrastructure machine. It's about growth. If there's to be slums, to be shantytowns--**and there will be--** they should be the best they could be.
It grows like a fungus. A cancer. That sounds sinister, yeah?
In any developing city that slow creep is always there. This city doesn't hide it. In a perverse way, it's honest. It's like Lego for grown-ups.
It's a city that treats the poor like grown-ups. It says "make what you want--we'll make it fit."
It's reactive. It's for surviving. It's…
…resilient.
It's not perfect, but it's better.
I don't trust Stark's future plans, but in terms of making today better than yesterday…
…this isn't bad. This is good, even.
And it's certainly not worth blowing up.
I SUPPOSE THAT BEGS THE QUESTION:
WHAT IS ***YOUR*** MOTIVATION TO TEAR IT DOWN, RING?
YOU MERELY HAD TO ASK, MANDARIN.
MISSION PARAMETERS: ELABORATION FOLLOWS.

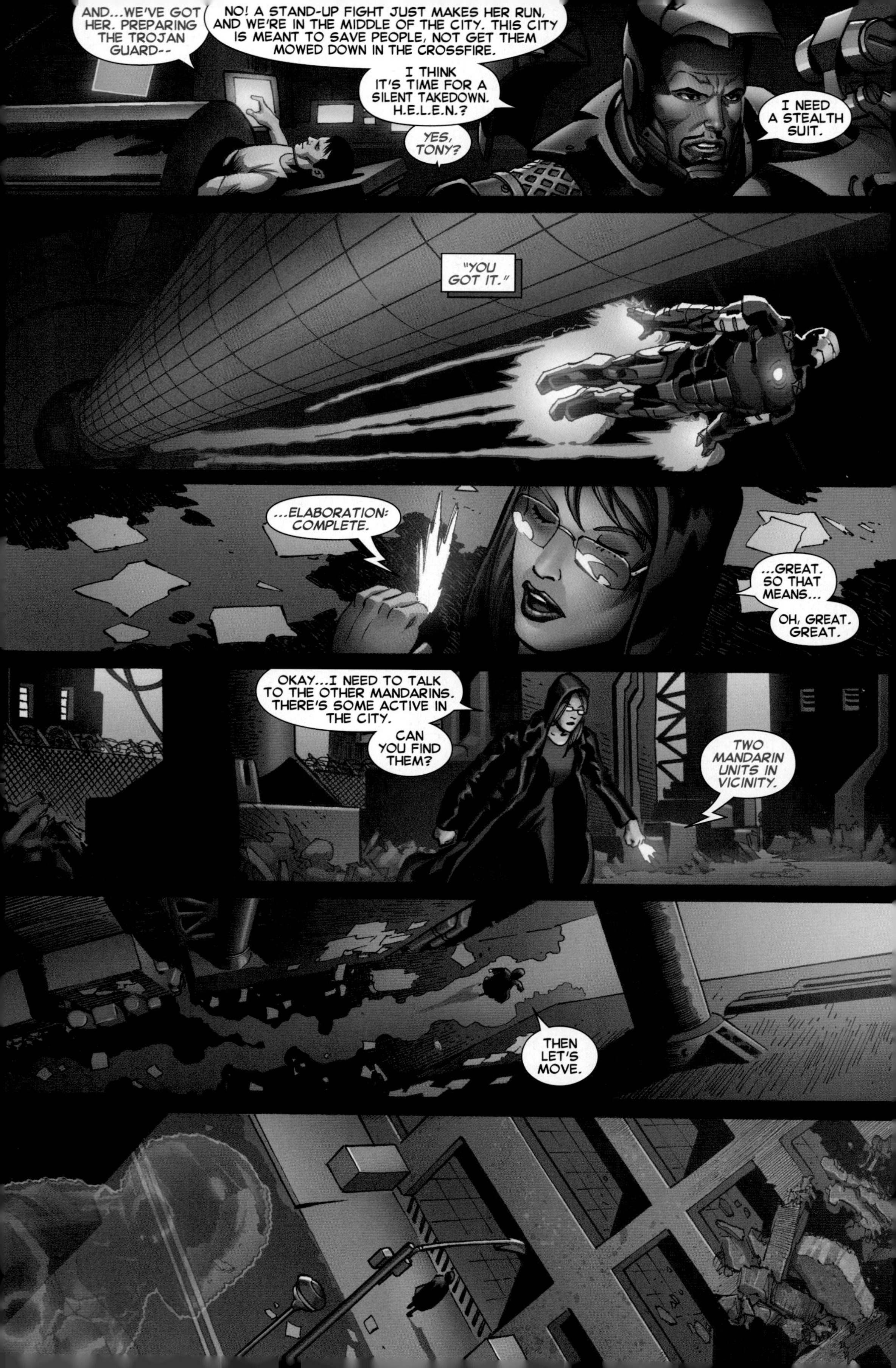
AND...WE'VE GOT HER. PREPARING THE TROJAN GUARD--
NO! A STAND-UP FIGHT JUST MAKES HER RUN, AND WE'RE IN THE MIDDLE OF THE CITY. THIS CITY IS MEANT TO SAVE PEOPLE, NOT GET THEM MOWED DOWN IN THE CROSSFIRE.
I THINK IT'S TIME FOR A SILENT TAKEDOWN. H.E.L.E.N.?
YES, TONY?
I NEED A STEALTH SUIT.
"YOU GOT IT."
...ELABORATION: COMPLETE.
...GREAT. SO THAT MEANS...
OH, GREAT. GREAT.
OKAY...I NEED TO TALK TO THE OTHER MANDARINS. THERE'S SOME ACTIVE IN THE CITY.
CAN YOU FIND THEM?
TWO MANDARIN UNITS IN VICINITY.
THEN LET'S MOVE.

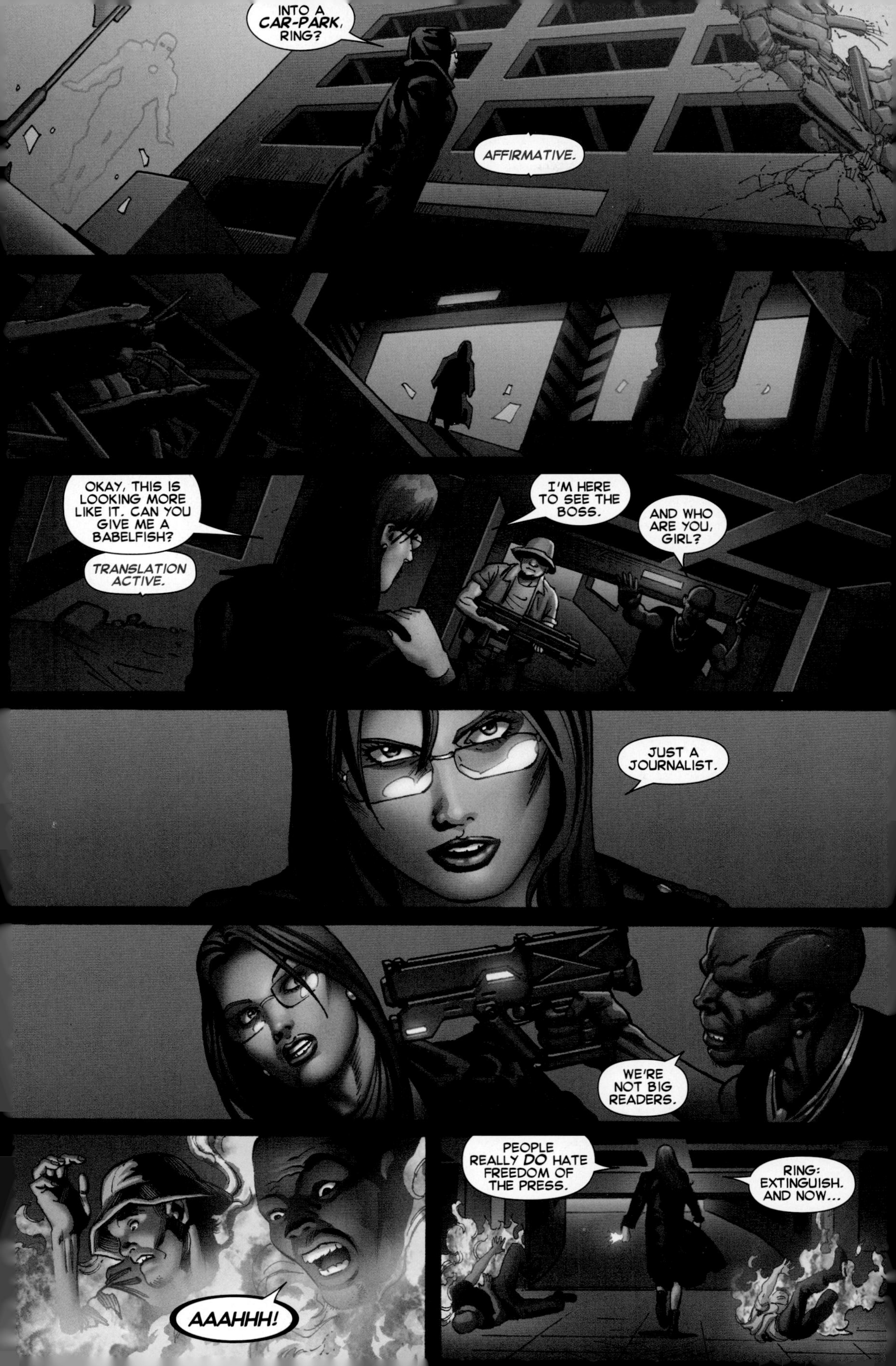
INTO A CAR-PARK, RING?
AFFIRMATIVE.
OKAY, THIS IS LOOKING MORE LIKE IT. CAN YOU GIVE ME A BABELFISH?
TRANSLATION ACTIVE.
I'M HERE TO SEE THE BOSS.
AND WHO ARE YOU, GIRL?
JUST A JOURNALIST.
WE'RE NOT BIG READERS.
AAAHHH!
PEOPLE REALLY DO HATE FREEDOM OF THE PRESS.
RING: EXTINGUISH. AND NOW...

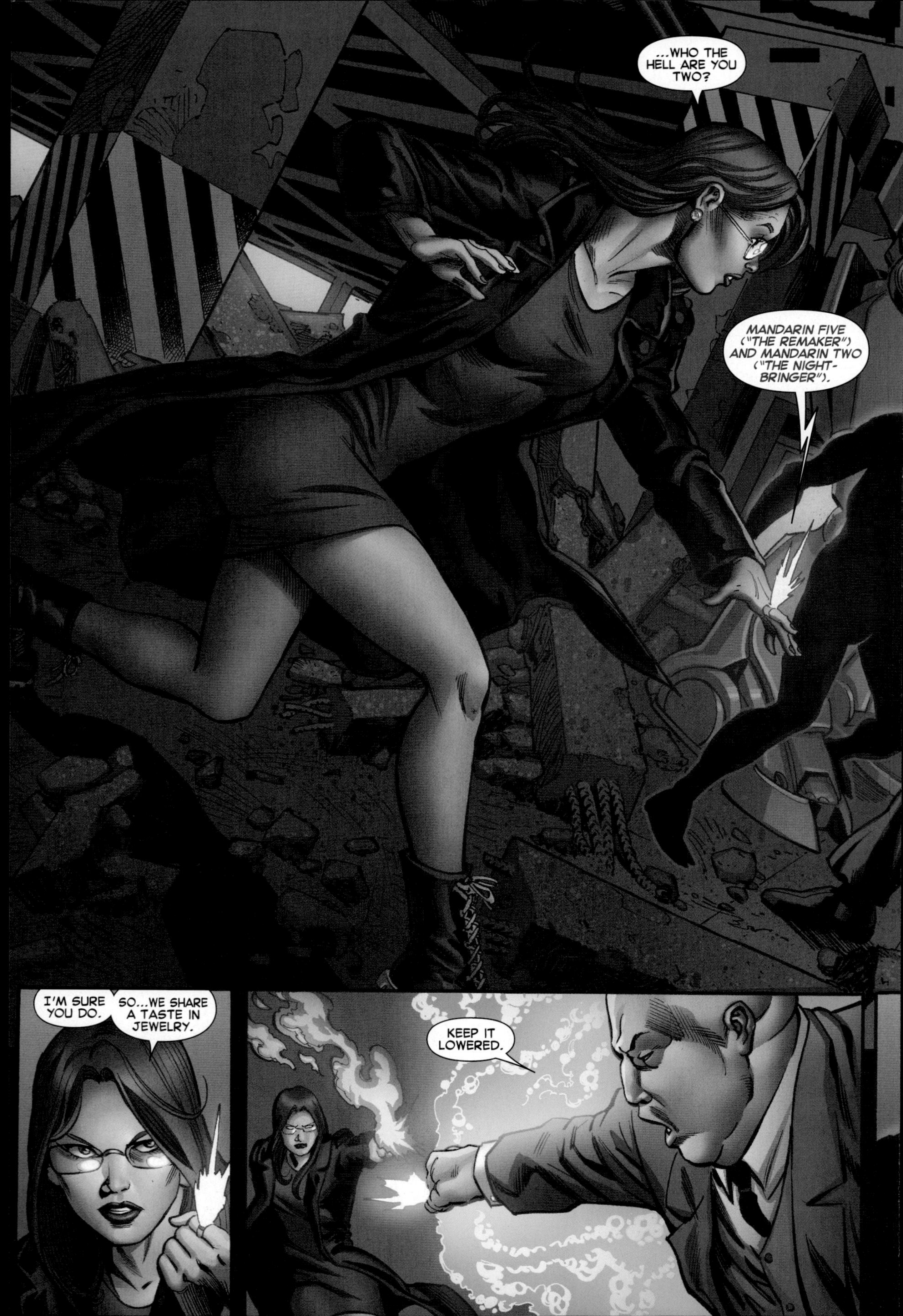
...WHO THE HELL ARE YOU TWO?
MANDARIN FIVE ("THE REMAKER") AND MANDARIN TWO ("THE NIGHT-BRINGER").
I'M SURE YOU DO.
SO...WE SHARE A TASTE IN JEWELRY.
KEEP IT LOWERED.

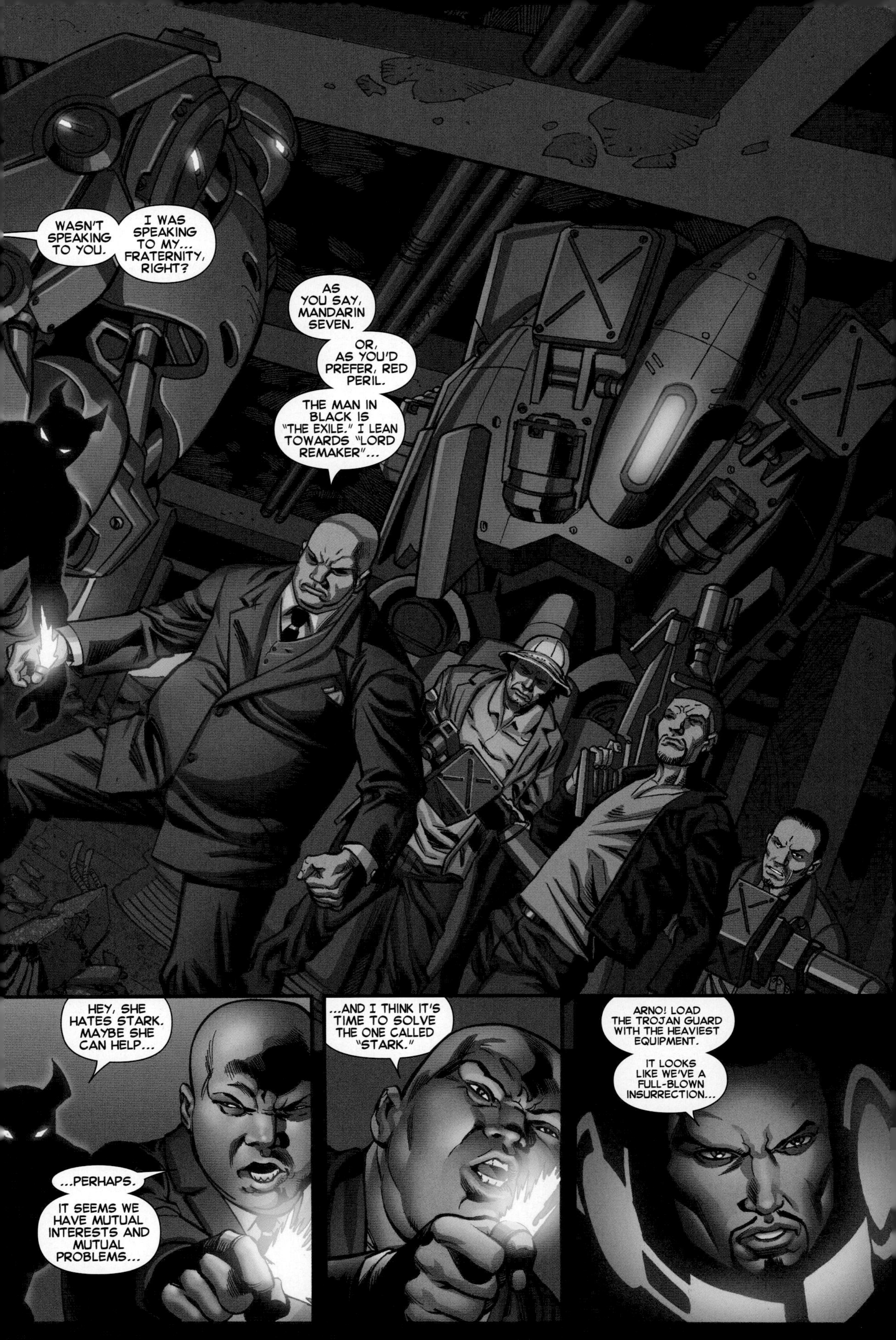
WASN'T SPEAKING TO YOU.
I WAS SPEAKING TO MY... FRATERNITY, RIGHT?
AS YOU SAY, MANDARIN SEVEN.
OR, AS YOU'D PREFER, RED PERIL.
THE MAN IN BLACK IS "THE EXILE." I LEAN TOWARDS "LORD REMAKER"...
HEY, SHE HATES STARK. MAYBE SHE CAN HELP...
...PERHAPS.
IT SEEMS WE HAVE MUTUAL INTERESTS AND MUTUAL PROBLEMS...
...AND I THINK IT'S TIME TO SOLVE THE ONE CALLED "STARK."
ARNO! LOAD THE TROJAN GUARD WITH THE HEAVIEST EQUIPMENT.
IT LOOKS LIKE WE'VE A FULL-BLOWN INSURRECTION...

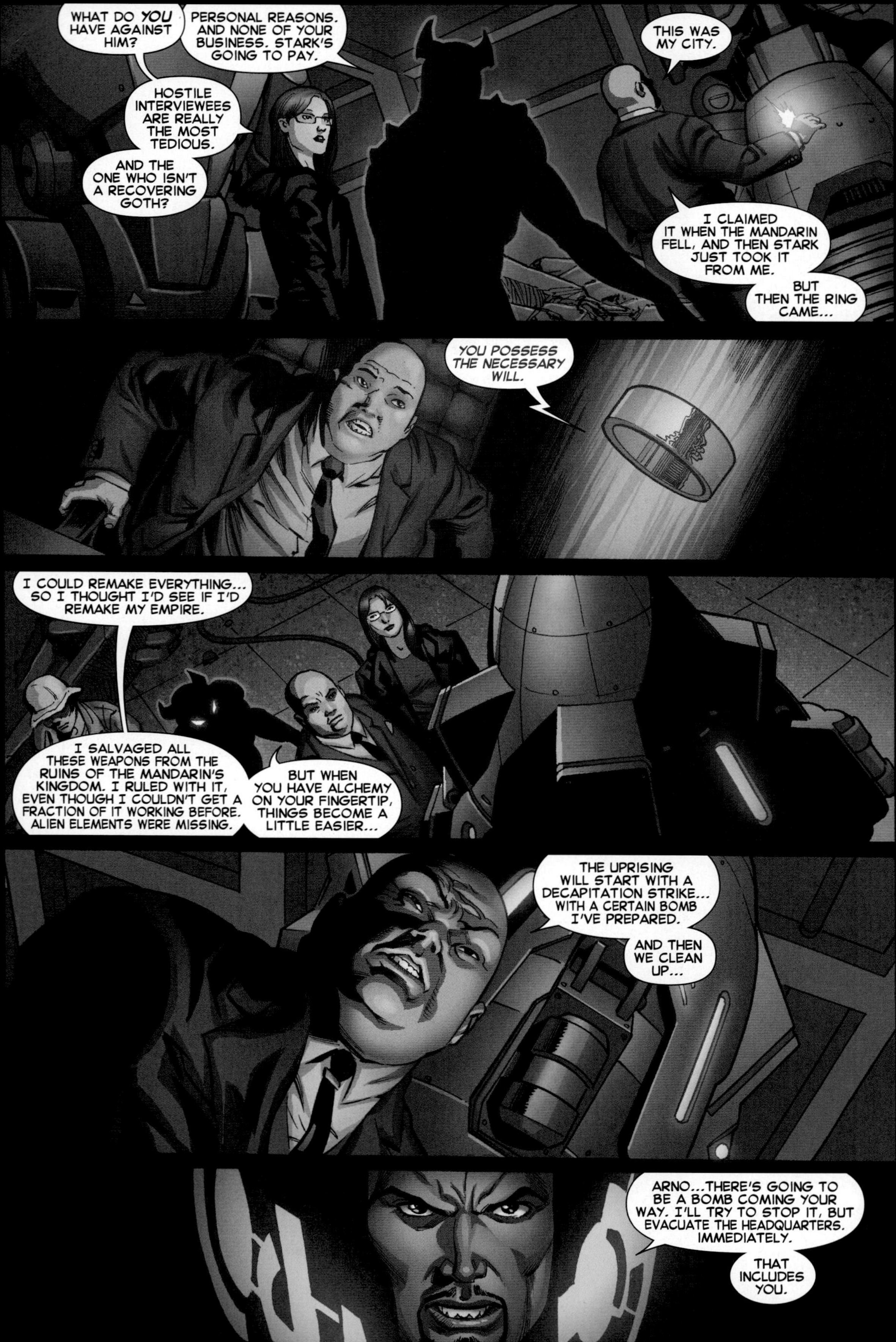
WHAT DO YOU HAVE AGAINST HIM?
PERSONAL REASONS. AND NONE OF YOUR BUSINESS. STARK'S GOING TO PAY.
HOSTILE INTERVIEWEES ARE REALLY THE MOST TEDIOUS.
AND THE ONE WHO ISN'T A RECOVERING GOTH?
THIS WAS MY CITY.
I CLAIMED IT WHEN THE MANDARIN FELL, AND THEN STARK JUST TOOK IT FROM ME.
BUT THEN THE RING CAME...
YOU POSSESS THE NECESSARY WILL.
I COULD REMAKE EVERYTHING... SO I THOUGHT I'D SEE IF I'D REMAKE MY EMPIRE.
I SALVAGED ALL THESE WEAPONS FROM THE RUINS OF THE MANDARIN'S KINGDOM. I RULED WITH IT, EVEN THOUGH I COULDN'T GET A FRACTION OF IT WORKING BEFORE. ALIEN ELEMENTS WERE MISSING.
BUT WHEN YOU HAVE ALCHEMY ON YOUR FINGERTIP, THINGS BECOME A LITTLE EASIER...
THE UPRISING WILL START WITH A DECAPITATION STRIKE... WITH A CERTAIN BOMB I'VE PREPARED.
AND THEN WE CLEAN UP...
ARNO...THERE'S GOING TO BE A BOMB COMING YOUR WAY. I'LL TRY TO STOP IT, BUT EVACUATE THE HEADQUARTERS. IMMEDIATELY.
THAT INCLUDES YOU.

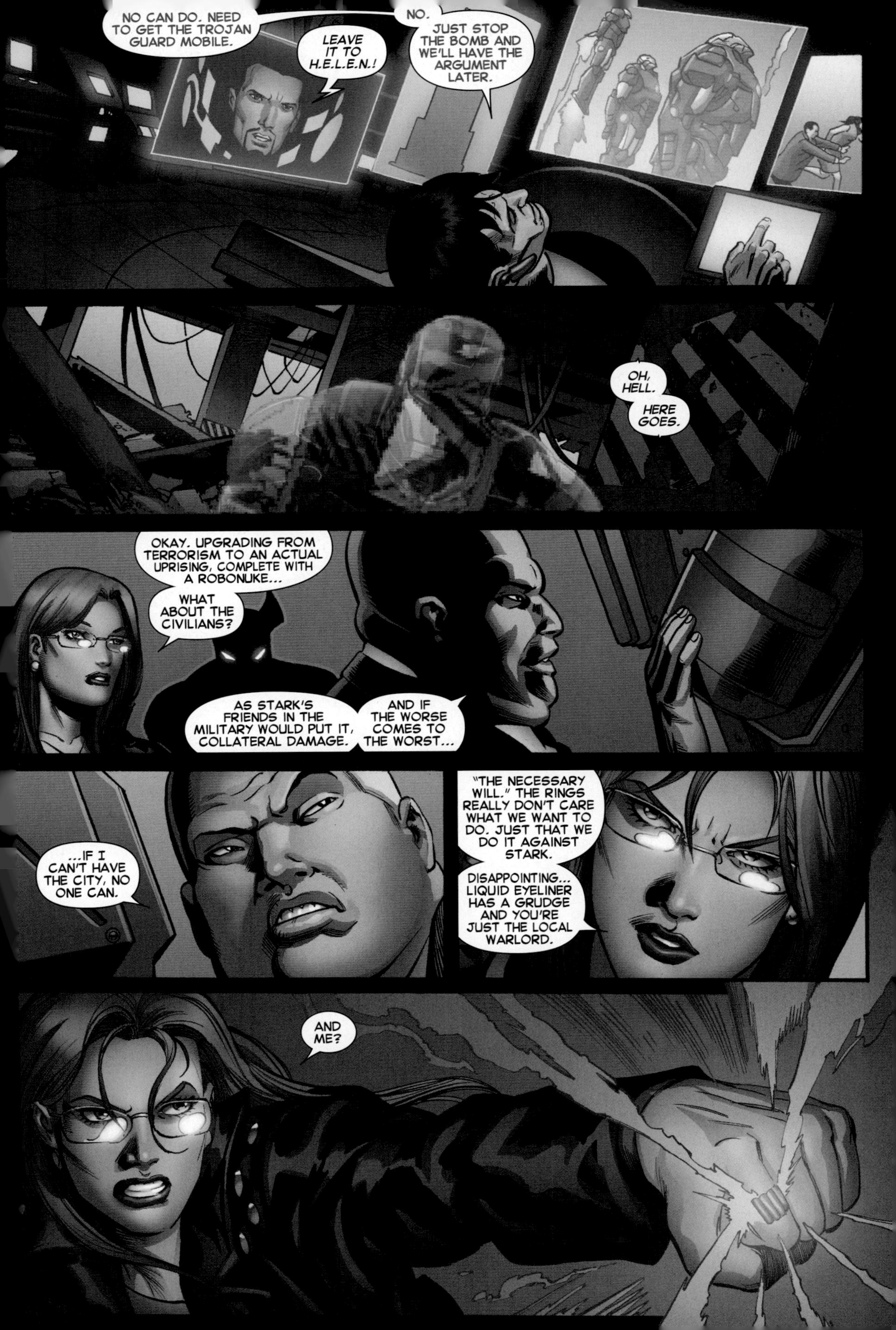
NO CAN DO. NEED TO GET THE TROJAN GUARD MOBILE.
LEAVE IT TO H.E.L.E.N.!
NO.
JUST STOP THE BOMB AND WE'LL HAVE THE ARGUMENT LATER.
OH, HELL.
HERE GOES.
OKAY. UPGRADING FROM TERRORISM TO AN ACTUAL UPRISING, COMPLETE WITH A ROBONUKE...
WHAT ABOUT THE CIVILIANS?
AS STARK'S FRIENDS IN THE MILITARY WOULD PUT IT, COLLATERAL DAMAGE.
AND IF THE WORSE COMES TO THE WORST...
...IF I CAN'T HAVE THE CITY, NO ONE CAN.
"THE NECESSARY WILL." THE RINGS REALLY DON'T CARE WHAT WE WANT TO DO. JUST THAT WE DO IT AGAINST STARK.
DISAPPOINTING... LIQUID EYELINER HAS A GRUDGE AND YOU'RE JUST THE LOCAL WARLORD.
AND ME?

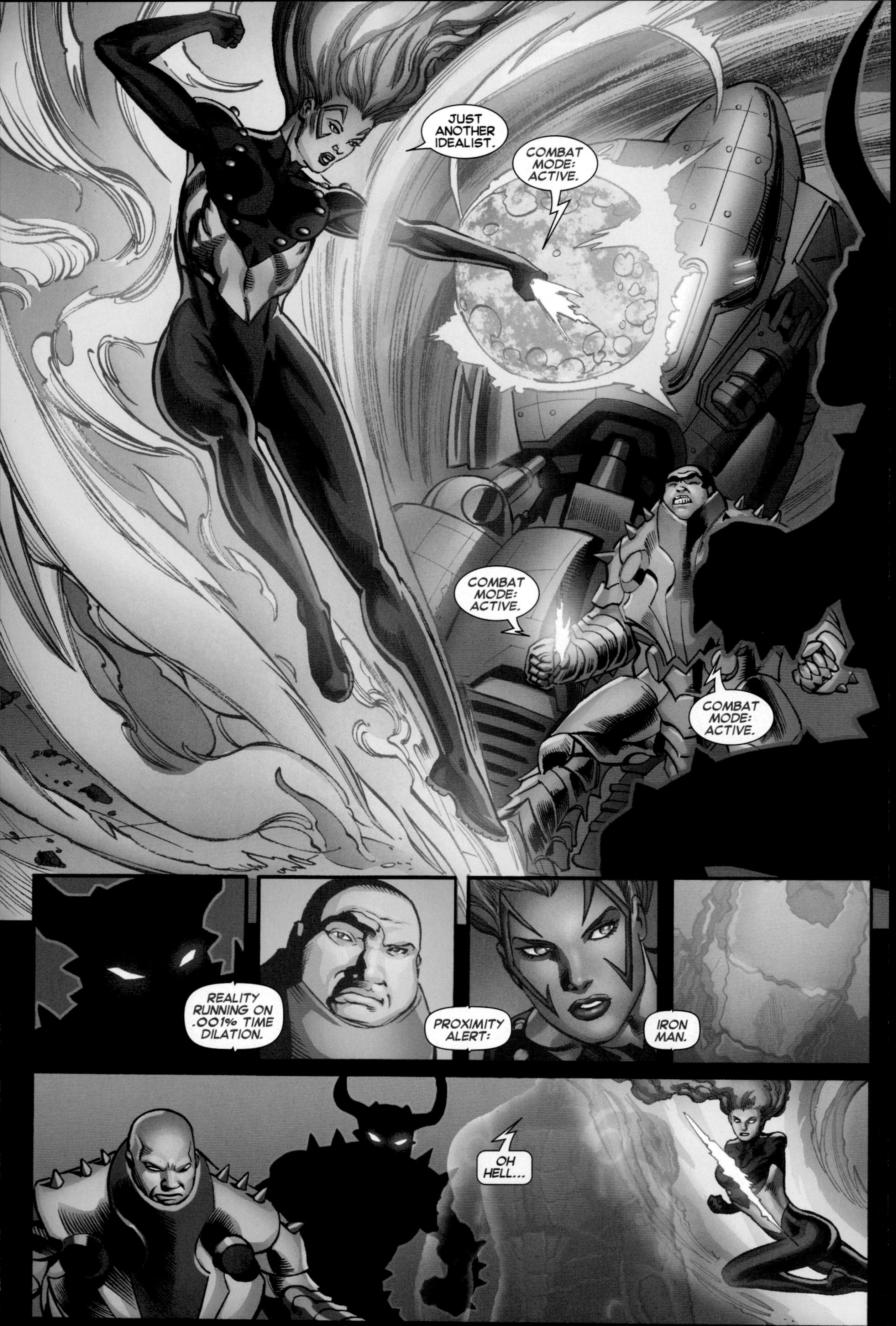
JUST ANOTHER IDEALIST.
COMBAT MODE: ACTIVE.
COMBAT MODE: ACTIVE.
COMBAT MODE: ACTIVE.
REALITY RUNNING ON .001% TIME DILATION.
PROXIMITY ALERT:
IRON MAN.
OH HELL...

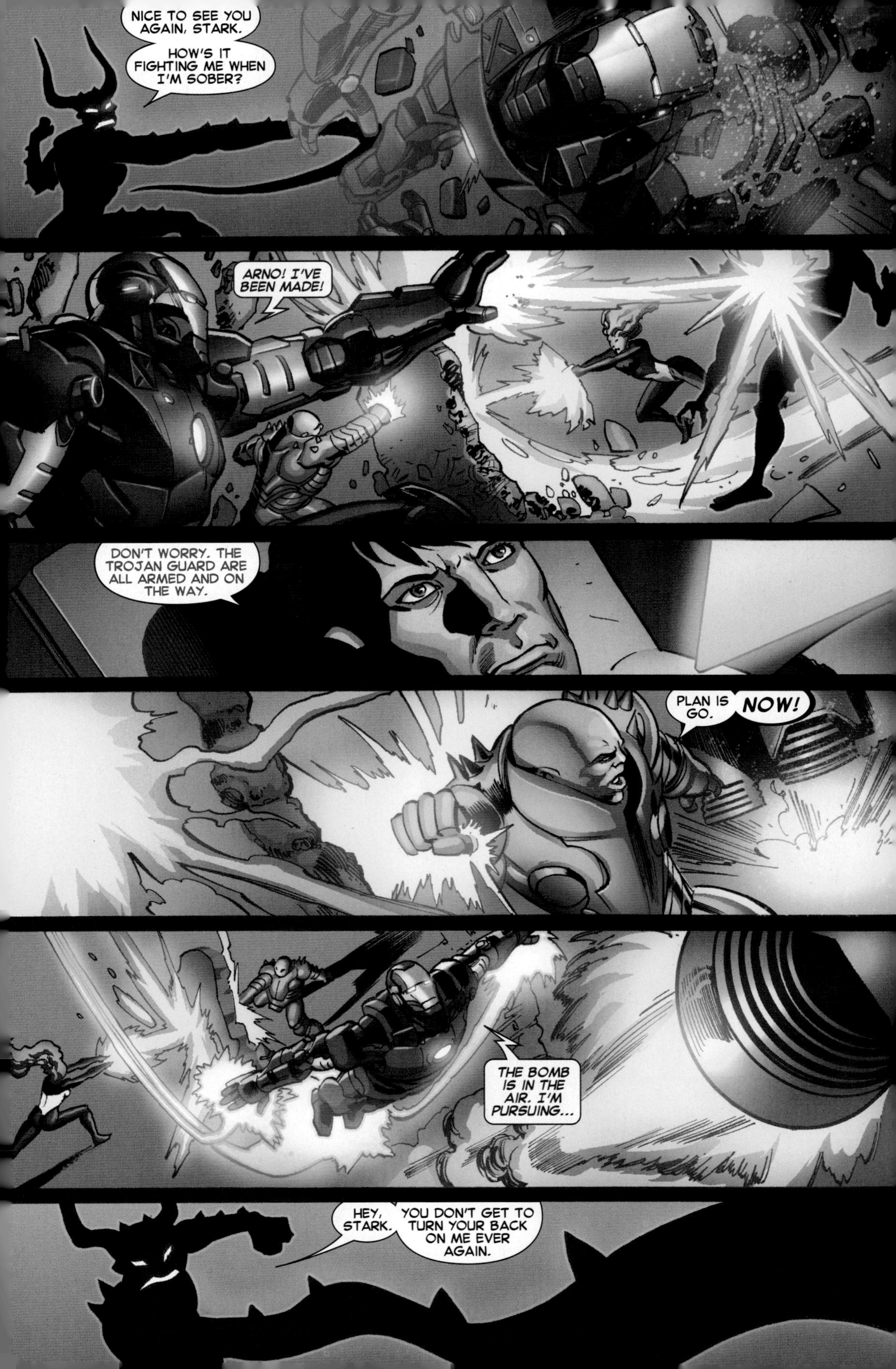
NICE TO SEE YOU AGAIN, STARK.
HOW'S IT FIGHTING ME WHEN I'M SOBER?
ARNO! I'VE BEEN MADE!
DON'T WORRY. THE TROJAN GUARD ARE ALL ARMED AND ON THE WAY.
PLAN IS GO.
NOW!
THE BOMB IS IN THE AIR. I'M PURSUING...
HEY, STARK.
YOU DON'T GET TO TURN YOUR BACK ON ME EVER AGAIN.

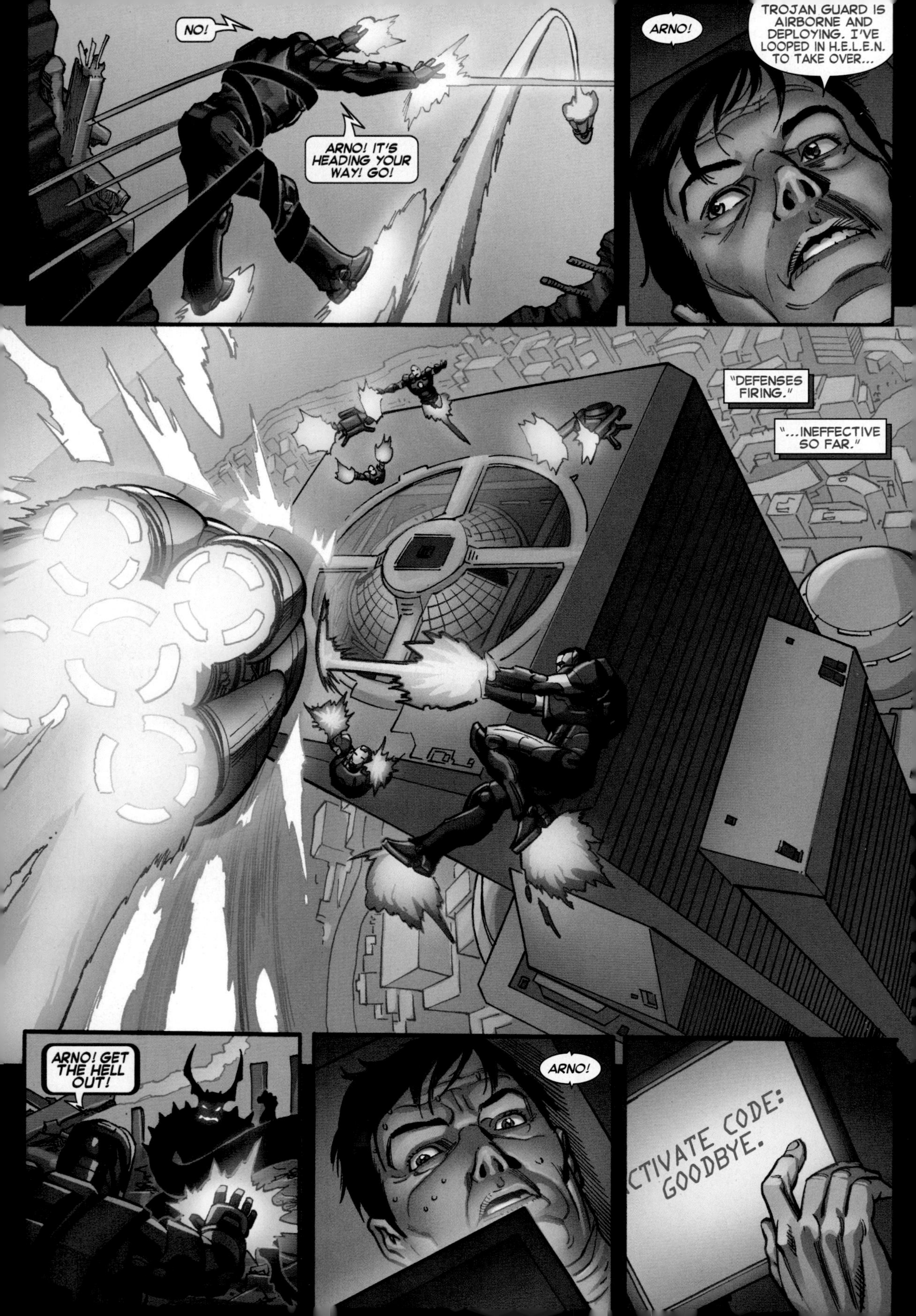
NO!
ARNO! IT'S HEADING YOUR WAY! GO!
ARNO!
TROJAN GUARD IS AIRBORNE AND DEPLOYING. I'VE LOOPED IN H.E.L.E.N. TO TAKE OVER...
"DEFENSES FIRING."
"...INEFFECTIVE SO FAR."
ARNO! GET THE HELL OUT!
ARNO!
CTIVATE CODE: GOODBYE.

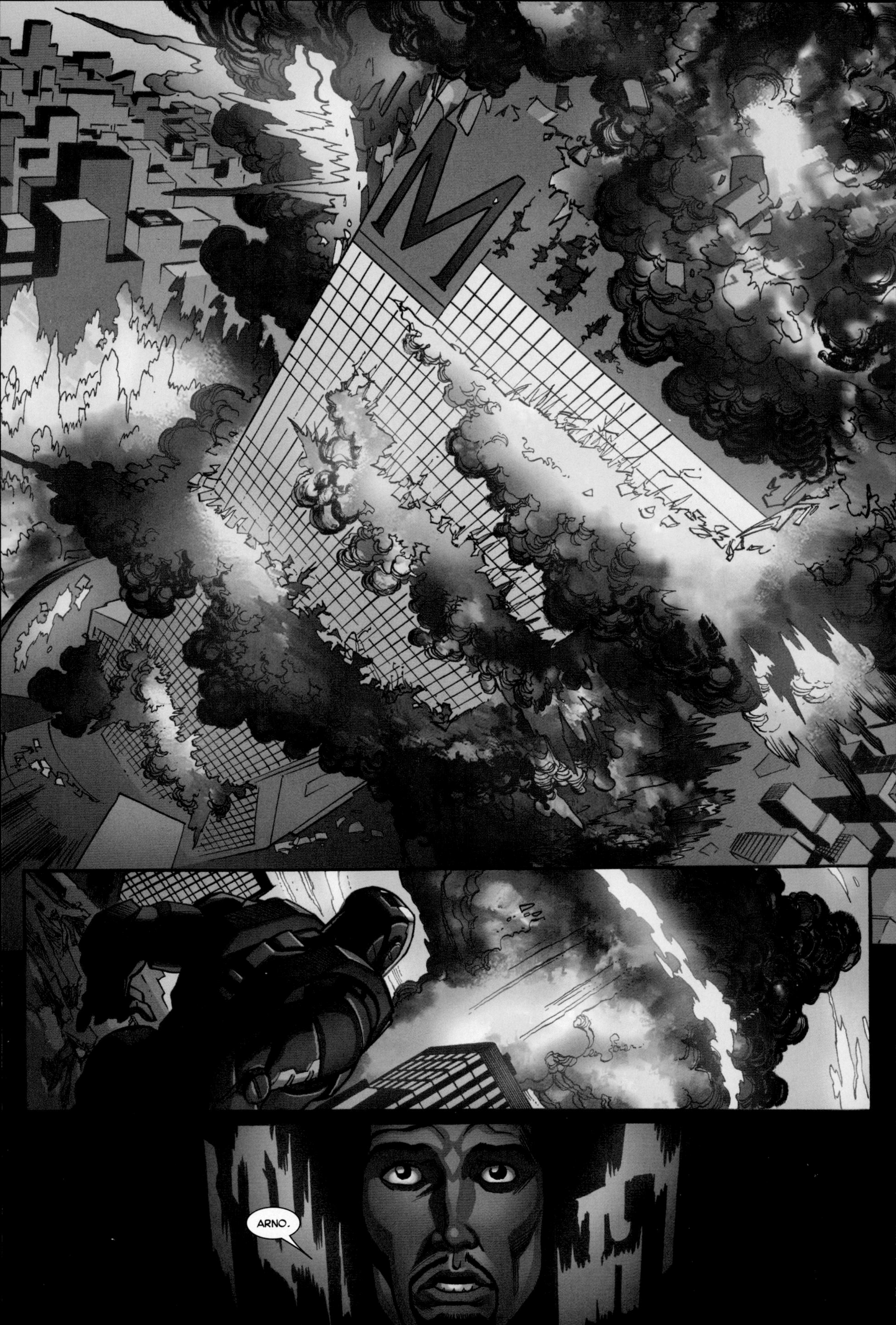
ARNO.

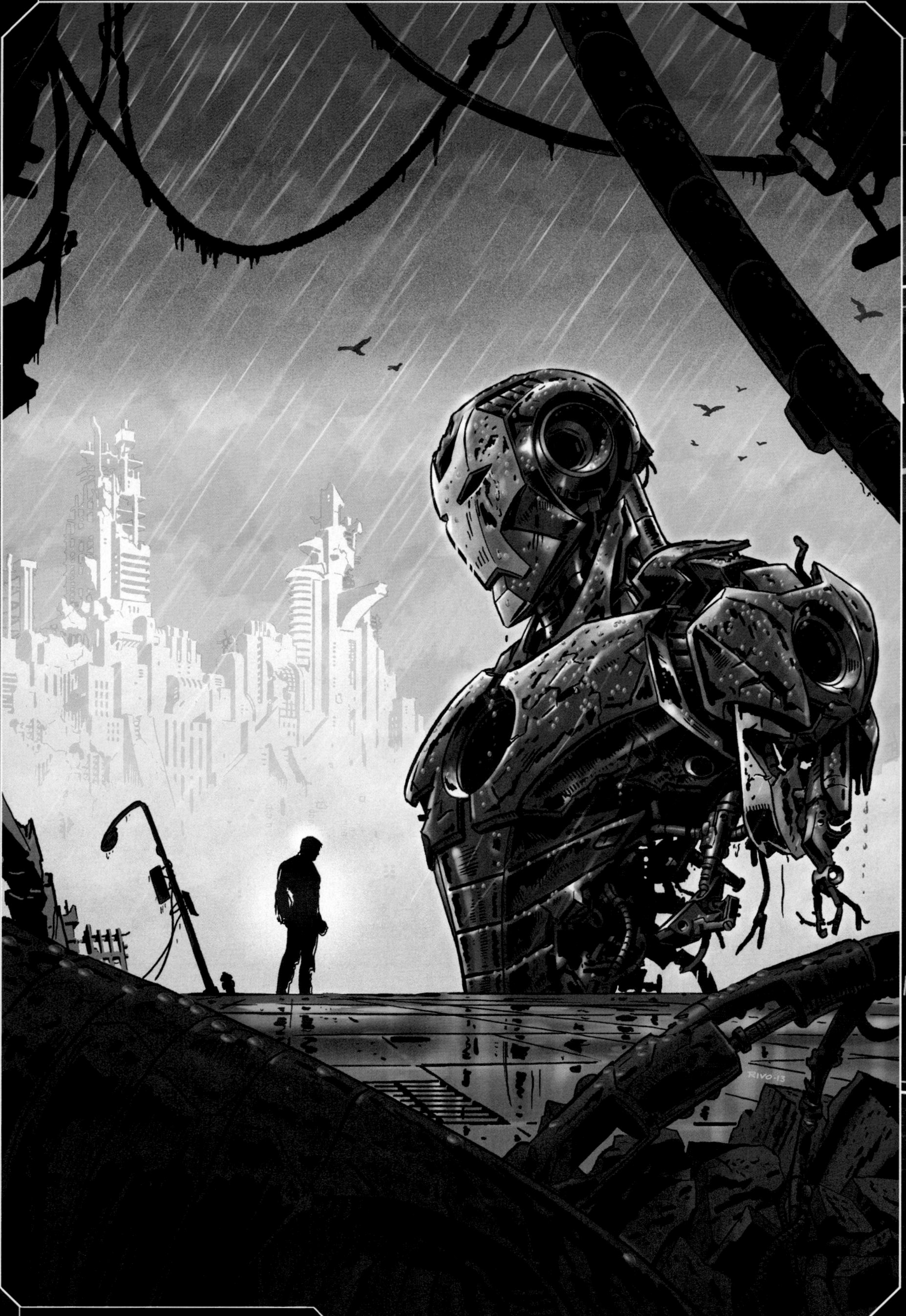
RIVO-13

22 IRON METROPOLITAN PART 5

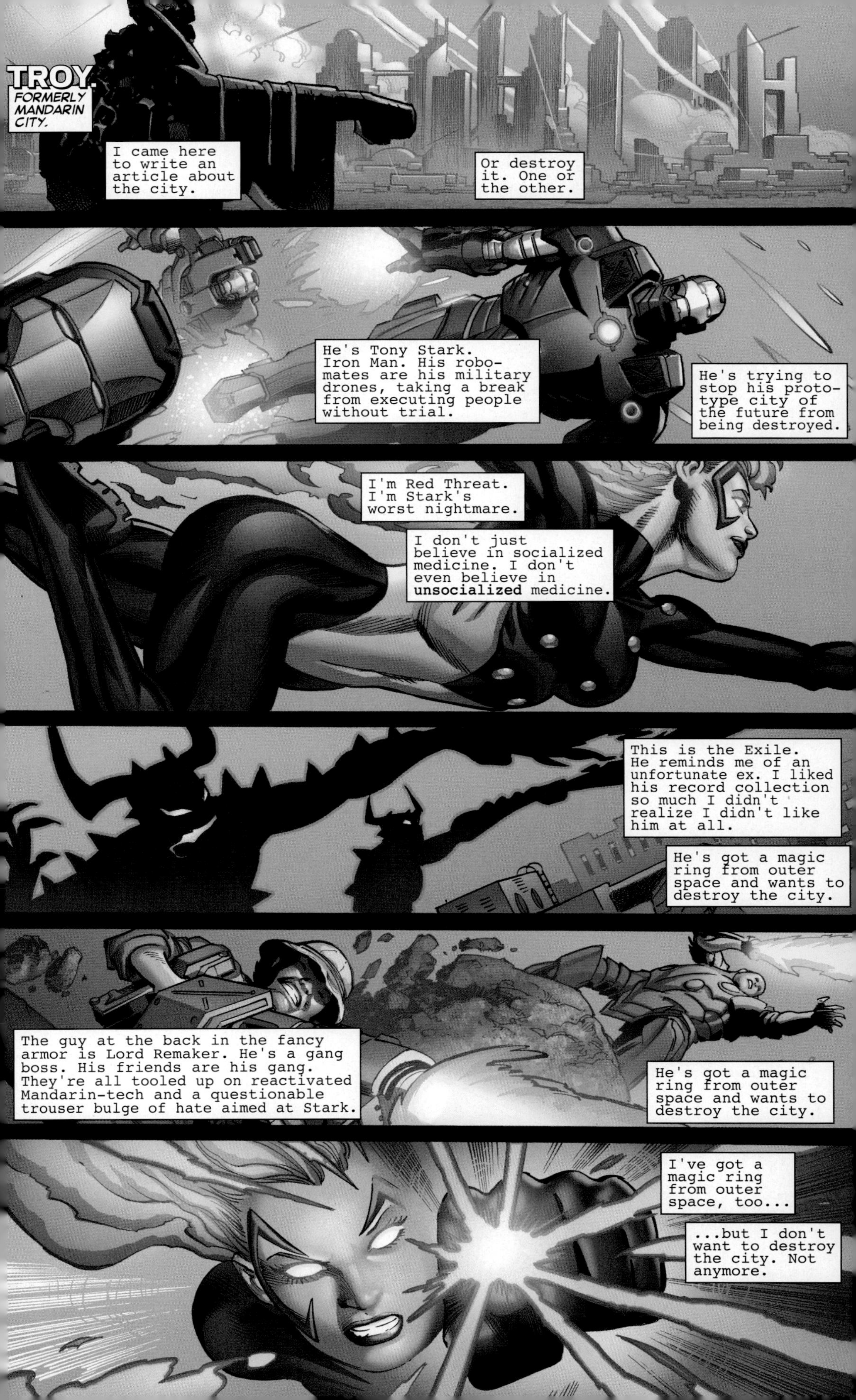
TROY. FORMERLY MANDARIN CITY.
I came here to write an article about the city.
Or destroy it. One or the other.
He's Tony Stark. Iron Man. His robo-mates are his military drones, taking a break from executing people without trial.
He's trying to stop his proto-type city of the future from being destroyed.
I'm Red Threat. I'm Stark's worst nightmare.
I don't just believe in socialized medicine. I don't even believe in **unsocialized** medicine.
This is the Exile. He reminds me of an unfortunate ex. I liked his record collection so much I didn't realize I didn't like him at all.
He's got a magic ring from outer space and wants to destroy the city.
The guy at the back in the fancy armor is Lord Remaker. He's a gang boss. His friends are his gang. They're all tooled up on reactivated Mandarin-tech and a questionable trouser bulge of hate aimed at Stark.
He's got a magic ring from outer space and wants to destroy the city.
I've got a magic ring from outer space, too...
...but I don't want to destroy the city. Not anymore.

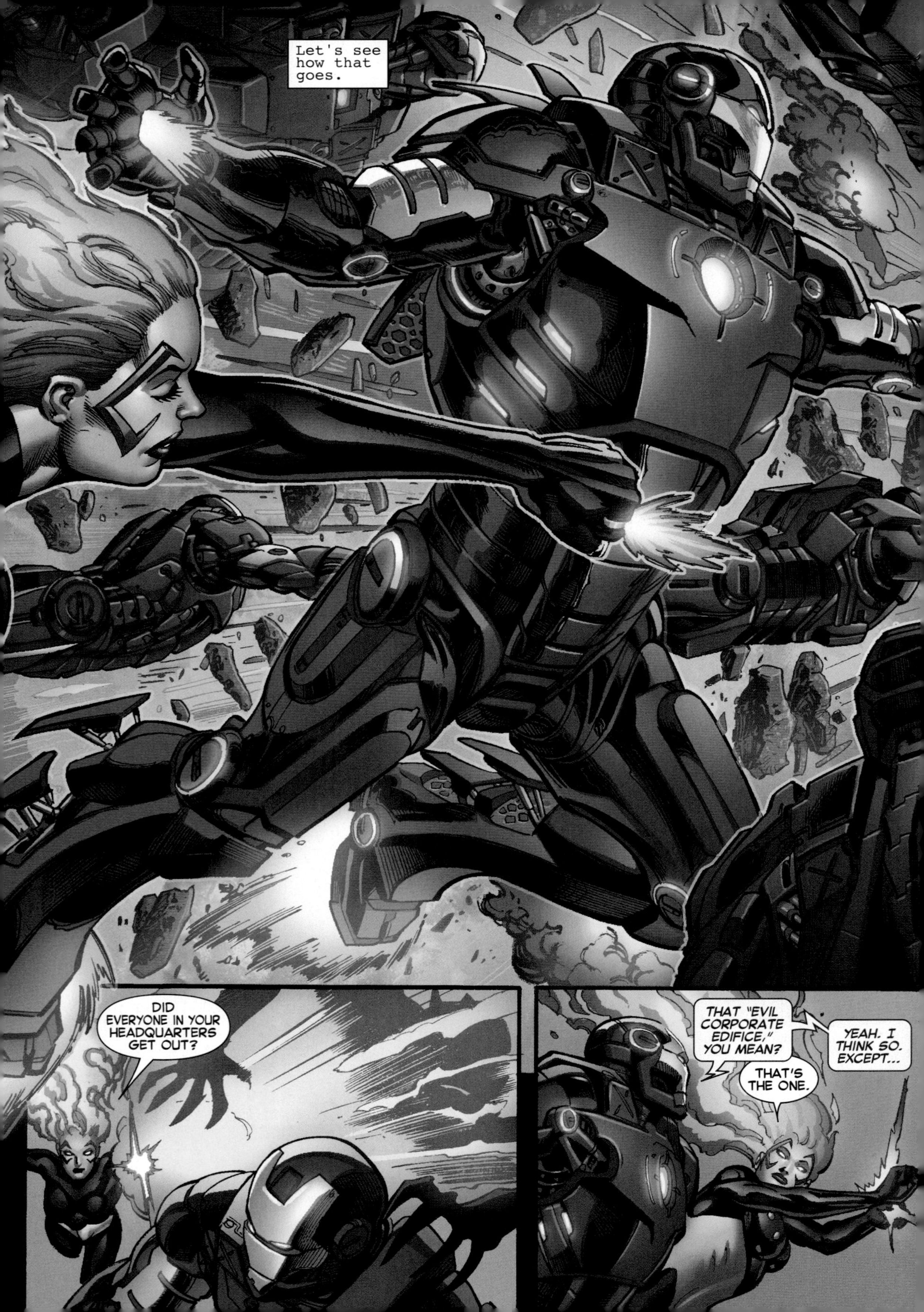
Let's see how that goes.
DID EVERYONE IN YOUR HEADQUARTERS GET OUT?
THAT "EVIL CORPORATE EDIFICE," YOU MEAN?
THAT'S THE ONE.
YEAH. I THINK SO. EXCEPT...

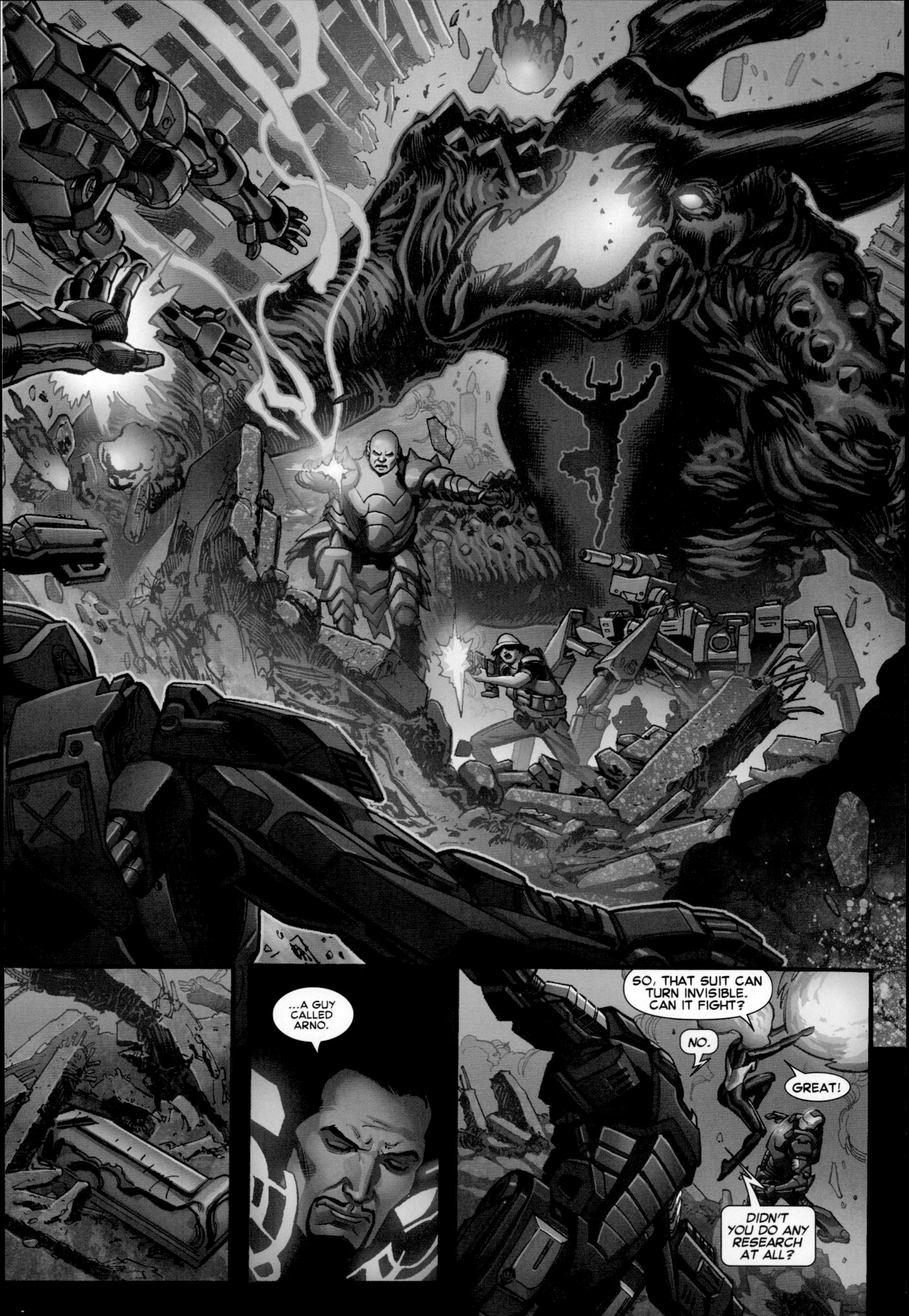
...A GUY CALLED ARNO.
SO, THAT SUIT CAN TURN INVISIBLE. CAN IT FIGHT?
NO.
GREAT!
DIDN'T YOU DO ANY RESEARCH AT ALL?

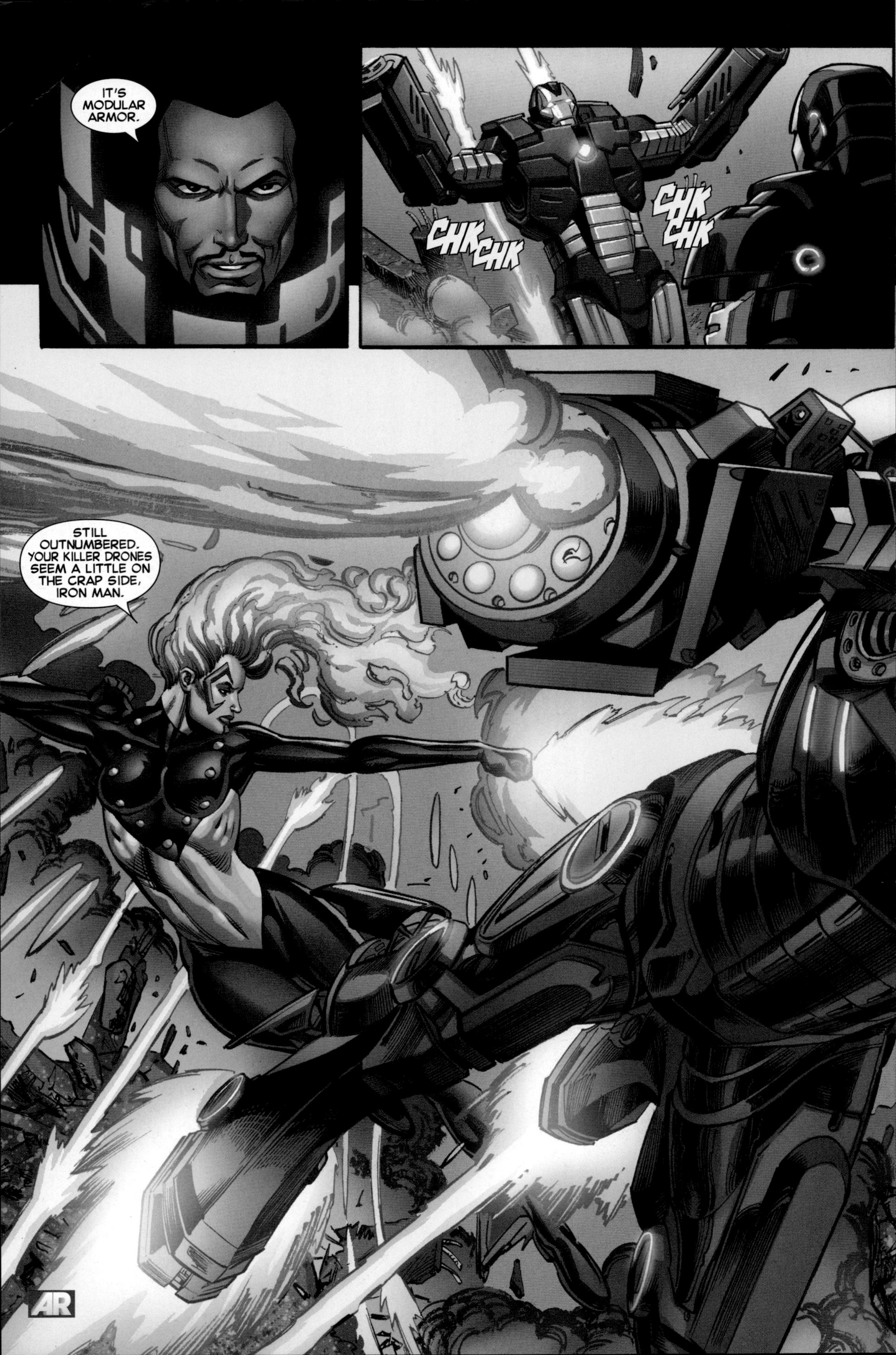
IT'S MODULAR ARMOR.
CHKCHK
CHK CHK CHK
STILL OUTNUMBERED. YOUR KILLER DRONES SEEM A LITTLE ON THE CRAP SIDE, IRON MAN.
AR

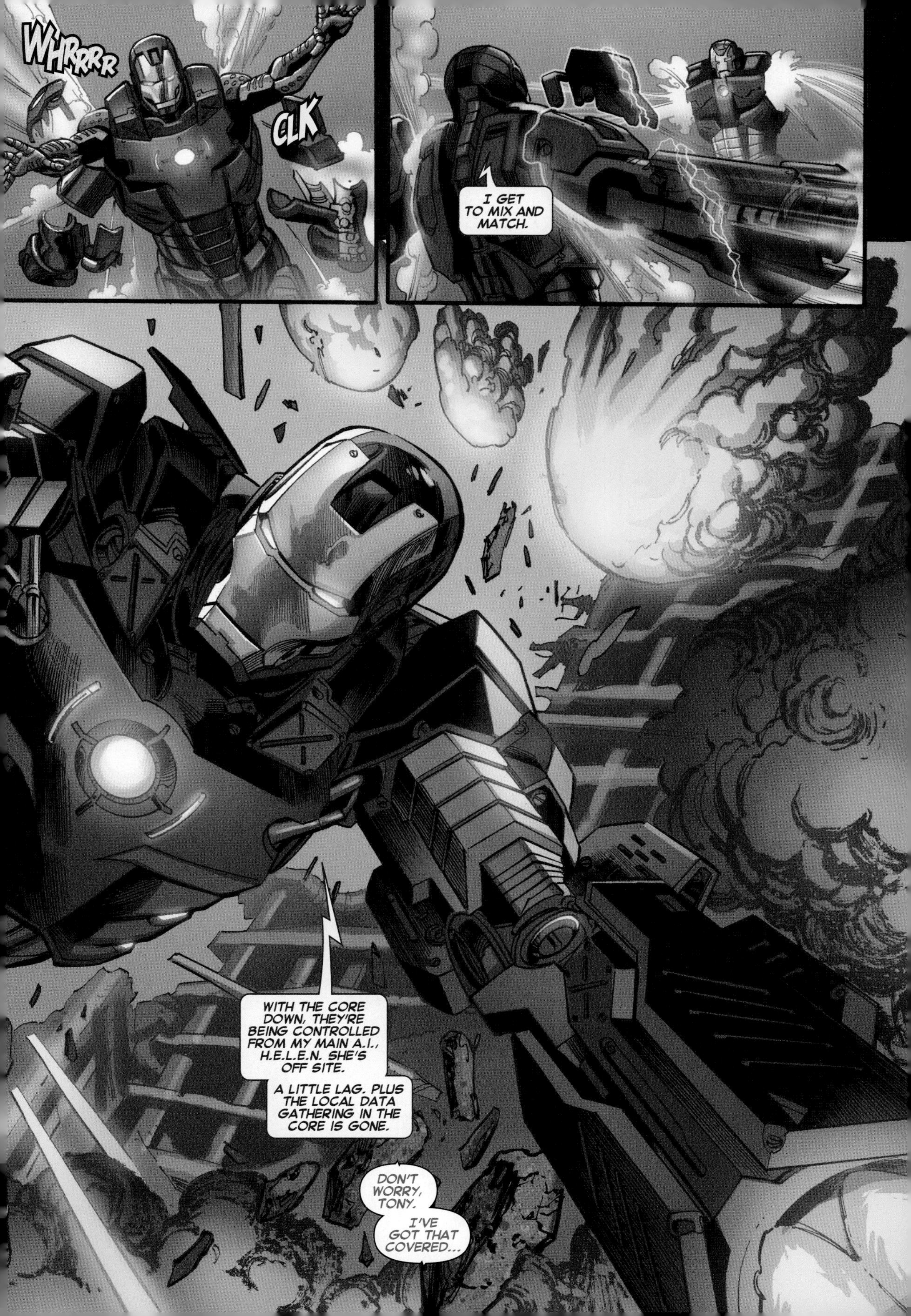
WHRRRR
CLK
I GET TO MIX AND MATCH.
WITH THE CORE DOWN, THEY'RE BEING CONTROLLED FROM MY MAIN A.I., H.E.L.E.N. SHE'S OFF SITE.
A LITTLE LAG. PLUS THE LOCAL DATA GATHERING IN THE CORE IS GONE.
DON'T WORRY, TONY.
I'VE GOT THAT COVERED...

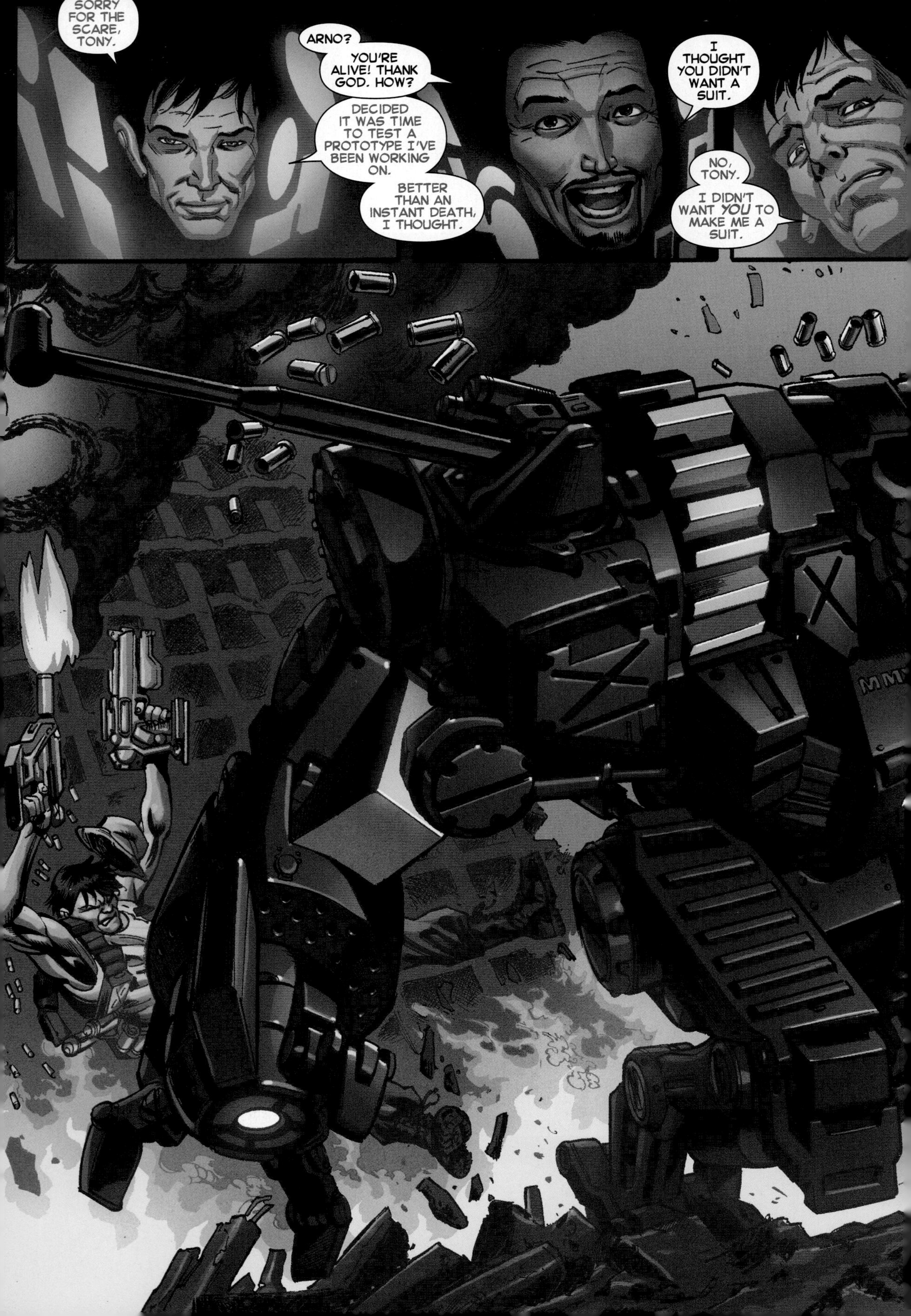
SORRY FOR THE SCARE, TONY.
ARNO?
YOU'RE ALIVE! THANK GOD. HOW?
DECIDED IT WAS TIME TO TEST A PROTOTYPE I'VE BEEN WORKING ON.
BETTER THAN AN INSTANT DEATH, I THOUGHT.
I THOUGHT YOU DIDN'T WANT A SUIT.
NO, TONY.
I DIDN'T WANT *YOU* TO MAKE ME A SUIT.

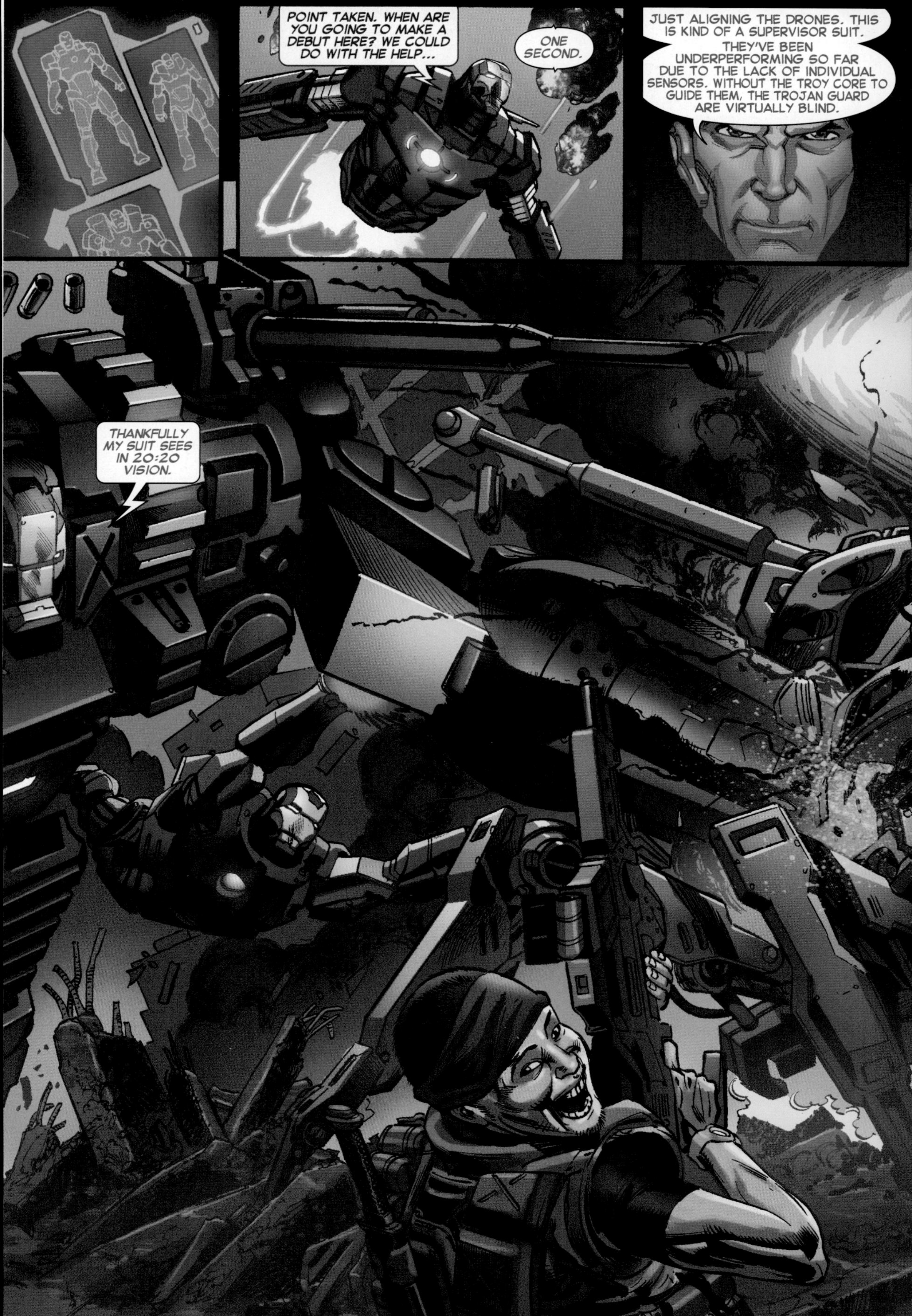
POINT TAKEN. WHEN ARE YOU GOING TO MAKE A DEBUT HERE? WE COULD DO WITH THE HELP...
ONE SECOND.
JUST ALIGNING THE DRONES. THIS IS KIND OF A SUPERVISOR SUIT.
THEY'VE BEEN UNDERPERFORMING SO FAR DUE TO THE LACK OF INDIVIDUAL SENSORS. WITHOUT THE TROY CORE TO GUIDE THEM, THE TROJAN GUARD ARE VIRTUALLY BLIND.
THANKFULLY MY SUIT SEES IN 20:20 VISION.

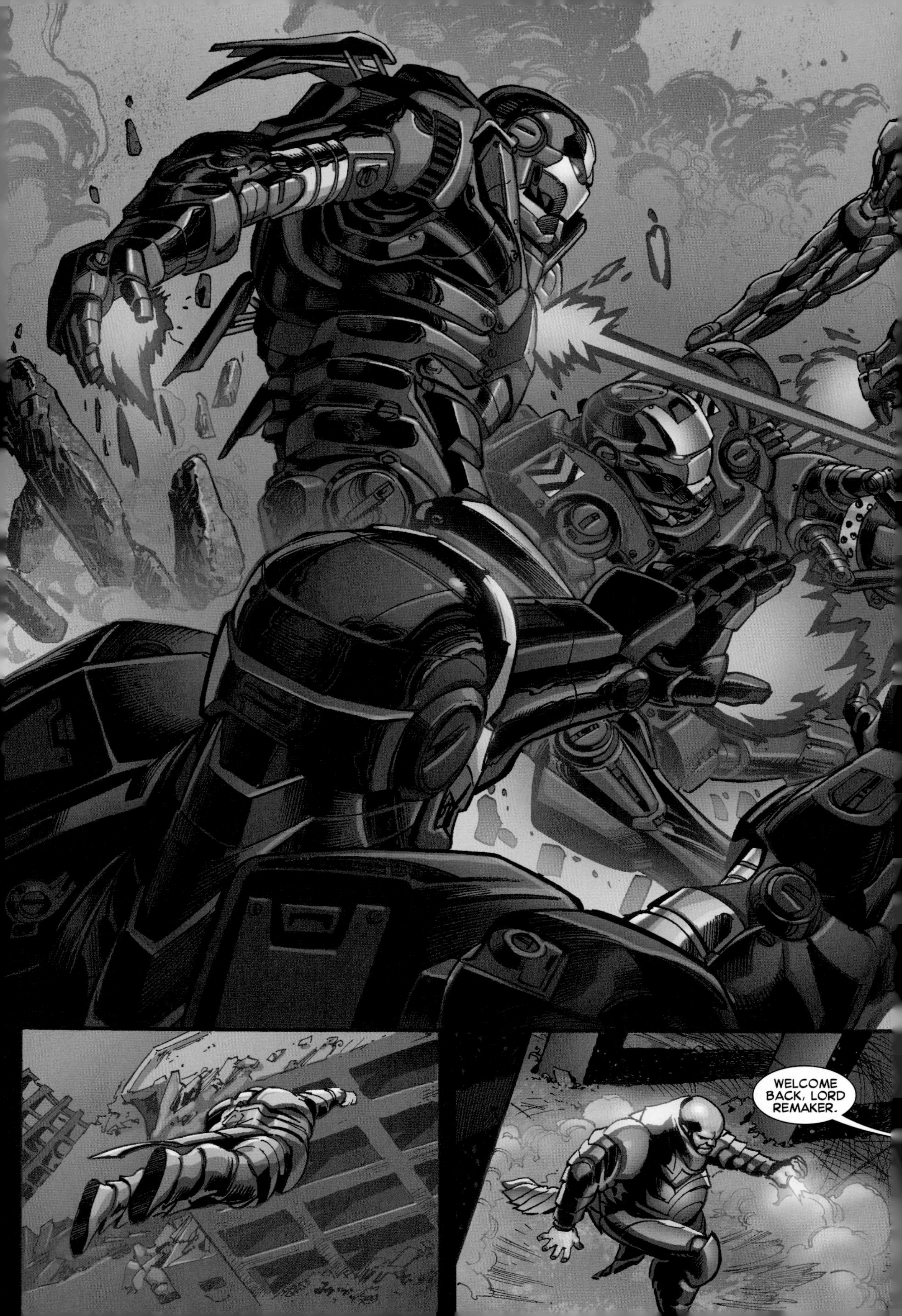
WELCOME BACK, LORD REMAKER.

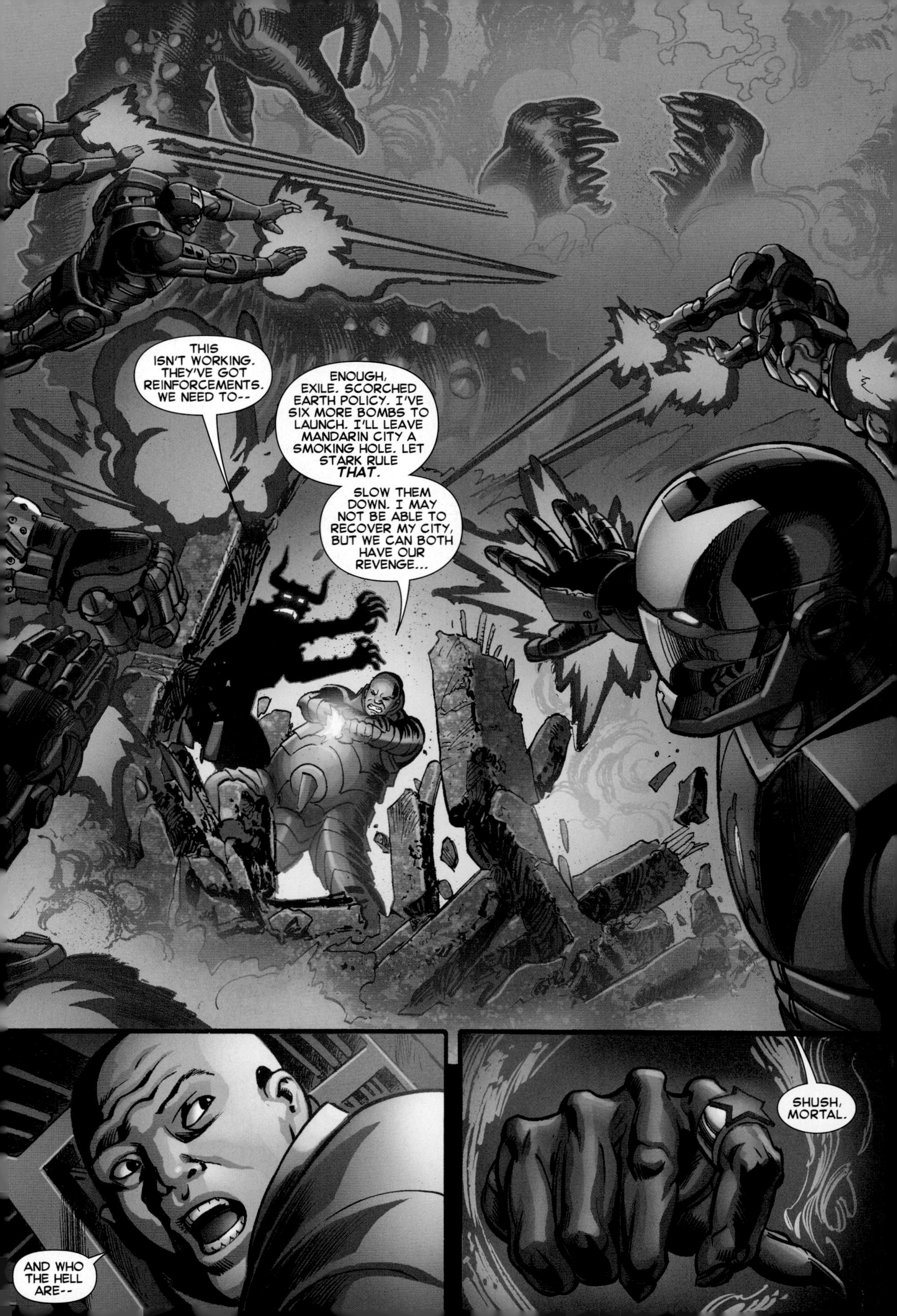
THIS ISN'T WORKING. THEY'VE GOT REINFORCEMENTS. WE NEED TO--
ENOUGH, EXILE. SCORCHED EARTH POLICY. I'VE SIX MORE BOMBS TO LAUNCH. I'LL LEAVE MANDARIN CITY A SMOKING HOLE. LET STARK RULE *THAT*.
SLOW THEM DOWN. I MAY NOT BE ABLE TO RECOVER MY CITY, BUT WE CAN BOTH HAVE OUR REVENGE...
AND WHO THE HELL ARE--
SHUSH, MORTAL.

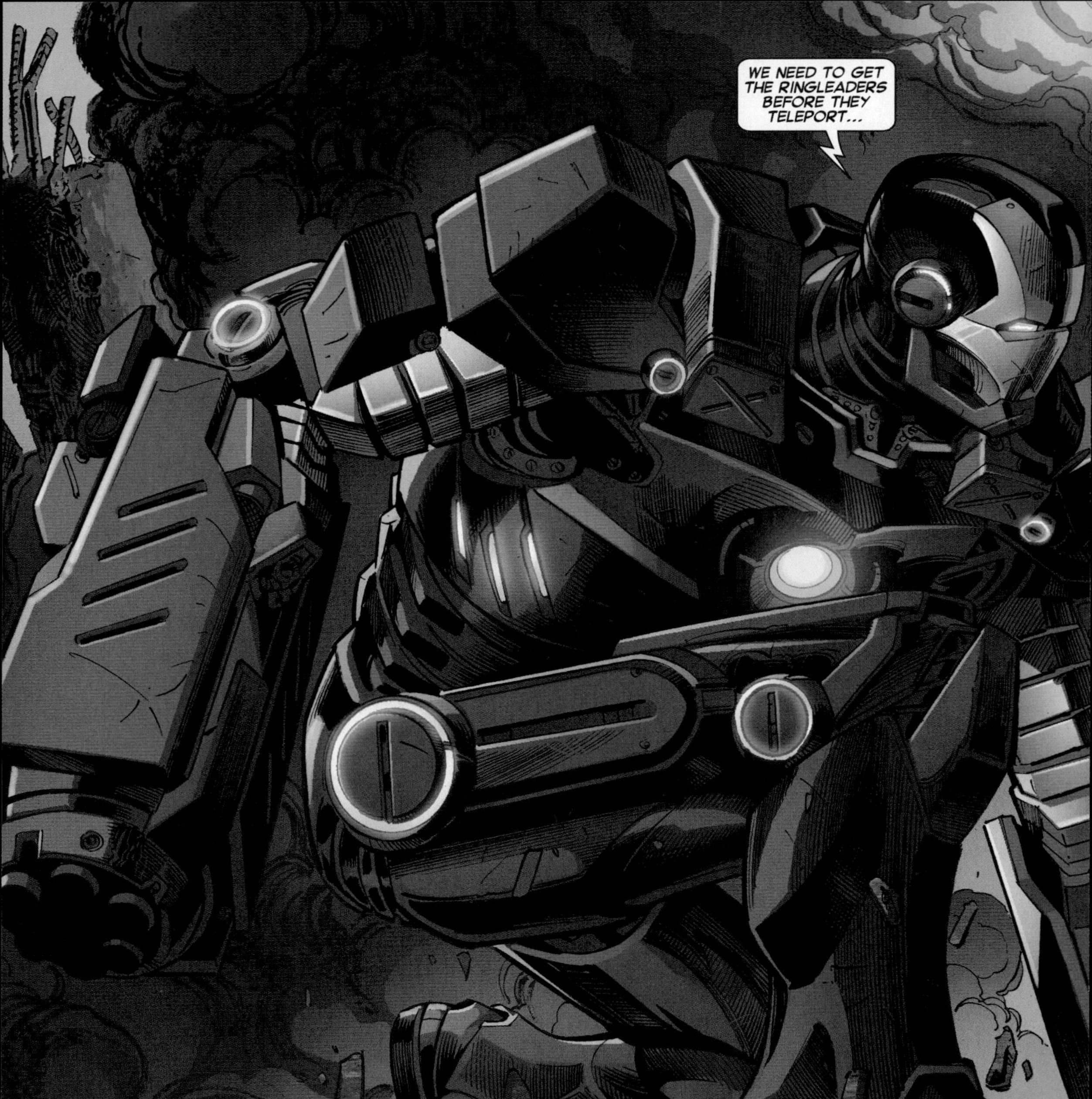
WE NEED TO GET THE RINGLEADERS BEFORE THEY TELEPORT...

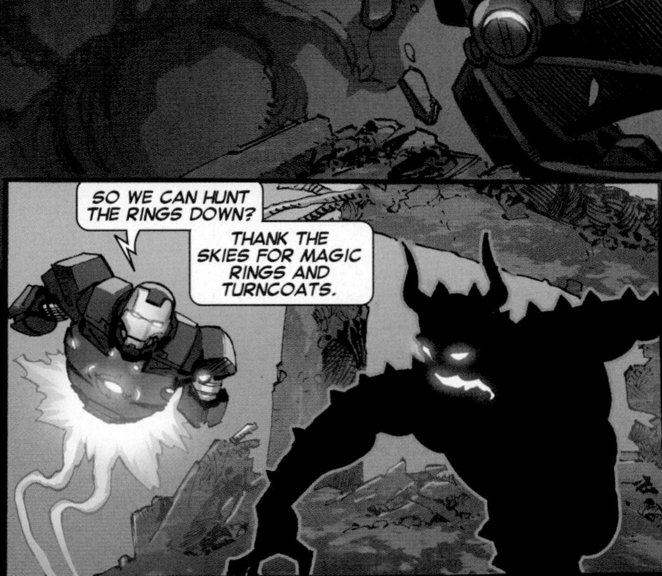
SO WE CAN HUNT THE RINGS DOWN?
THANK THE SKIES FOR MAGIC RINGS AND TURNCOATS.

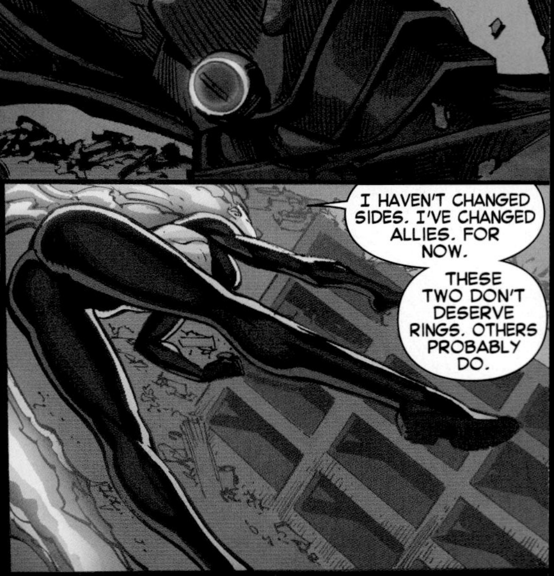
I HAVEN'T CHANGED SIDES. I'VE CHANGED ALLIES. FOR NOW.
THESE TWO DON'T DESERVE RINGS. OTHERS PROBABLY DO.

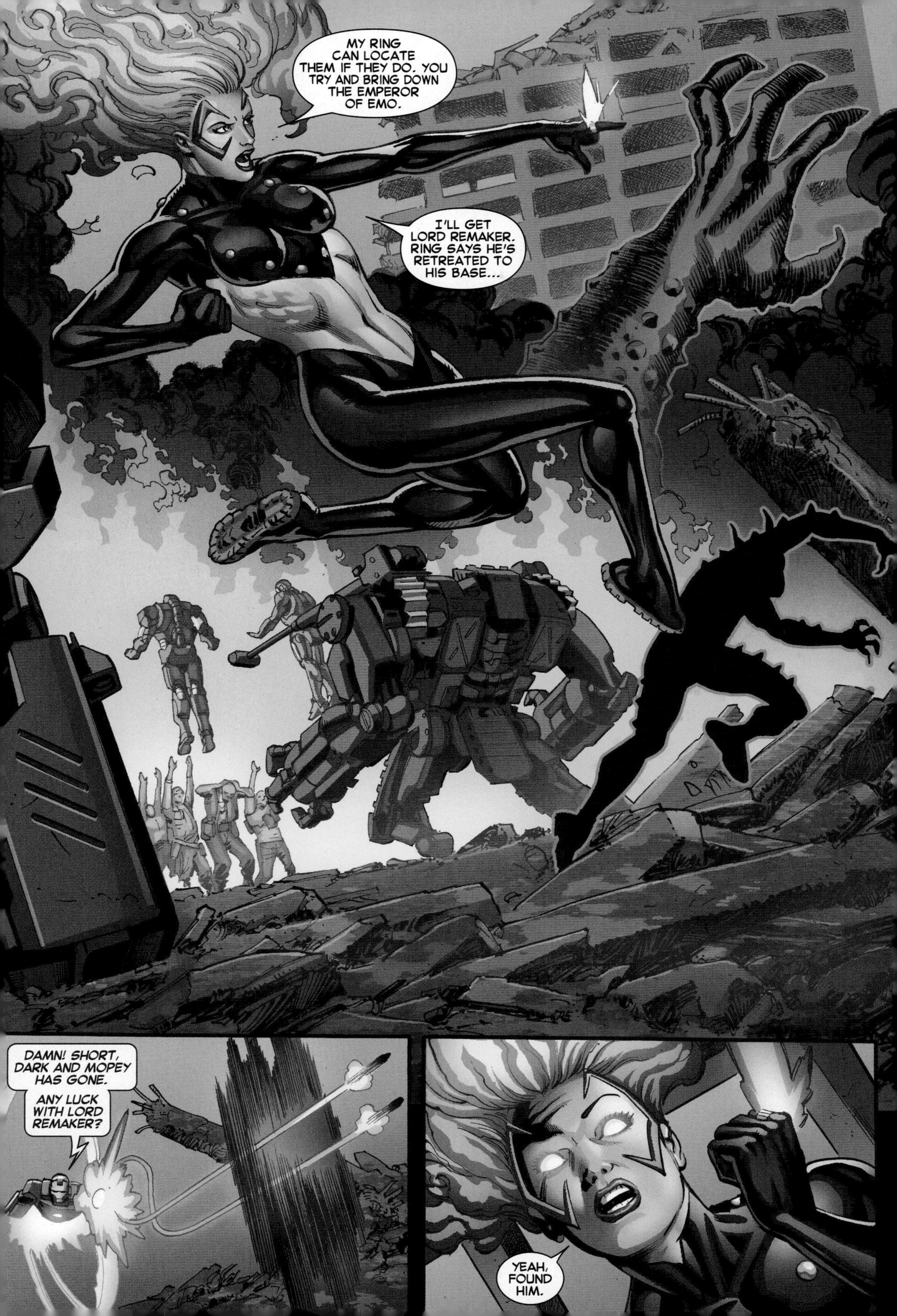
MY RING CAN LOCATE THEM IF THEY DO. YOU TRY AND BRING DOWN THE EMPEROR OF EMO.
I'LL GET LORD REMAKER. RING SAYS HE'S RETREATED TO HIS BASE...
DAMN! SHORT, DARK AND MOPEY HAS GONE.
ANY LUCK WITH LORD REMAKER?
YEAH, FOUND HIM.

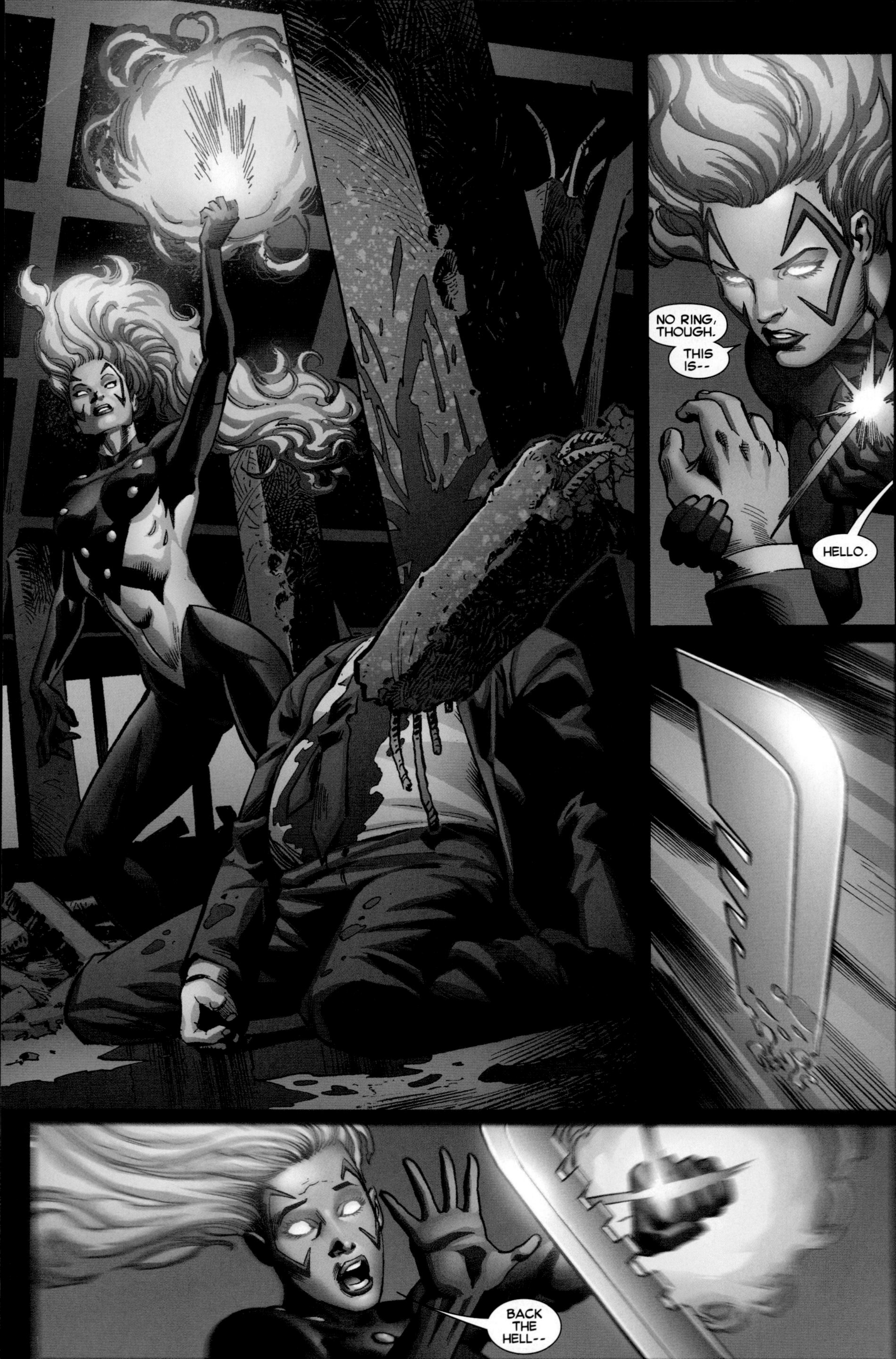
NO RING, THOUGH.
THIS IS--
HELLO.
BACK THE HELL--

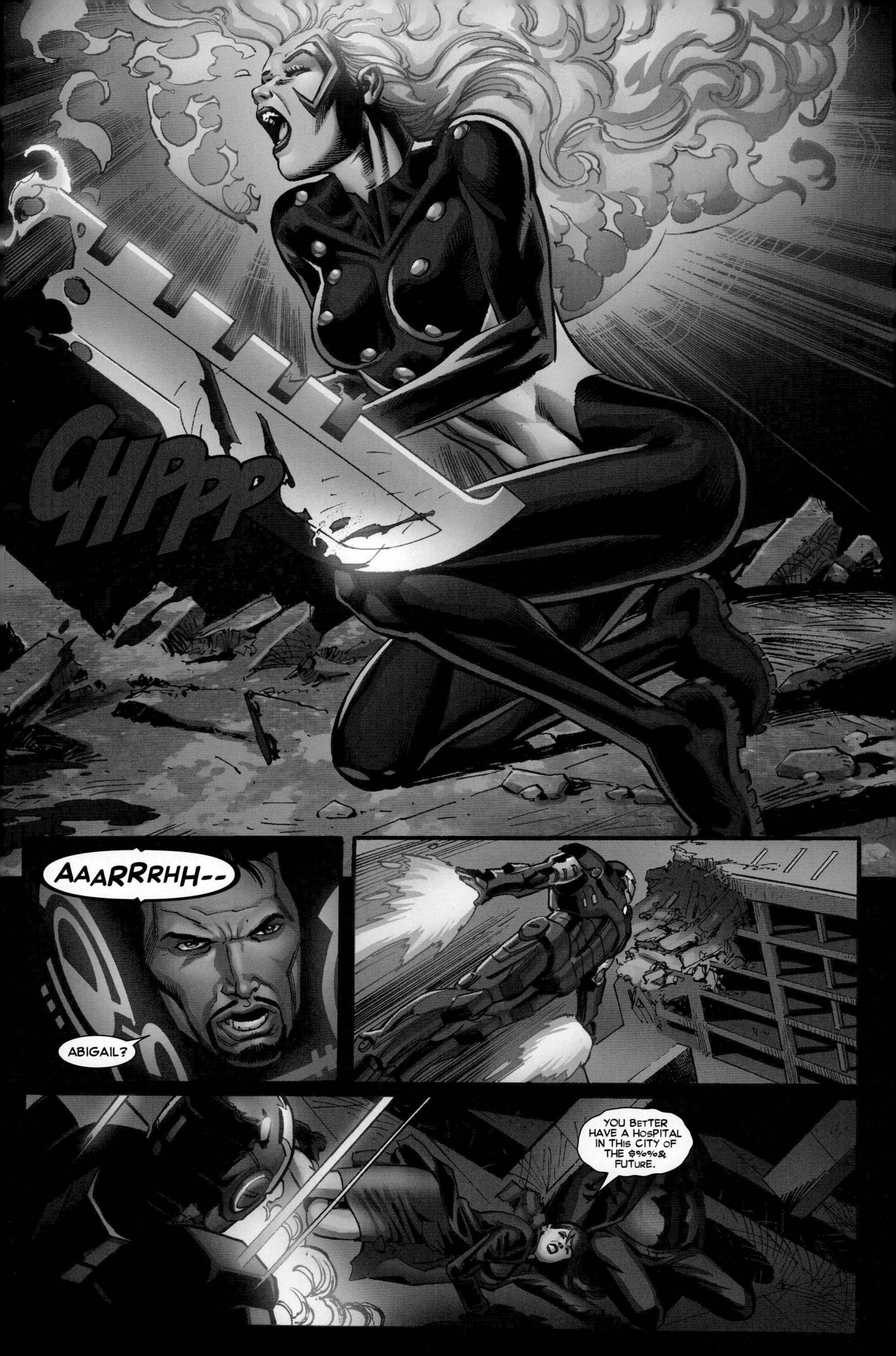
CHPPP
AAARRRHH--
ABIGAIL?
YOU BETTER HAVE A HOSPITAL IN THIS CITY OF THE $%%& FUTURE.

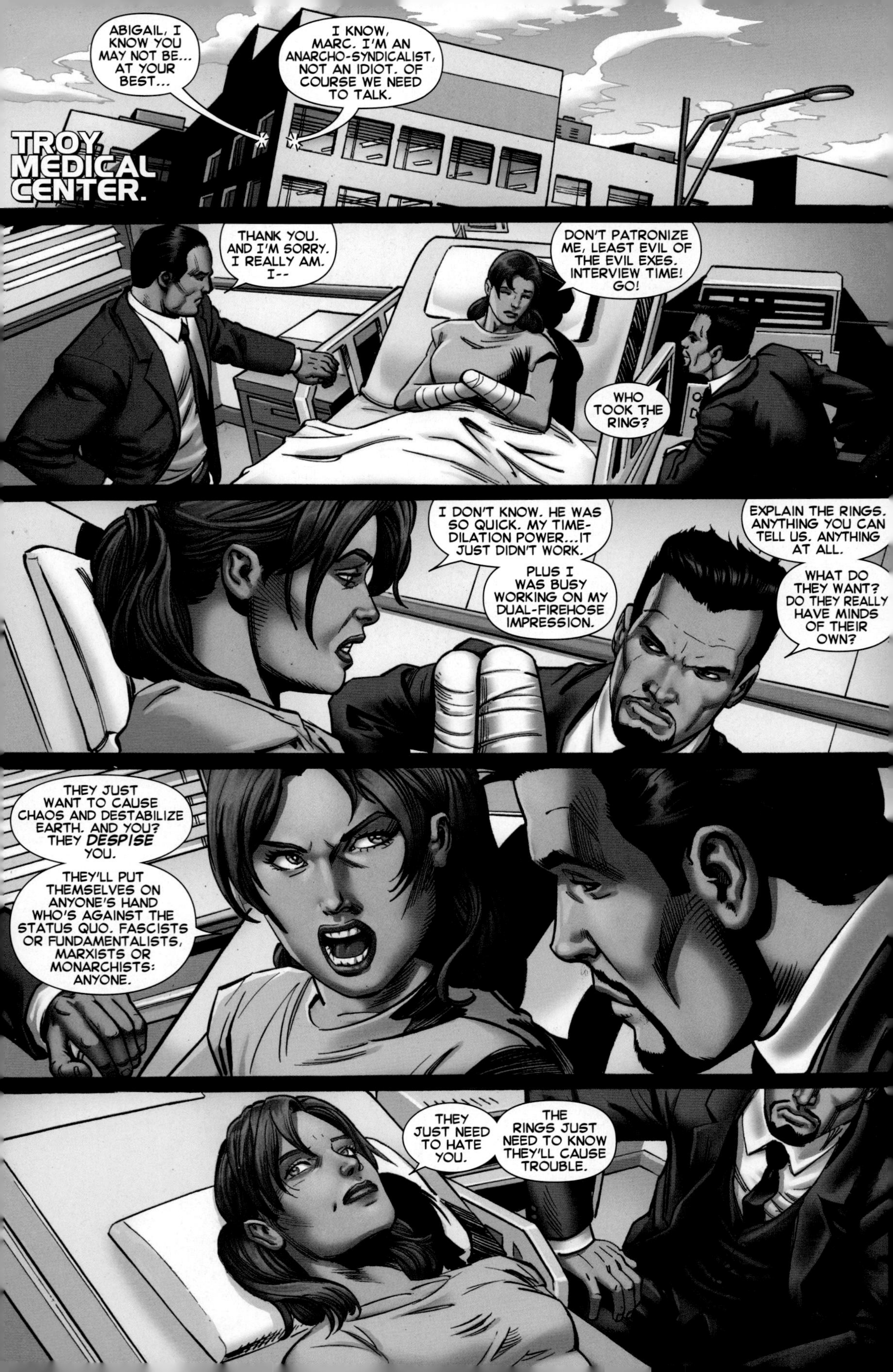
ABIGAIL, I KNOW YOU MAY NOT BE... AT YOUR BEST...
I KNOW, MARC. I'M AN ANARCHO-SYNDICALIST, NOT AN IDIOT. OF COURSE WE NEED TO TALK.
TROY MEDICAL CENTER.
THANK YOU. AND I'M SORRY. I REALLY AM. I--
DON'T PATRONIZE ME, LEAST EVIL OF THE EVIL EXES. INTERVIEW TIME! GO!
WHO TOOK THE RING?
I DON'T KNOW. HE WAS SO QUICK. MY TIME-DILATION POWER...IT JUST DIDN'T WORK.
PLUS I WAS BUSY WORKING ON MY DUAL-FIREHOSE IMPRESSION.
EXPLAIN THE RINGS. ANYTHING YOU CAN TELL US. ANYTHING AT ALL.
WHAT DO THEY WANT? DO THEY REALLY HAVE MINDS OF THEIR OWN?
THEY JUST WANT TO CAUSE CHAOS AND DESTABILIZE EARTH. AND YOU? THEY *DESPISE* YOU.
THEY'LL PUT THEMSELVES ON ANYONE'S HAND WHO'S AGAINST THE STATUS QUO. FASCISTS OR FUNDAMENTALISTS, MARXISTS OR MONARCHISTS: ANYONE.
THEY JUST NEED TO HATE YOU.
THE RINGS JUST NEED TO KNOW THEY'LL CAUSE TROUBLE.

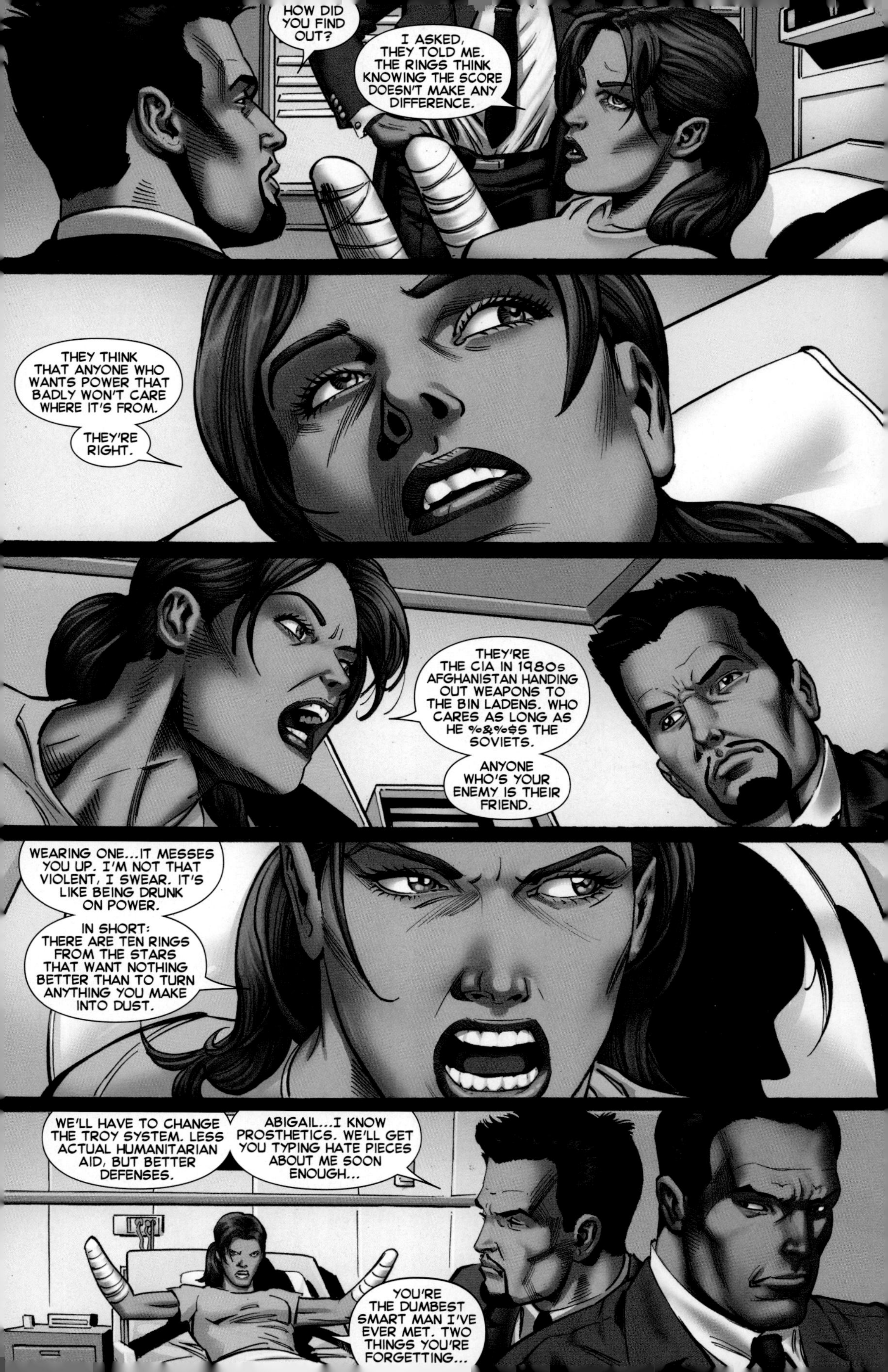
HOW DID YOU FIND OUT?
I ASKED, THEY TOLD ME. THE RINGS THINK KNOWING THE SCORE DOESN'T MAKE ANY DIFFERENCE.
THEY THINK THAT ANYONE WHO WANTS POWER THAT BADLY WON'T CARE WHERE IT'S FROM.
THEY'RE RIGHT.
THEY'RE THE CIA IN 1980s AFGHANISTAN HANDING OUT WEAPONS TO THE BIN LADENS. WHO CARES AS LONG AS HE %&%$S THE SOVIETS.
ANYONE WHO'S YOUR ENEMY IS THEIR FRIEND.
WEARING ONE...IT MESSES YOU UP. I'M NOT THAT VIOLENT, I SWEAR. IT'S LIKE BEING DRUNK ON POWER.
IN SHORT: THERE ARE TEN RINGS FROM THE STARS THAT WANT NOTHING BETTER THAN TO TURN ANYTHING YOU MAKE INTO DUST.
WE'LL HAVE TO CHANGE THE TROY SYSTEM. LESS ACTUAL HUMANITARIAN AID, BUT BETTER DEFENSES.
ABIGAIL...I KNOW PROSTHETICS. WE'LL GET YOU TYPING HATE PIECES ABOUT ME SOON ENOUGH...
YOU'RE THE DUMBEST SMART MAN I'VE EVER MET. TWO THINGS YOU'RE FORGETTING...

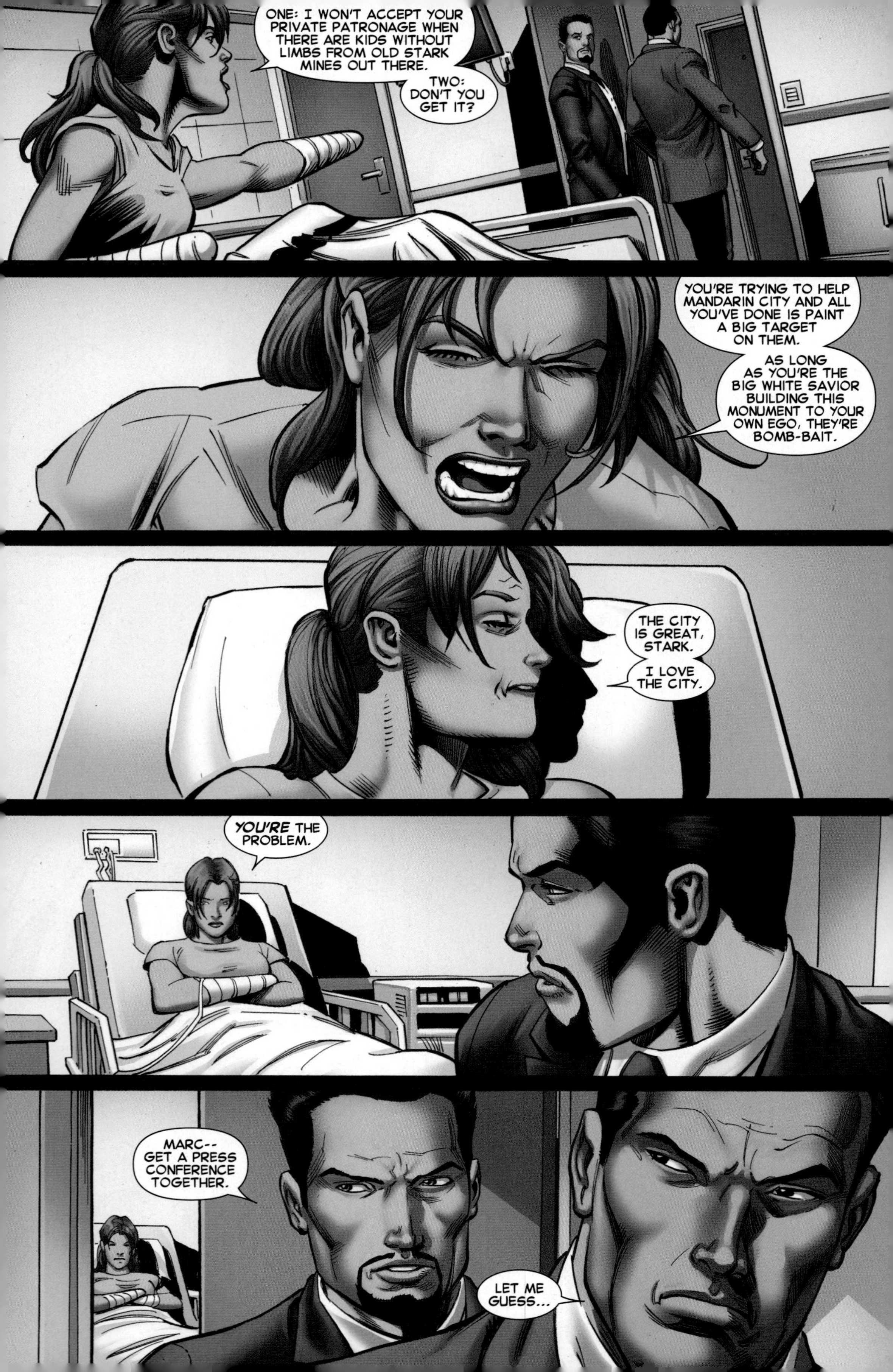
ONE: I WON'T ACCEPT YOUR PRIVATE PATRONAGE WHEN THERE ARE KIDS WITHOUT LIMBS FROM OLD STARK MINES OUT THERE.
TWO: DON'T YOU GET IT?
YOU'RE TRYING TO HELP MANDARIN CITY AND ALL YOU'VE DONE IS PAINT A BIG TARGET ON THEM.
AS LONG AS YOU'RE THE BIG WHITE SAVIOR BUILDING THIS MONUMENT TO YOUR OWN EGO, THEY'RE BOMB-BAIT.
THE CITY IS GREAT, STARK.
I LOVE THE CITY.
YOU'RE THE PROBLEM.
MARC-- GET A PRESS CONFERENCE TOGETHER.
LET ME GUESS...

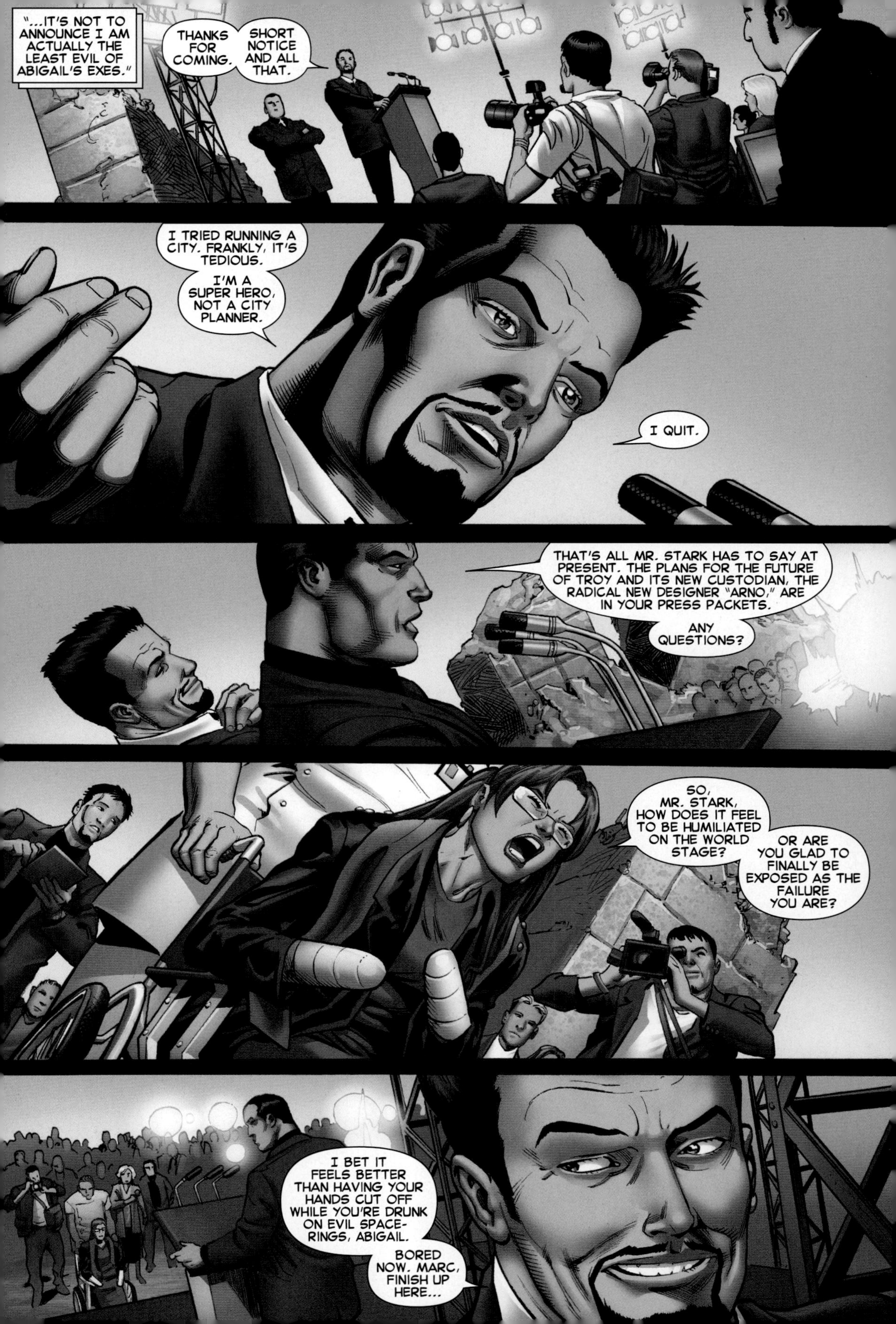
"...IT'S NOT TO ANNOUNCE I AM ACTUALLY THE LEAST EVIL OF ABIGAIL'S EXES."
THANKS FOR COMING.
SHORT NOTICE AND ALL THAT.
I TRIED RUNNING A CITY. FRANKLY, IT'S TEDIOUS.
I'M A SUPER HERO, NOT A CITY PLANNER.
I QUIT.
THAT'S ALL MR. STARK HAS TO SAY AT PRESENT. THE PLANS FOR THE FUTURE OF TROY AND ITS NEW CUSTODIAN, THE RADICAL NEW DESIGNER "ARNO," ARE IN YOUR PRESS PACKETS.
ANY QUESTIONS?
SO, MR. STARK, HOW DOES IT FEEL TO BE HUMILIATED ON THE WORLD STAGE?
OR ARE YOU GLAD TO FINALLY BE EXPOSED AS THE FAILURE YOU ARE?
I BET IT FEELS BETTER THAN HAVING YOUR HANDS CUT OFF WHILE YOU'RE DRUNK ON EVIL SPACE-RINGS, ABIGAIL.
BORED NOW. MARC, FINISH UP HERE...

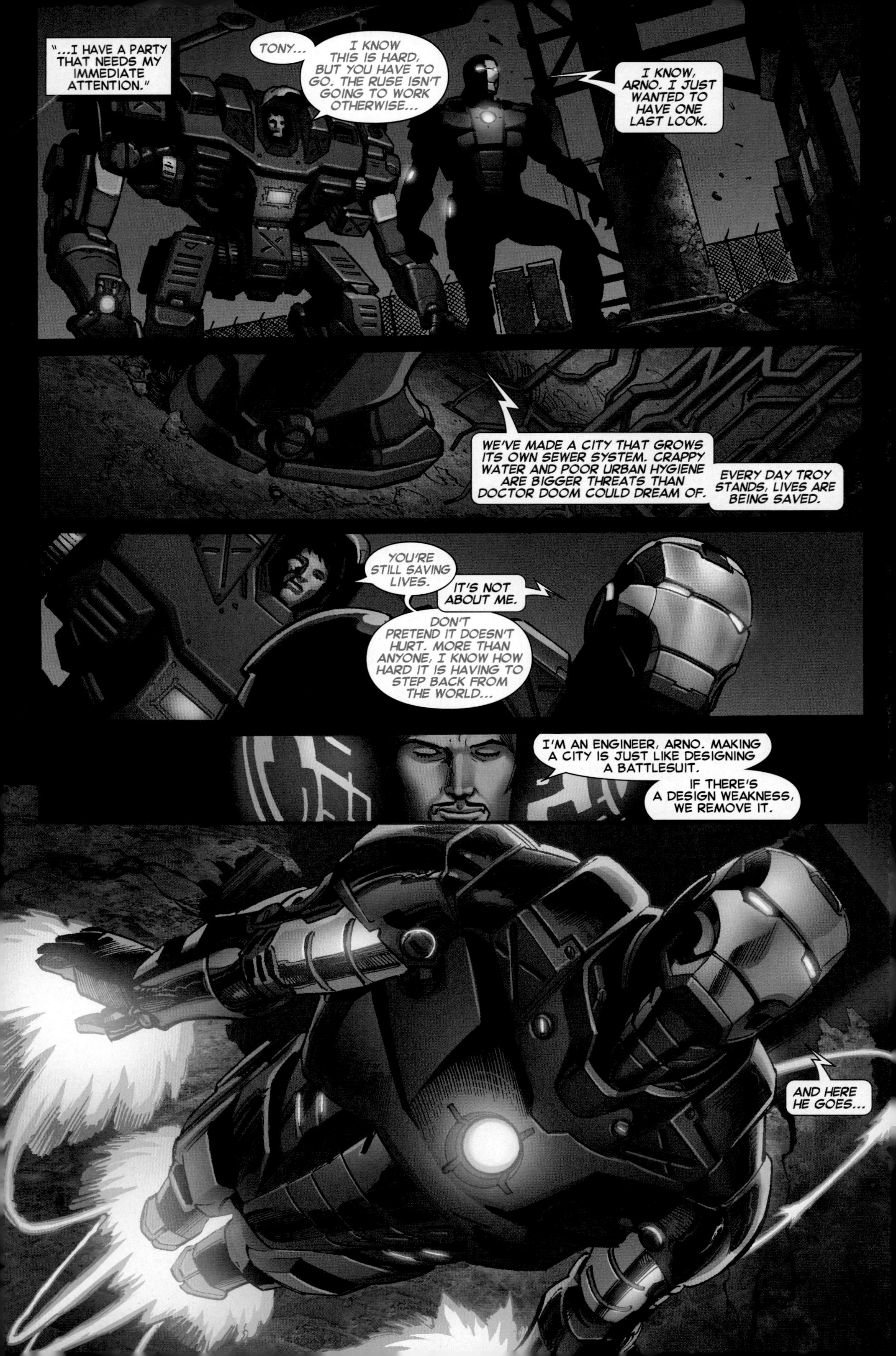
"...I HAVE A PARTY THAT NEEDS MY IMMEDIATE ATTENTION."
TONY...
I KNOW THIS IS HARD, BUT YOU HAVE TO GO. THE RUSE ISN'T GOING TO WORK OTHERWISE...
I KNOW, ARNO. I JUST WANTED TO HAVE ONE LAST LOOK.
WE'VE MADE A CITY THAT GROWS ITS OWN SEWER SYSTEM. CRAPPY WATER AND POOR URBAN HYGIENE ARE BIGGER THREATS THAN DOCTOR DOOM COULD DREAM OF.
EVERY DAY TROY STANDS, LIVES ARE BEING SAVED.
YOU'RE STILL SAVING LIVES.
IT'S NOT ABOUT ME.
DON'T PRETEND IT DOESN'T HURT. MORE THAN ANYONE, I KNOW HOW HARD IT IS HAVING TO STEP BACK FROM THE WORLD...
I'M AN ENGINEER, ARNO. MAKING A CITY IS JUST LIKE DESIGNING A BATTLESUIT.
IF THERE'S A DESIGN WEAKNESS, WE REMOVE IT.
AND HERE HE GOES...

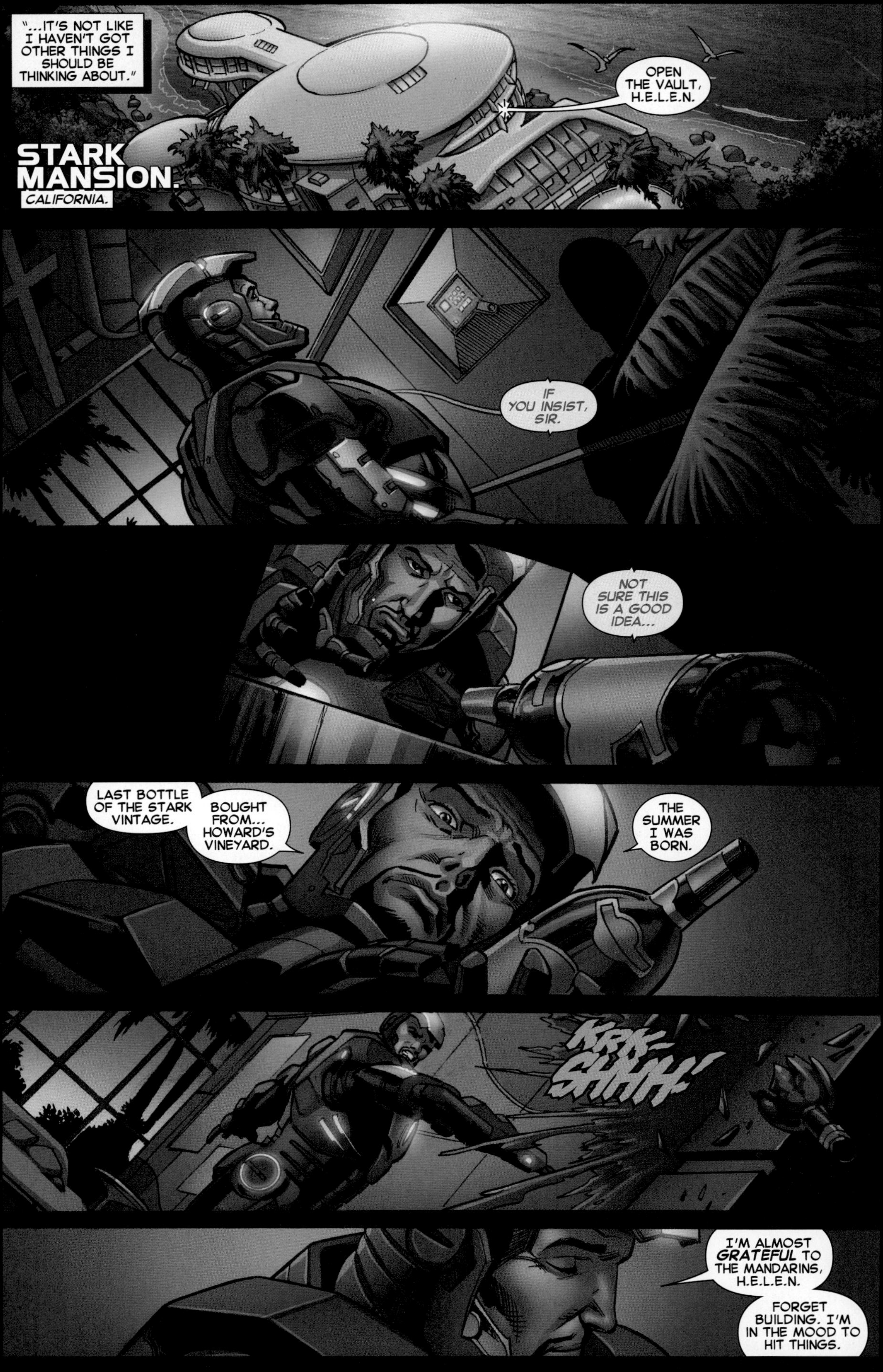
"...IT'S NOT LIKE I HAVEN'T GOT OTHER THINGS I SHOULD BE THINKING ABOUT."
OPEN THE VAULT, H.E.L.E.N.
STARK MANSION.
CALIFORNIA.
IF YOU INSIST, SIR.
NOT SURE THIS IS A GOOD IDEA...
LAST BOTTLE OF THE STARK VINTAGE.
BOUGHT FROM... HOWARD'S VINEYARD.
THE SUMMER I WAS BORN.
KRK-SHHH!
I'M ALMOST GRATEFUL TO THE MANDARINS, H.E.L.E.N.
FORGET BUILDING. I'M IN THE MOOD TO HIT THINGS.

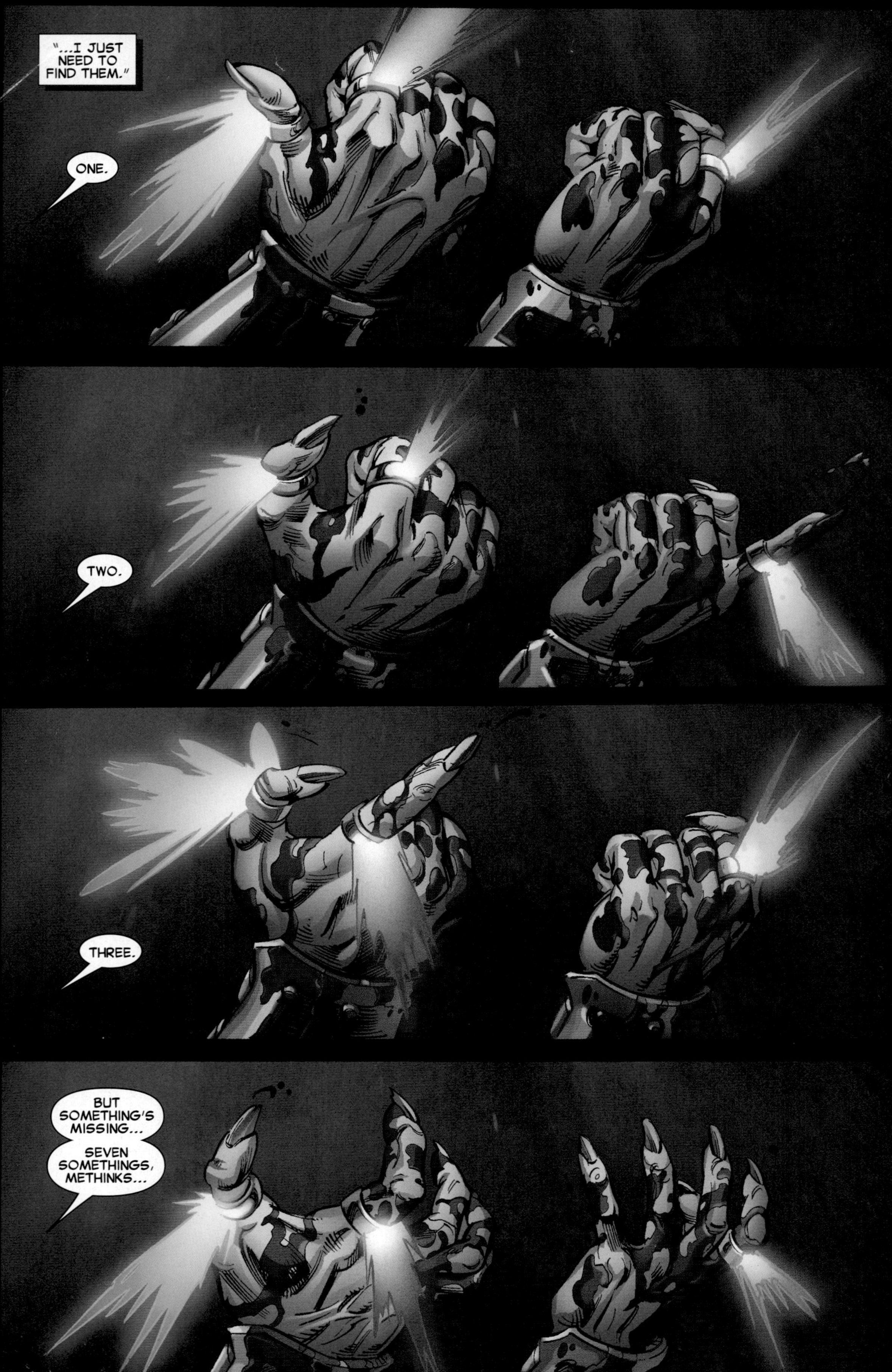
"...I JUST NEED TO FIND THEM."
ONE.
TWO.
THREE.
BUT SOMETHING'S MISSING...
SEVEN SOMETHINGS, METHINKS...

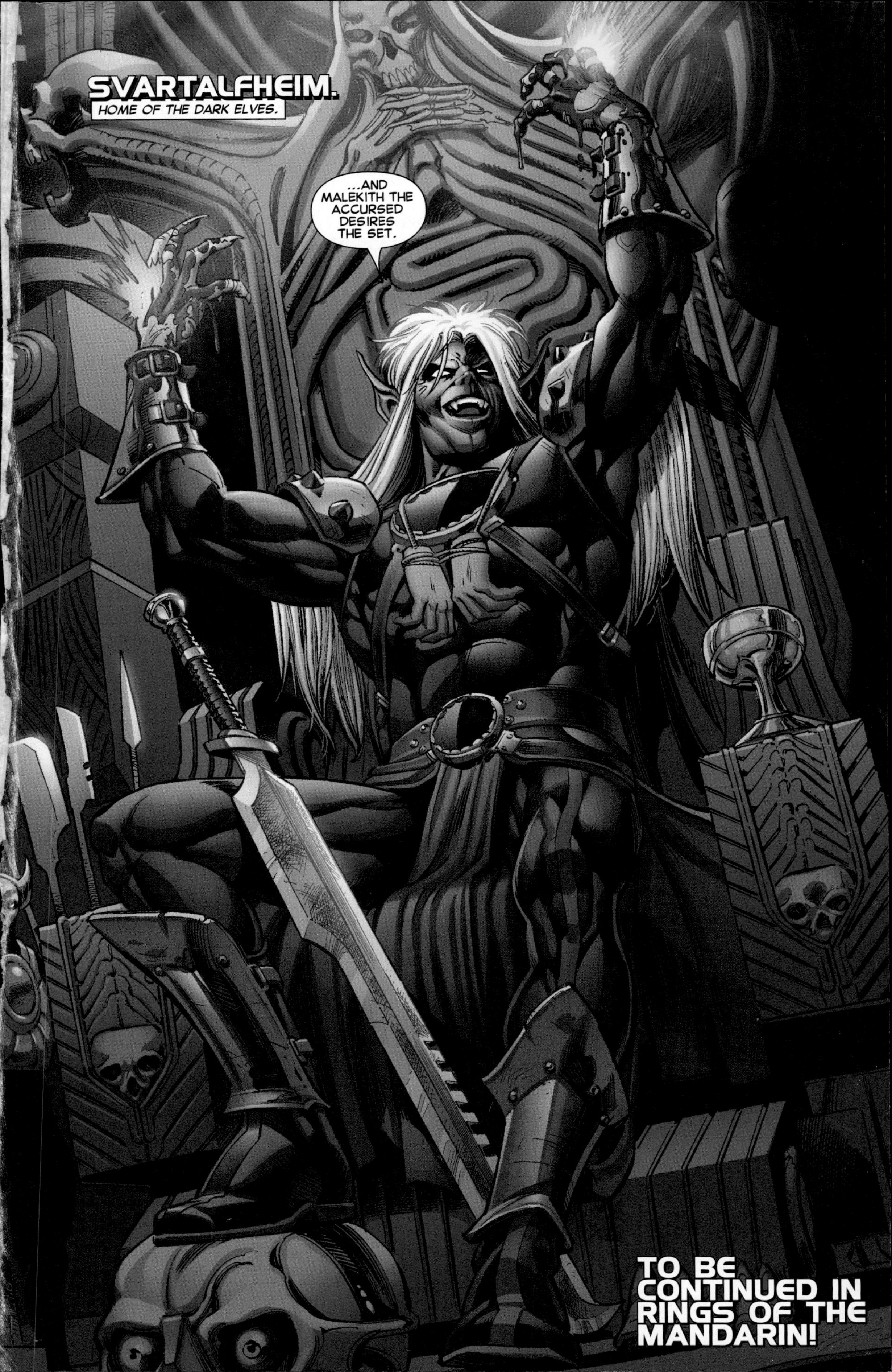
SVARTALFHEIM.
HOME OF THE DARK ELVES.
...AND MALEKITH THE ACCURSED DESIRES THE SET.
TO BE CONTINUED IN RINGS OF THE MANDARIN!